"This Book is absolutely phenomenal! Dave Hutchins does an outstanding job of bridging the gap between the ancient text of Scripture and the everyday challenges of parenting teens. If you desire godly courage as a Christian parent, this book is for you."

—REV. JEFF GANNON, SENIOR PASTOR,
CHAPEL HILL FELLOWSHIP, WICHITA, KS

"*Courageous Parenting* is the culmination of Dave Hutchins years of experience working with youth and their parents. This practical teaching program is a must for every parent who desires to be wise and godly in raising children, and for every pastor who longs to help parents in their God-ordained role and responsibility."

—MARK R. HARDY, PASTOR-TEACHER
COEURD'ALENE BIBLE CHURCH, COEURD'ALENE, IDAHO

"Thanks to what Dave Hutchins has written, we are accomplishing more by influencing our daughters than we ever achieved by trying to control them. Hutchins gently and convincingly exposed us to truths of Scripture and hard truths about ourselves that resulted in fundamental changes in the way we now parent."

—GARY PREHN, MINISTER OF ADULTS,
NORTHVIEW BIBLE CHURCH, SPOKANE, WA

"Rather than give formulas or fixes, Dave Hutchins encourages us to struggle for intimacy with our children. Being involved in the process requires hard work, but brings satisfaction and peace in parent-child relationships."

—DOUG WIEBER, SENIOR PASTOR,
"HIS PLACE" EVANGELICAL FREE CHURCH, POST FALLS, IDAHO

"The desperate need of our youth today is to have parents who will love and guide them with the power of Jesus Christ. *Courageous Parenting* has met that need for many parents and teens—even those inside the Juvenile Justice system."

—MARK LEWIS, JUVENILE PROBATION ADMINISTRATOR,
SPOKANE COUNTY JUVENILE COURT

COURAGEOUS PARENTING

The Passionate Pursuit of Your Teen's Heart

DAVID HUTCHINS

A WORKBOOK FOR GROUPS OR INDIVIDUALS

NAVPRESS ◖
Bringing Truth to Life
P.O. Box 35001, Colorado Springs, Colorado 80935

OUR GUARANTEE TO YOU

We believe so strongly in the message of our books that we are making this quality guarantee to you. If for any reason you are disappointed with the content of this book, return the title page to us with your name and address and we will refund to you the list price of the book. To help us serve you better, please briefly describe why you were disappointed. Mail your refund request to: NavPress, P.O. Box 35002, Colorado Springs, CO 80935.

The Navigators is an international Christian organization. Our mission is to reach, disciple, and equip people to know Christ and to make Him known through successive generations. We envision multitudes of diverse people in the United States and every other nation who have a passionate love for Christ, live a lifestyle of sharing Christ's love, and multiply spiritual laborers among those without Christ.

NavPress is the publishing ministry of The Navigators. NavPress publications help believers learn biblical truth and apply what they learn to their lives and ministries. Our mission is to stimulate spiritual formation among our readers.

Cover illustration by Brad Wilson/Photonica
Cover design by Jennifer Mahalik
Creative Team: Karen Lee-Thorp, Deena Davis, Darla Hightower, Tim Howard

Some of the anecdotal illustrations in this book are true to life and are included with the permission of the persons involved. All other illustrations are composites of real situations, and any resemblance to people living or dead is coincidental.

Contents

Acknowledgments

Special thanks to Kevin Huggins, M.Div., M.A., writer, speaker, counselor and, most importantly, parent of adolescents. His work on teenagers, *Parenting Adolescents* (NavPress), provides much of the conceptual framework that guides this course. With Kevin's permission, the *Courageous Parenting* curriculum uses his concepts and graphs that highlight key components in understanding adolescents. Formerly director of Adolescent Ministries of the Institute of Biblical Counseling and director of a two-year training program for parents of adolescents in Akron, Ohio, and now professor of Christian counseling at Philadelphia College of the Bible, Kevin has extensive experience in helping parents of teens. He has been used by God to impact many parents to courageously pursue their own teenagers with a greater degree of love and compassion.

I would also like to thank the men and women I had the opportunity to colabor with at Spokane Youth For Christ. For nearly twelve years I had the wonderful privilege of learning from and working with caring ministers to adolescents and parents. Many of my experiences of working with families and adolescents came out of this "training camp" of dedicated people. This workbook reflects the combined wisdom and efforts of these mission-oriented people.

I feel a deep sense of gratitude toward Drs. Larry Crabb, Dan Allender, and Tom Varney, all of whom taught at Colorado Christian University's Master in Biblical Counseling program when I was a student there. These men, more than being just teachers, became mentors in the richest sense of the word as they freely shared their lives. Each man uniquely compelled me to think about God and people in ways that, paradoxically, both confound me and encourage my heart to seek God with a more honest passion. I have been forever altered by inclusion in their spiritual journeys.

A humble thanks to the publisher and editors at NavPress for the vision and desire to see this project completed when they saw potential in the early manuscript. Kent Wilson's early words of encouragement and Paul Santhouse's forbearance were so affirming in the early stages. But most importantly, my deepest thanks to Karen Lee-Thorp, the editor who guided my ideas and words into a final version that hopefully will encourage parents in loving their kids more courageously. Karen's thoughtful, probing words of affirmation and plain hard work helped bring the entire project together in ways I could never have done on my own. Working together has been a pleasure. Thank you, Karen.

Additional thanks are due to these people at the Genesis Institute, who gave freely of themselves to encourage others: Bob and Margaret Bishopp, Mark Cornelius, Dennis Roach, Ray Hopkins, Leroy Miller, Sherri Hopkins, Angie Alden, and many others. A special note of thanks to Beth Miller, who labored over her kitchen table editing the initial drafts of this manuscript. Thanks also to the dozens of other people who have contributed in one way or another to this work. If I have missed your name, know that there is Someone who knows and remembers.

I'm especially grateful to my wife, Cathy, as we actively parent our adolescent son, Seth. She lovingly continues to believe in me, challenges me to be more as a man and father, and labors to see Christ formed in me. No other person has ventured so deeply into my soul. Lastly, my thanks to Seth, who continues to believe passionately that, as a son, "he teaches me more than anyone." He just may be right. The Lord uses him relentlessly, often compelling me as few other people do, to look at my heart and love more. My life is richer because of you.

How Does This Course Work?

What Is the Course Content?

Courageous Parenting is a sixteen-week training course designed for parents of kids ten to twenty years old. Based on biblical principles, the course helps parents to develop deeper levels of influence (not control) through love and discipline fleshed out. The goal is to promote godliness in the hearts of their kids. The course focuses first on what wise parents need to understand about entering their kids' hearts, not merely on changing their behaviors. Second, the course focuses on what maturing parents need to do in terms of communicating love and discipline to their kids.

What Will I Learn?

You will learn to think more deeply and biblically about how you understand and relate to your kids. You will learn to deepen your relationship with them and become a more godly parent. You will have the opportunity, with feedback from other parents, to think about changing yourself by looking at the ways you relate to your kids in current family situations. These insights and feedback will be key components to help you move your kids toward maturity in Christ.

Why Meet in a Small Group?

Parents can give and receive invaluable feedback. By considering each other's varied points of view, parents can learn to think creatively about their kids. The group becomes a reflective, supportive community that encourages one another to continue to pursue relationship, even when loving a kid may be tough.

Can I Use This Workbook on My Own?

This workbook is written in such a way that any parent who is reading it alone, honestly reflecting on the Scriptures, and interacting with the materials will make progress in deepening a relationship with his or her kids.

What Time Commitment Is Involved?

Ideally, the small group will meet two hours per week to cover the material in each session. If necessary, a group can complete the material in ninety-minute sessions. A parent who is using the workbook independently should be able to work through each session in ninety minutes.

How Are the Meetings Structured?

Each meeting is divided into two parts. In the first hour, the whole group discusses the text of the session to make sure everyone understands the concepts. Discussion questions are interspersed throughout the text to allow participants to tell their own experiences about the topic being presented.

In the second hour, parents discuss the Reflection questions and exercises, which help them to apply the concepts of the session to their relationships with their kids.

An ideal group will have about twelve to fifteen parents and two leaders. The entire group will meet together during the first hour. The group will divide into subgroups for the second hour, with six to eight parents and a leader in each subgroup. Other sizes of groups will also work, but six to eight people per leader is a good ratio.

What Will I Have to Do Outside the Group?

Each parent is expected to read the material for the weekly session before the group meeting. The actual reading time averages about twenty to thirty minutes per session. The supplemental reading is recommended but not essential to benefit from the course.

Is This Course Intended Only for People Who Go to Church?

Any parent can benefit from this course. It has been used extensively not only in church groups but in community and support groups. The workbook is written in ordinary language so that any parent can participate and find help. Theological terminology and key concepts are explained either in the text or in the glossary (page 159).

Who Leads the Meetings?

Any parent who wants to learn with other parents in an interactive, supportive process can be a leader. However, the best leaders are parents who are willing to be honest and flexible, who are able to provide feedback to the other parents out of their own stories with their kids, and who are committed to personal integrity. If you have access to an experienced small-group leader, take advantage of his or her skills.

What Is the Purpose of the Pregroup Interview?

Parents who enter this course expecting to receive simple formulas for fixing their kids will be disappointed. This course asks parents to look at their own hearts. Experience has shown that if parents have a chance before they join a group to consider the basic assumptions of the course and its approach, they are more likely to invest themselves in the group and have a positive experience.

Pregroup Interview

It's a good idea for the leader of the course to spend an hour with prospective group members before the course begins. In this pregroup interview, parents will receive an overview of the course and decide if they want to participate. Experience with this material has shown that parents are much more likely to commit themselves to the group and to the process of growth if they are able to make an informed decision about the course before they begin. This interview can be conducted one-on-one between a parent and the leader, or it can be a group meeting between several parents and the leader. The interview need not be long; parents will cover course philosophy again when they meet with the group.

The pregroup interview should cover the following issues:

1. A Brief Overview of the Course Philosophy

Parents need a chance to read over the key philosophical issues outlined on pages 3-4 of session 1:

- Parent-focused and biblically based
- Moves beyond traditional formulas
- Leaders are growing parents, not experts

At this stage, a thorough discussion of these points isn't necessary, but parents need the opportunity to decide if this sounds like a course in which they want to participate.

2. Group Covenant

Parents need to understand and buy into the ground rules by which the course will be conducted, as follows:

We agree to participate in the following areas to help make the group successful:

- The reason our group exists is to learn how to be more encouraging and godly with our kids.
- The group will meet for sixteen sessions, once a week for two hours. At the end of the covenant period, we will evaluate our progress and growth.

- Our group will be open to new members until the third week and then will be closed.
- We will meet on the ____ (day of the week), from ___ until ___ (beginning and ending times).
- Our meeting will be held at _____ (place).
- We will use the *Courageous Parenting* workbook as the basis for the group.
- We will spend the first hour discussing material from the workbook.
- We will spend the second hour discussing and applying the Reflection exercises to our own families.

We will agree on the following expectations to help make the group meaningful:
- *Attendance:* We will be here whenever possible (only emergencies will keep us away).
- *Courtesy:* We will come to the group meetings on time.
- *Acceptance:* We will affirm one another's verbal contributions.
- *Confidentiality:* What is spoken in the group remains in the group. However, the confidential relationship between leader and parent-participant does not apply when there is knowledge of sexual abuse, physical abuse, suicidal threats, or extreme neglect of kids. Such incidents often are reportable offenses according to state statutes. Confidentiality may not be guaranteed in these exceptions to the normal limits of confidentiality.
- *Self-discipline:* When we agree to do homework by reading the workbook, we will come prepared.
- *Honesty:* We will be forthright and truthful when we speak.
- *Openness:* We will be candid with others in appropriate ways. We will allow feedback from others in the group and give appropriate feedback in return.
- *Respect:* We will not judge, give quick advice, or criticize parents in the group. We will help make the group experience a safe place for parents to talk freely.

3. Questions and Answers
The pregroup interview concludes with a chance for parents to ask questions about the philosophy and group covenant and to clarify any concerns not addressed.

One

An Internal Shift

PARENTING teens is a tough job, even in the best of homes. A letter I received from a friend named Mark captures what most of us experience at times as parents. He and his wife are raising four kids.

> "Dad, I'm not sure I'm a Christian anymore. In fact, I wonder if the whole Bible is just made up."
>
> "Dad, would it be all right if I went to a movie and the dance with Brittany and another couple next weekend?"
>
> "Dad, can I subscribe to *Teen* magazine?"
>
> "Dad, I don't like coming home anymore. I'd rather stay with my friends."
>
> "Dad, there was a bomb scare today at school."
>
> "Dad . . . Dad . . . Dad . . . "

We are in the teen years. All of a sudden. Three of our four are in preadolescent or adolescent stages, with all the dynamic chaos I've heard older parents talk about. And at 3:00 in the morning a few days ago, I identified the predominant feeling provoked in me as this teenage kettle is boiling—PANIC.

What causes you to panic? What is panic? The *American Heritage Dictionary* defines it as "a sudden, overpowering terror, often affecting many people at once."

I don't know if raising teens affects "many people at once," but it sure affects me and all of our friends with teenage kids!

I don't think I've ever felt less in control of a situation, or more powerless, at times, to do much about it. The forces of our culture loom large. Just last week, a teacher at a local Christian school was arrested for photographing eighth-grade girls in the nude. He used Bible texts to convince them it was okay. My daughter's request to get *Teen* magazine seemed innocent enough until I read some of the articles, one in particular about the epidemic of self-mutilation among teenage girls.

In addition to our culture's chaos are the daily changes in my kids! I spent a wonderful few days with one of our kids in November, talking about the upcoming high-school years, what it meant to walk with God, the simplicity of the gospel. I came away impressed with her deep convictions about God. She now wonders if He even exists (at least she did yesterday; today in church she wanted to take communion!). A couple of my kids are doing worse in school than even six months ago. I don't always like how they dress, how they talk, who they hang out with, what music they like, what they find amusing, what they want to watch on TV and in the movie theater. . . . Whew!

Panic nudges me toward action *(I've got to do something!),* the kind of impulsive action that will at best not be very helpful and at the worst will blow up in my face. I'm reading my fourth book since September on parenting teens. Nothing wrong with that, right? Perhaps not, but maybe I am looking for answers to the wrong question.

The antidote for panic is not to somehow calm myself down. If it were, I could do deep breathing, exercises, meditative prayer—or just eat a nice meal, get some alcohol, or find some other diversion. No, panic is more of an indicator of something deep that is trembling in my own soul. I fear that something vital is about to be lost, and that if I don't do something about it, no one else will. But could there be a subtle attitude of "God, I don't have what I want right now. You're in charge of the universe, so I'm going to 'trust' You to fix this situation"? God may or may not relieve that chaos of three adolescents under the same roof! But can I trust Him to be good, wise, powerful, and working on my behalf, no matter what happens with my kids or in any other circumstance in my life?

Don't panic! Well, I can't help it sometimes, and neither can you, probably. May God use these uncomfortable times in our lives to reveal our lack of trust and to nudge us toward a deeper confidence in Him in the midst of uncertainty and upheaval.

Mark's letter captures the courage needed by parents today. "Confusion," "change," "chaos," "pressure," and even "PANIC" seem to be part of a parent's landscape. Perhaps, as Mark says, part of maturing as a parent is allowing God "to nudge us toward a deeper confidence in Him in the midst of uncertainty."

1. What part of Mark's letter most affected you? How did it affect you?

OBJECTIVE: In this session you will get acquainted with the other members of your parenting group and discuss the basic outlook of this course.

Not in the Concrete!

Surviving as a parent means different things to different people. And being an effective parent often seems out of reach for many of us. Yet, becoming an effective parent is one of the most rewarding tasks in life. It is also one of the most challenging. Part of the challenge involves sorting through the conflicting theories of childrearing we find in books, newspapers, on television, and those we receive from friends, relatives, and teachers. It's so easy to become confused!

Mr. Brown just loved all the neighborhood children. He had a reputation for being kind to all of them. One day, Mr. Brown poured a new cement driveway. After dark, some mischievous kids discovered the fresh cement and decided to leave their footprints and initials. The next morning, when he discovered their handiwork, Mr. Brown was furious. He shouted threats that could be heard for blocks. He couldn't wait to get his hands on the culprits.

The neighbors were puzzled by Mr. Brown's intense reaction to the kids' prank. Mrs. Greene, next door, finally got up the nerve to ask the question on all their minds: "I thought you loved the kids. Why are you suddenly so angry at them?"

Mr. Brown replied, "I love them in the abstract, not in the concrete."

Okay, it's a terrible pun. But the moral of this story applies to all those theories on child-rearing. It's one thing to learn about some *abstract* theory; it's another thing to make a *concrete* application and put the theory into practice!

With so many conflicting ideas on child-rearing, parents need a firm foundation. They can't afford to change their approach every time a new trend or theory surfaces. They need an approach that makes sense, has stood the test of time, and is true regardless of the situation.

The Bible gives that foundation. It also serves as a corrective force to balance the whims of theories that look only at the outcome and forget the reasons behind the actions. By combining the practical insights of professionals with the lasting truth of the Bible, we have a solid and balanced approach to the challenges of parenting in the twenty-first century.

Courageous Parenting is designed to help you in the concrete, everyday world of parenting. It has been developed to make application as easy as possible. Read each session, using the questions and charts to check your understanding of the principles. Then take time each week to practice what you've learned. Success will depend on your commitment and involvement.

What's Different About Courageous Parenting?

The *Courageous Parenting* program is unique for three reasons.

It's Parent-Centered.

Our focus will be on *you,* the parent. We'll look at what kind of parent loves and disciplines wisely.

When my son, Seth, was ten years old, I took him out for a hamburger and a relaxing father-son evening. I just wanted to enjoy my son, chat a little, and have some good moments together. It should have been an easy, fun evening. It wasn't. Seth began to complain about the menu, the slow ordering, the cold food, and the slower server. My anticipated joy turned to frustration in a matter of twenty minutes. I became angry and sullen. I somewhat righteously "corrected" him at the table. Seth lowered his head and drifted away, deaf to any more of my helpfulness.

I felt defeated. Something was going on in my mind and heart that caused me to require Seth to change. It was a strong influence and it damaged my ability to relate well with my son. What was it? How could I have changed that scene from one of defeat to hope? This course will focus on issues like the hidden problems that occurred between Seth and me at that table. As parents, most of us have done things we don't like thinking about, yet it's worthwhile to think deeply about our effect upon our kids.

After all, the only person we can really control and change is ourselves. Rather than concentrating on our kids' actions ("Dad, I won't eat this lousy hamburger!"), we will deal with our responses to them.

___

2. What do you think was going on in my way of relating to Seth at the restaurant table that weakened my relationship with him?

___

It's Heart-Directed, Not Formula-Oriented.

Many parents, especially those dealing with rebellious teens, just want someone to give them a sure-fire formula to help and motivate their kids. This course will help you to think through your unique situations. Formulas may help in the short run, but most of us need help for the long haul. We can manage budgets, money, time, and schedules, but we can't manage relationships—especially when it comes to our kids' lives.

We need to learn ways to *enter relationships,* not just manage them. Entering a relationship requires more than a quick-fix formula. We are in a marathon with our kids, not a hundred-meter dash. It is essential to communicate to our kids that they are loved human beings, not just problems to be solved.

---

3. What goes through your mind when you think about *entering* a relationship with your teen, not just managing it?

It Goes Beyond the Superficial, Requiring Wisdom and Courage.

Many parenting techniques seek to produce an immediate behavior change or provide a quick fix. But it's naïve to tell an anorexic girl to "just eat," or to tell a suicidal boy to "look on the bright side." Parents and counselors who focus only on kids' external behaviors risk ignoring the deeper, more subtle emotional realities of a teen's world. This doesn't give parents much chance of developing the kind of deep love that ultimately stimulates kids to repentance. Our aim in *Courageous Parenting* is to help parents develop new levels of love and justice that touch the souls of their teenagers.

Bon Voyage!

In this course you will learn about a model of parenting that shifts the focus from what you can *never* control (the kind of person your teenager becomes), to what you *can* control (the kind of parent you choose to become). Parenting from this model gives you a sense of hope and strength that you may never have dreamed possible.

Through study and application, as well as working with a group, you will become a more effective parent. If you're willing to stick with it, *Courageous Parenting* will help you reap the rewards of parenting and deepen your influence with your teen.

Blessings on you as you begin this challenging but rewarding journey.

Parenting Pairs Exercise

In future sessions, you will divide into small groups to discuss how the material applies to your own family. In this first session, you'll spend the rest of your meeting getting to know each other through the following exercise.

INSTRUCTIONS: Pair up with someone you don't know or don't know well. That person will be your partner for this exercise.

You will have twenty minutes to discuss the worksheet below with your partner. Each of you will take ten minutes to answer the questions while your partner writes notes about your answers. The leader(s) will keep track of time, announcing when ten minutes are up (and the first person needs to stop talking) and when twenty minutes are up (and the second person needs to be finished).

At the end of the pair time, the leader will gather the group back into the circle. Each person will introduce his or her partner to the rest of the group, using the information from the worksheet. Limit your introductions to three minutes each.

1. What is your name? What are the names and ages of your kids? (Include your spouse's name if you are married.)

2. What are your hobbies or recreational activities? What do you enjoy about these activities?

3. What do your kids like to do with the family? What do they like to do on their own?

4. What do you hope to gain by taking the *Courageous Parenting* course with these other parents?

Two

A Look at Ourselves

A DRAMA is unfolding in the principal's office at Anytown High School:

Dad: Don't think you're going to get any help from us, young man. You're ungrateful. First you start hanging around with those creepy friends of yours. Then you get messed up on drugs. Then you blow it at school and get suspended. Then you run away and don't tell us a blessed thing for two days. Now you have the nerve to tell your counselor that your mom and I don't understand you and don't care about you. Great! I've got nothing better to do than get called in here and—

Graham: But Dad . . .

Dad: You can't even wait till I'm through talking! You always talk back and give me and your mother nothing but crap. Well, now you're going to listen to what I have to say. All this talk about young people's rights, their problems, their poor abused feelings. What about my rights and my feelings?

Mom: Honey, maybe you should let Graham tell you—

Dad: Shut up! So, your dear old Dad is supposed to come down here and tell everyone he's sorry his son is such a screw-up. I'm supposed to say, "Boy, your mom and I really want to help you. We'll forget the whole thing and start over."

Forget it! Don't bother coming home. The place is quieter without you anyhow. You can tell the counselor, the principal, and anybody else that your old man walked in here and disowned you. But you'd be wrong! I didn't disown you. You disowned me. We give you everything you need.

I work myself to the bone for you and get absolutely nothing in return. Well, no more! I don't care. It's all yours from now on. You made your bed, now lie in it. Come on, Sally. Let's get out of here!

Graham: Who cares?!

There is no such thing as a perfect parent. It's easy to read about Graham and his dad and know that you would have done it differently, isn't it? But sooner or later, all parents make mistakes.

Unfortunately, we are often unaware of why we parent the way we do. Any adolescent can stir strong feelings within his or her parents. Yet parents often don't understand how strongly these feelings control their actions and decisions. We may be dictatorial, indulgent, or mature. Or we may swing back and forth between several parenting styles. We may even disagree on parenting practices. No matter what our current parenting style is, it is important for all of us who want to be effective parents to take a serious look at ourselves before we work on becoming the kind of parents we want to be.

OBJECTIVE: This session will help you take a look at yourself as you decide what kind of parent you want to become.

Sometimes you feel all alone; you feel that you are the only one doing such a bad job. This perception can bring discouragement when you start to take a hard look at the effect you are having and then consider why you parent as you do. The truth is, there are no perfect parents. All of us have the opportunity to improve if we are willing to face the truth. As we look at our lives and how we relate, both positively and negatively, God can begin to free us to relate in more mature ways.

An Estranged Son

Long ago, there lived a father and son who didn't get along any better than Graham and his dad. The father was King David; the son, Absalom. David was known for his courage and passion; indeed, the Bible called David a man after God's heart (see Acts 13:22). Yet David lacked critical areas of understanding as a father. He didn't know his own heart well enough to deal wisely with his children. In this area of his life he was operating in blindness.

Our modern culture isn't the only society to deal with abuse, hatred, and even murder within families. David's eldest son, Amnon, raped his beautiful half-sister Tamar. Absalom, Tamar's full brother, was furious with Amnon and wanted David to take action to deal with this family crime.

What did David do when he received news of his daughter's rape? "When King David heard all this, he was furious" (2 Samuel 13:21). He got mad. He raged but then did nothing. He grew strangely quiet about the rape and avoided dealing with his son's crime and his daughter's shame. For over two years, Absalom waited patiently for his father to avenge his sister's rape. Nothing happened. Absalom finally took matters into his own hands by having Amnon murdered. He then went into hiding, fleeing from his father's wrath.

Again Absalom waited. This time he waited three years for his father to send some message to him, good or bad, about whether he would be disowned or received back into the family. Again David did nothing. Finally, in desperation, the king's general, Joab, devised a way to ensure that David would bring Absalom home. Joab used a wise woman to confront the king and help him look at his blind spots. She pretended to be the mother of a son who had killed his brother, and she begged David to pardon her surviving son so that she would not be left a widow. When he did so, she turned the tables on him, showing him his own heart: "When the king says this, does he not convict himself, for the king has not brought back his banished son. . . . But God does not take away life; instead he devises ways so that a banished person may not remain estranged from him" (2 Samuel 14:13-14). Even then, David allowed Absalom to return to the capital city, but he did not fully receive his son back into his heart.

King David had everything the world could offer, but he was still having problems with his son. He desperately wanted Absalom home. Yet he would not meet or talk with Absalom for two more years. David just compounded his problems with his children. Why?

David had never come to grips with his own problems. Years earlier, he had committed adultery and then murdered the woman's husband. Now there was rape and murder among his children, and he couldn't face it. Without reflecting upon his past he would never be able to handle his problems with Absalom in a redemptive way.

A Look in the Mirror

There are hidden dynamics in every family that control how parents look at themselves and their children. For example, our upbringing influences our present behavior as parents. If we have been brought up to believe we must be the best at everything we do, then we may push our kids to be brilliant successes. If we have come to believe we are entitled to have our own way, we may try to force our kids to cater to our wishes or expect them to get others to cater to theirs. However, the results of our parenting efforts are often disappointing. Like it or not, it is the kid, not the parent, who decides how the kid responds.

Because parents are often unaware of why they parent as they do, it is important to take the time to consider what might be going on beneath the surface. We call this process of looking at the hidden dynamics *parental reflection.*

1. What does it mean to reflect as a parent?

2. What are some questions King David might have asked himself if he had begun to reflect as a parent?

Do you remember the first time you saw yourself in a mirror? Probably not. And there's a good chance you didn't care much about how you looked. But as you grew older and continued to watch your reflection, you probably found certain changes you wanted to make. Then you became a teenager, and studying your reflection became second nature. Your hair, your clothes, your complexion (those *pimples!*) — you thought your whole life depended on how you looked. As you searched that mirror, nothing was supposed to be hidden from your gaze.

We need that same kind of teenage zeal to find out the truth about how we're parenting our kids. Without reflecting, parents operate on "automatic pilot." They often end up reacting to their kids on the basis of their own needs. As parents try to protect their personal interests, their own goals and desires become top priority. Graham's dad reacted on automatic pilot when Graham didn't meet his desires. Even godly King David showed little awareness of the forces driving him in his relationships with his children.

When parents do not utilize reflection they lose the opportunity to grow and are limited to addressing their kids on a superficial level. Underlying problems continue to develop unchecked, and all a parent has succeeded in doing is to control the situation for a moment. The unwillingness of parents to look at the truth about themselves and their kids is called *nonreflection.* Operating nonreflectively (with little or no awareness of motivational forces within) is the single most important obstacle to effective parenting.

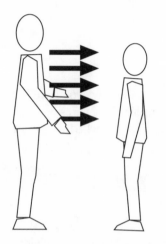

A nonreflective parent operates on autopilot

---

3. What is a nonreflective parent like? How would you describe such a person?

The Causes of Nonreflective Parenting

If reflection is so important, you might wonder why it is so hard for parents to take a serious look at themselves. It's because we don't want to acknowledge the causes of nonreflective parenting. Adolescent specialist Kevin Huggins says there are at least three strong reasons why people flee from facing the truth about themselves:[1]

Disappointment

We are often unwilling to experience disappointment. We have high hopes for our kids, and it's often easier simply to react to a situation. Parents often fail to look honestly at disappointments in themselves and their kids. When we take a look inside, we are often compelled to look at changing something that could take us into new, uncomfortable areas.

Failure

We don't like failure. It's easier to pretend that everything is working out just as we had planned. If we honestly acknowledge failure, we must be willing to take risks and change. Change is difficult for most parents, so it's easier to ignore things that push us to change.

Fear

We are often unwilling to experience the possibility that we can't control or protect what's most important to us. Control is a goal in the hearts of many parents, and the lack of control strikes fear. We frequently don't know what's going to occur next between us and our kids. Fear provokes powerful emotions that drive us in harmful ways unless we deal with it honestly.

Consequences of Nonreflective Parenting

Unfortunately, the consequences of refusing to look inside only get worse the longer parents put it off. Here's why:

No Growth

Nonreflective parents seldom mature. They never get to know why they feel the way they do or how effective they could be. They never enlarge their capacity to love their kids and in turn stimulate their kids to deeper levels of love.

Automatic Responses

Nonreflective parents react to their kids on the basis of their own needs. Automatic responses are only temporary and usually have no long-term impact on the adolescent. Parents who respond automatically often continue in their ineffective approach, decreasing their influence with their kids.

Distance

Nonreflective parents remain at an emotional distance from their kids. The parent-child relationship suffers. When parents refuse to be truthful about themselves, teens see no need to be truthful about their own feelings and actions with mom and dad. Parents ultimately forfeit influence with their teens when they allow distance to remain in the relationship.

Remember

If you want to become an effective parent, you begin by taking a serious look at the way you parent and its impact on your kids. This process is called *parental reflection*. A healthy curiosity about yourself and your teen, honesty with yourself, and ongoing feedback from others are vital parts of this reflection process.

Reflection

1. List some desires you are aware of feeling with regard to your adolescent.

2. List some of the ways you have been most disappointed (desires not met) or frustrated (plans blocked) by your teen.

3. When you look at yourself, what problems in thinking or relating do you see?

4. Talk about your experience of emotional distance with your kids.

4. How are your problems (question 3) related to your desires and frustrations (question 2)?

Action Lab

As you look at your teen(s) this week, identify one or two areas in which you feel disappointment. Mentally make notes to discuss these at your next group meeting.

NOTES
1. Adapted from Kevin Huggins, *Parenting Adolescents* (Colorado Springs, CO: NavPress, 1989), pp. 93–110.

Three

How Teens See the World

A RELATIVE of mine told me about her relationship with her son Aaron a number of years ago. Here are the main details:

When Aaron was ten years old, he suffered a terrible tragedy: his father, with whom he had been very close, was killed in a freak drowning accident. While he cried at the funeral and told his mother he missed his dad, he handled the death without a great deal of trauma. He was able to get on with his life right away, seemingly with few long-term emotional effects.

Five years later another tragedy struck: the girl Aaron was dating broke up with him for another boy. It was his first "true love" that went bad. This time Aaron was not able to get on with his life. In fact, he attempted suicide. He was rushed to a local hospital, where the doctors performed emergency medical services to save his life from a first-time drug overdose. He was within minutes of death by the time his mother got him to the emergency room.

Apparently he could take his dad's death in stride at age ten and then fall apart at age fifteen when a girl dumped him. Some powerful shift had taken place in him.

---

1. What might have been occurring within the teenage Aaron to cause such a destructive reaction?

OBJECTIVE: In this session, you will learn how adolescents perceive the world around them. In doing so, you will gain insight into Aaron's behavior and the many other baffling behaviors for which teens are known.

As you think about Aaron and your own kids (and just about any teen you know), you may be shaking your head and saying, "Kids are *impossible* to figure out! Why in the world wouldn't Aaron be more upset about losing his dad than about losing a girl he probably knew only a few months and wouldn't even remember a few years later?"

Believe it or not, *kids aren't impossible to figure out.* A proverb says, "The purposes in a man's heart are deep waters, but a man of understanding draws them out" (Proverbs 20:5). This proverb teaches us that it is indeed possible to figure out what's going on inside other people (in this case, adolescents), but *we must become people of understanding* in order to do so. Another proverb says, "He who gets wisdom loves his own soul; he who cherishes understanding prospers" (Proverbs 19:8). Seeking deeper understanding of our kids is a wise thing to do. Indeed, our own soul "prospers" over time. Adolescent behavior is always purposeful, even when on the surface it seems irrational or destructive.

There are a couple of areas we need to examine in order to understand how teens look at the world and how what they see affects their feelings and actions.

Even those teens who don't seem obsessed in these ways experience a great deal of pressure about appearance. They're also learning to judge others by their appearance. From seductive ads for Calvin Klein jeans to Air Jordan athletic shoes, the message is the same to kids in our culture: You must have "the look" to be accepted.

Our son, Seth, is now fourteen. He spends nearly twenty minutes getting himself ready for school by standing in front of the hall mirror. My wife and I call it "The Ritual"— standing in front of the mirror, grooming his hair, meticulously placing strands in just the right order, creating just the right look before he leaves for school. From what his friends' parents tell me, it seems his classmates nearly all have adopted the same ritual. I once made the mistake of playfully running my hand through his hair after the ritual. This was met by a howling shriek and protests never to touch his hair again. Sadly, he feels the pressure to look a certain way to be accepted.

---

2. Give an example of how one of your kids deals with expectations to look right.

Changes in What the World Expects of Kids

First, we must realize that *adolescence brings on changes in what the world expects from a person.*[1] As a child begins to look more like an adult on the outside, the world responds by heaping adult-sized expectations on him or her that are hard for the adolescent to meet.

Expectation #1: How They're Supposed to Look

Unfortunately, our world believes you're only as good as you look. The emphasis on appearance causes some teens to become obsessed with clothes, hair, weight lifting, or dieting.

Expectation #2: How They're Supposed to Think

Children and adults think very differently. Some psychologists refer to the way children think as "concrete thinking." This means young children take things pretty much at face value. Adults, on the other hand, use what Swiss psychologist Jean Piaget called "formal thinking." This means that adults are able to use abstract principles and reasoning in addition to their concrete experiences. During adolescence, children begin to use more adultlike, or "formal," thought processes. The adolescent can now perceive more subtle cause-and-effect relationships and can understand and feel them more than he did as a child.

Aaron provides a good example of this. One reason he was able to carry on after his father's death is that he looked at it in concrete terms: His dad wasn't around anymore. His mom was around. Ice cream still tasted good. He could still go to Boy Scout camp. As a teen, he saw the breakup with his girlfriend in the light of formal thinking: If he were better looking, she would still want to date him. Probably no one would ever want to date him. He was worthless and painfully alone, so why bother living?

Formal thinking is an essential process on the road to adulthood. It enables a person to reflect honestly on how and why she affects and is affected by her world. This eventually allows her to operate by personal choice rather than simple obedience to what others tell her. Of course, these personal choices can be either wise or foolish, but we'll address that in a later session. The point here is that the transition from concrete to formal thinking is necessary but rocky for teens.

Why is it so rocky? The main reason is that it's gradual. Parents and teachers would like kids to wake up one day suddenly able to grasp abstract concepts, such as algebra and long-range planning. Unfortunately, it usually takes years for a child's brain to make the full transition. Also, a teen has to learn to use his new abilities through trial and error. Aaron's early attempt at abstract thinking (*No one will ever want to date me.*) was not as sophisticated as an adult might want from him.

Parents might wish that the onset of formal thinking was as predictable and obvious as the onset of teething in a baby, but it isn't. Some kids begin to use formal thinking as early as ten years of age, while others don't begin until they are fifteen or even older. Stress can delay the process. Some twenty-year-olds continue to have difficulty seeing the subtle connections between cause and effect. The process can frustrate adults, who know that a young person faces increasingly important decisions (whether to work hard in school, what life goals to set, how to handle money and sexuality) and needs to approach them with adult thinking skills.

---

3. In your own words, what is the difference between "formal" and "concrete" thinking? Can you give some examples?

Expectation #3: How They're Supposed to Relate to Others

As a child begins to look like an adult, the world (including his parents!) usually saddles him with the burden of behaving like an adult in his relationships with other people.

To illustrate this idea, let's look at a model of relationships created by Dr. Ross Campbell called *The Emotional Gas Tank.*[2] In order to function in healthy ways, children and adolescents need to have their emotional gas tanks kept full by others—typically by parents. So parents are the emotional "fuelers," and kids are the "drainers."

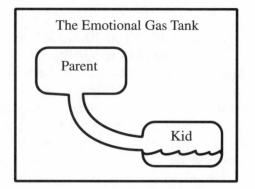

The Emotional Gas Tank

Parent

Kid

A teen finds himself in a painful situation when he is pushed prematurely into the position of "fueler" (perhaps by a parent or a partner in an intense dating relationship) when he is still desperately in need of being fueled himself.

It's important to remember that adults are fuelers and kids are drainers. And teens are still kids when it comes to their emotional gas tanks! As you may have discovered by now, teens can "drain your tank" in ways you've never been drained before. This isn't wrong in any way; it simply comes with the territory of parenting an adolescent and dealing with all the changes he or she is going through. What once filled your kid's tank ("kissing it better," a big cuddle in the rocking chair) doesn't work anymore. It's a tough job, but still an essential one.

Some parents feel drained by the pressures of their lives, and if they have no healthy, intimate relationships to fuel them, they may begin turning to their adult-looking teenage kids to fill their tanks. Or at the very least, they may begin to resent the fact that someone who is taller than they are and increasingly demanding adult privileges still needs so much fuel. These are natural parental feelings, but however tall or demanding teens are, they are still kids when it comes to their need for emotional fuel.

Now that we've looked at the changes teens experience in what the world expects from them, let's examine another change to help us understand how teens look at their world.

Changes in What Kids Notice About Their World

As a child enters adolescence, he begins to observe a few things he never noticed before.[3] His new awareness grows with his increasing ability to use formal thinking. His observations have an enormous impact on the way he sees his world.

Observation #1: How Things Really Are

We learned earlier that young children accept most events in their lives at face value. That is concrete thinking. For instance, when Aaron's father was killed, Aaron was able to observe that his dad was no longer around. This made him sad, but he was able to accept it. Teens, however, *see how things really are in comparison to how things should be.* A teen in Aaron's situation will be sad that his dad is not there, but he will also be anguished when he thinks about how much better it would be to have his dad around. Adolescents experience a lot of disappointment and pain when reality doesn't measure up to their ideals. And they have very high ideals of how their parents should respond to them!

Observation #2: How Things Can Turn Out

During adolescence, kids develop a capacity to visualize the future and foresee painful events on the horizon. The reality teens see doesn't come close to what they long for (unfailing love, for example, as we'll see in session 3). Kids can spend enormous amounts of time and energy thinking about, dreading, and scheming to avoid these negative realities they anticipate happening.

Charles, a single parent who lived in an apartment building, awoke to hear a fire alarm blaring and distant sirens howling. It was early in the morning, and his twelve-year-old daughter, Amber, stood trembling beside his bed. Amber confessed to pulling the fire alarm on a whim. When the fire truck arrived, Charles had the "privilege" of telling the fireman what his daughter had done. The 6'4" fireman, bending low, stared into Amber's panicked eyes and said sternly, "Young lady, don't do that again." Later, Amber said, "Daddy, don't tell anyone at church what happened." She experienced the pain of how things can turn out, and powerful emotions surfaced in her to avoid experiencing more shame with the kids at church.

Observation #3:
How Things Can Be Avoided

It's easy to get a small child to think that mom and dad have eyes in the backs of their heads. How else could parents know you've just stuffed all your clothes in the toilet when they're not in the bathroom with you? As kids become more sophisticated, they come to realize that it's possible to hide things from their parents and others. In fact, it is frequently the easiest way to get along in life. Deceptive relating often becomes the usual path for kids if they anticipate pain.

Proverbs 26:23-26 captures the way deception affects people, including our kids:

> Like a coating of glaze over earthenware
> are fervent lips with an evil heart.
> A malicious man disguises himself with
> his lips,
> but in his heart he harbors deceit.
> Though his speech is charming, do not
> believe him,
> for seven abominations fill his heart.
> His malice may be concealed by decep-
> tion,
> but his wickedness will be exposed in the
> assembly.

Often kids living in a fallen world come to the conclusion that they (not God) must meet their deepest needs. Such thinking ultimately backfires with kids, yet they can stubbornly hang on to these ways of relating.

Seth was ten when we traveled to Denver for graduate training in biblical counseling. My wife and I believed that God was clearly directing us. Our son disagreed. He loved his school, his friends, and his extended family — staying put in our hometown was his sole pas-sion. School in Denver was agonizing for him. He didn't fit in with new friends. He became angry, bored, sullen, often weeping and thinking about how much he missed friends back home. The year after we returned home, he came to my wife and me, sheepishly telling us "confessions" about his time in Denver. "Dad, I used to swear at school, just to fit in. The other kids swore all the time, and I felt so alone with no friends. The only way I knew I could make friends was to be like them. But I kept my swearing away from you and Mom because I knew you wouldn't like it. I felt bad then and I wanted to tell you now." Our son fundamentally has a good heart. He loves God, and we believe deeply in him. Yet in Denver, Seth was able to see only how *pain might be avoided* by fitting in with his peers through swearing. In his thinking, his deceptive ways seemed justified because his emotional pain was so strong. Furthermore, we, his parents, could not fully relieve his pain.

---

4. What desires do you think Seth was trying to meet?

5. Do you see your kids trying to meet their needs in some of the same ways? Explain.

Teens learn that it's easy to avoid conflict with parents by hiding things from them. As kids get older, they find they can keep their true feelings and thoughts private from the adults in their world. They also learn that in many cases, their parents may not want to know the truth. Many parents find the reality of their kids' thoughts and actions so painful that they would rather not know about them.

All Those Changes Pack Quite a Punch!

As adolescents experience the inevitable changes in what the world expects of them and what the world is like, these experiences affect them profoundly. The resulting ongoing process is painful but important; it greatly influences the person a teen grows up to be. Thus, it's important for parents to understand how these changes affect their teens.

Stability

While a child views his world as fairly predictable, an adolescent sees nothing but threat to his environment on all fronts: at school, at home, and among friends. He comes to realize his parents can't protect him from the bad things out there. Seth knew that even though we loved him, we couldn't protect him fully from his classmates' verbal jabs at him. School became an unstable place.

Esteem

As the world changes in the way it treats kids, and as kids perceive these changes, they suffer a serious crisis in the way they feel about themselves. Like many adults, teens today usually find their self-esteem in two areas: appearance (how good they look) and performance (how well they do). During childhood, adults often look at the "darling little girl" or the "class clown" with appreciation. During adolescence, the cute kid and the class clown don't have the same attractiveness for adults.

In fact, those same behaviors are often annoying to adults when exhibited by teens.

Security

Proverbs 14:26 says, "He who fears the LORD has a secure fortress, and for his children it will be a refuge." Our kids have a built-in need to experience security; parents are the ones whom God charges to model this sense of "refuge" or security. The biblical metaphor of a "fortress" is a good picture of parents who try to keep kids spiritually secure in a hostile world. Yet even the best parents can't completely meet their kids' needs for security. So much of what teens once found safe and predictable now appears uncertain. Peers, siblings, school, and a host of other forces are unpredictable. Often kids feel a need to gain control of their world and create a sense of security. This can be a destructive path. Teens learn that they live in a world of selfish people and they feel afraid that they won't be able to find love in such a world.

Why Do These Changes Hit Kids So Hard?

As you read this, you might be thinking to yourself, *Hey, all this is true for me, too! I struggle with stability, esteem, and security. Why do adolescents tend to "lose it" emotionally instead of finding a way to deal with it, as I do?*

There are a few reasons—all related to the fact that adolescents aren't adults yet:

1. The first time a person experiences disappointment in personal relationships at a very high intensity is usually in adolescence. As with Aaron's failed dating relationship and his attempted suicide, teens often experience much greater frequency and intensity of relational disappointment, but they haven't yet learned the skills to respond well.

2. While teens haven't completely developed formal thinking skills, concrete thinking is too simplistic for the painful world in which they find themselves.

3. Their peers and the media teach teens that the stress they're experiencing can be relieved by the excitement of dirty movies, the effects of alcohol or drugs, or the closeness (however short-lived) of sexual relationships. The fact that parents usually don't approve of these things or they forbid kids to participate in them, sets parents up as the bad guys: "Why won't they let us do these things if these things relieve the pain and stress we're experiencing?" Adolescents see parents as actively interfering in what appears to give them stability, esteem, and security.

Three Styles of Parents

1. rescuers
2. adversaries
3. allies

As we've seen in this session, kids entering adolescence experience major changes in the way they see the world. The way they view their parents also changes. At this time in a kid's life, parents come in three styles: rescuers, adversaries, and allies.

> Rescuers: Will they bail me out every time I run into difficulty?
>
> Adversaries: Will they oppose my every move?
>
> Allies: Will they stand beside me as I go through crisis after crisis?

This third path—that of the Allied Parent—is the one we want to walk. Parents who consistently focus on changing themselves first will have the greatest positive influence on their teens. The more that parents find active ways to stand beside their kids during their struggles, the more their biblical influence will increase over time.

6. Does your teen see you as a rescuer, an adversary, or an ally?

Remember

To understand the way teens see the world, parents must understand some changes their kids are going through. Adolescence changes what the world expects from kids and enables them to observe things in their world that they hadn't seen before. These changes have painful effects on kids. Teens also change in the way they view their parents, seeing them as rescuers, adversaries, or allies.

Reflection

1. In your Action Lab from session 2, you noted one or two areas in which you felt disappointment about your kid(s). What were those areas of disappointment?

   In order to understand the changes your kids are going through, it can be helpful to recall what life was like for you as a teenager.

2. What are two or three significant, painful events you experienced as an adolescent?

3. What made them so painful? How did these events threaten you?

Sometime this week, find someone you can talk to about what life was like for you as an adolescent. Write down some points from your discussion about what it was like to grow up in your home.

NOTES

1. Kevin Huggins, *Parenting Adolescents* (Colorado Springs, CO: NavPress, 1989), pp. 49–56.
2. Ross Campbell, *How to Really Love Your Teenager,* (Wheaton, IL: Scripture Press, 1981), pp. 28–30.
3. Huggins, pp. 57–62.

4. What lasting impact did these events have on you? How did these experiences affect the way you learned to cope with life?

5. What roles (rescuers, adversaries, allies) did your parents play as you went through these crises?

Four

Why Teens Do What They Do

April 14, 1912. The North Atlantic Ocean, off the coast of Newfoundland. The S. S. *Titanic,* the largest, most luxurious passenger ship ever built, was steaming toward New York on its maiden voyage. The captain was pleased with the way things were going; the passengers were in good spirits, enjoying a dinner dance in the elegant ballroom. The *Titanic* was a magnificent ship. It was a reassuring thought for the captain on that foggy evening. He noticed a few small chunks of ice in the water near the ship, but smiled, thinking, "It'll take a whole lot more than those little things to sink this ship!"

At 11:40 P.M., the passengers noticed a slight "nudge" but dismissed it as nothing important. After all, the *Titanic* could take care of itself among the tiny icebergs the crew could see. Even as the great ship began to tilt, apparently taking on water, the band played on, the people danced, and the captain didn't worry. Hours passed before the alarm was sounded. Desperate attempts to contain the flooding failed. At that point, nothing could be done to prevent tragedy. The S. S. *Titanic,* the ship that couldn't be sunk, slipped under the surface at 2:20 A.M. on

April 15. Although lifeboats were manned and launched, some 1,500 passengers and crew perished. Ironically, the dance band continued to play even as the ship went down. No one knows if the captain ever understood what happened; like all good sea captains, he went down with his ship.

Later, investigators concluded that the *Titanic* went down because the tiny icebergs the captain and crew hadn't taken too seriously were merely the tips of huge underwater ice mountains. It wasn't what the crew saw above the water that proved fatal to the *Titanic;* rather, the huge danger was lurking below the waterline, where they couldn't see it.

OBJECTIVE: In this session you will learn about the hidden forces (under the waterline) that drive teens to behave in foolish ways.

Like the captain of the *Titanic,* many parents sail happily along until their ship (shall we call it the S. S. *Parent*?) is wrecked. They collide with what looks like a tiny iceberg and the next thing they know, a huge hole is ripped in the hull of their parenting effectiveness. Our kids' outward behavior is just the tip of the iceberg; there's a huge ice mountain lurking under the waterline that explains a great deal about the little bit we can see. We need to learn from the *Titanic's* tragedy to look "below the waterline."

We'll continue using the "iceberg" theme in this session. Take a look at this diagram:

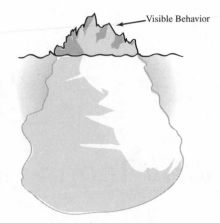

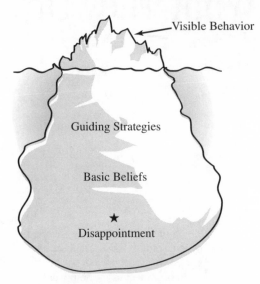

The Tip of the Iceberg: What Kids Do

The only thing parents can actually see that indicates what's going on inside their kids is their outward behavior. To parents, this behavior can be annoying, gratifying, frustrating, a source of shame, or a source of pride. It is this outward behavior that sometimes causes parents to fear that "something's wrong" with their kids. However, a teen is like an iceberg, and behavior is just the tip. Below the waterline lies a vast mountain that parents can't see. The Bible uses the term *heart* to describe the hidden part of the iceberg.

Performance and appearance are two of the major arenas in which teens act out in their behavior what is hidden in their hearts. Such behaviors include obsession with dieting or hair, a loss of interest in appearance, weird haircuts, and intense competitiveness in sports or academics. Many parents are frustrated that so many of these behaviors are driven by peer pressure. They begin to wonder, *If Johnny jumped off a bridge, would our own kid jump off after him?*

I was a typical teen in many ways. Then, as a high-school freshman, I stopped being the nice, clean-cut boy who had always enjoyed a close relationship with his mom. Although I didn't rebel violently or openly, I did pull away from my mother at this time and remained distant from her for years. I began to dress in the tattered-blue-jeans-and-flannel-shirt uniform of the cool crowd. To my parents' horror, I began wearing my hair long.

My mother was confused by my aloofness, while my father was just angry that I stayed out with my friends so much and projected an I-can-handle-life-myself attitude. My behaviors troubled my parents, but the behaviors alone didn't tell the whole story.

---

1. What are some of the behaviors your kids do that upset you or take up your attention?

2. How does it feel to know that below your teen's behaviors lie purposes that neither you nor your teen may fully understand?

parents and kids are victims of a fallen world where unfailing love is not fully available to them. Our kids desire unfailing love and significance, but even the best parents can't fully meet their kids' desires. Thus, all teens (and all parents) will experience some degree of disappointment in the parent-teen relationship.[1]

Below the Waterline: Why Kids Do What They Do

Thoughts and feelings that parents can't see are the causes of their teens' visible behavior patterns. Recall that Proverbs 20:5 says, "The purposes of a man's heart are deep waters, but a man [or parent] of understanding draws them out." A parent's task is to begin to help teens make sense of their own purposes. Because kids don't have adult maturity, they often can't see the connections between their outward behaviors and the forces or motives inside them that are driving their decisions. Many parents report asking their kids, "Why did you do that?" and receiving the response, "I don't know!" The frightening fact is that this is often the truth: kids frequently don't know why they do what they do.

The parents' job is to help teens connect their purposes to their behaviors. Teens need to learn that they are icebergs. Enormous ice mountains of disappointment, basic beliefs, and guiding strategies lie beneath their visible behaviors. Let's take a careful look at the parts of the mountain that lie beneath the waterline.

Disappointment

Disappointment is at the core of a kid's emotional iceberg; it drives all of his thoughts and ways of relating. "Many a man claims to have unfailing love, but a faithful man who can find?" (Proverbs 20:6). Every parent and every teen has a passionate longing to be loved unfailingly. Yet the sad reality is that both

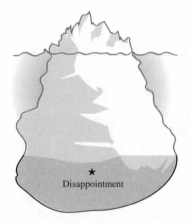

Disappointment

Here is how disappointment plays itself out for kids: In session 3 we discussed teens' Emotional Gas Tank. Parents are primarily responsible to provide emotional fuel for teens. The fuel that kids need comes in three forms:[2]

1. *Unfailing love*: Proverbs 19:22 says, "What a man [or teen] desires is unfailing love." Kids (and adults) yearn for relationships that don't fail them. Teens bring into their relationships with parents and others a passionate desire to be loved completely and unfailingly.
2. *Significance*: We all want to feel that what we do and say is important to other people.
3. *Security*: Relationships are supposed to be refuges where we can be safe.

People of all ages long for these things. Children learn at a very young age how to manipulate their relationships in order to get love, significance, and security from parents and others. Depending on the parents, a child might work hard at ballet lessons, get into Boy Scouts, or be a "Daddy's girl." Basically, children learn to meet the expectations of their parents in order to earn love and esteem.

When a child becomes an adolescent, however, the strategies that earned them love, significance, and security begin to fail. We discussed this change in session 3. When childhood strategies no longer work, an adolescent experiences a deep, heartfelt disappointment. Often multiple disappointments begin to pile up in a kid's heart and can overwhelm him or her.

I experienced a profound disappointment when I was fifteen. One day, I was banged up in a basketball accident and taken to the hospital emergency room. Once the initial patching up was taken care of, I had to wait for a final check-over by the doctor. While I waited, my mom told me at length and in detail how miserable her marriage was with my dad. She planned to leave our home and divorce my father. My world shifted to slow motion. I couldn't believe my mother's words: "I am leaving our home to be happy elsewhere." Something powerful occurred in my thinking that day as I listened stoically to my mom.

I was at a stage where I needed my mom to fill my emotional gas tank. Not only did she fail to do it, she tried to get me to fill her tank by confiding in me as one would to an adult. I was devastated, but I didn't let it show. I just quietly nodded, staring hard at my mother and not saying a word.

---

3. What can a parent do to reduce the risk of a kid experiencing the level of disappointment I experienced at fifteen?

Basic Beliefs

Disappointment is the core of the ice in a teen's heart. Around that core, another layer of ice accumulates: a layer of basic beliefs.

Kids come to trust certain life strategies to fuel their emotional tanks. They feel betrayed when those strategies fail them as they hit the teen years. They feel betrayed by their parents, their world, and God, and they feel a great deal of anger and contempt for all three. When this happens, kids develop a new basic belief about the world. This basic belief is an operational definition of adolescent foolishness:

> I know what it takes to get my deepest desires met. I don't need you, and I certainly don't need God. I will rely on myself to make what I need happen. I can come up with ways to gain love and acceptance all by myself (because my parents and God have failed me). I can meet my needs independently of God or anyone else.

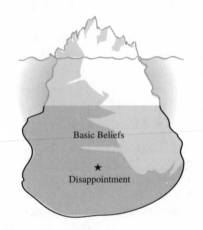

A second, related foolish belief is:

> I need to do everything I can to protect myself from pain.

Teens foolishly believe that pain relief is their strongest need. They believe more than anything else that they need relief from the pain of not being deeply loved and accepted. And they believe they don't need anyone but themselves to meet that need. Most of us adults can see how foolish these beliefs are. None of us, no matter how hard we try, can gain unfailing love and acceptance from others simply on the basis of our own efforts. We may come up with a strategy that works for a short time, but eventually it will leave us high and dry and more disappointed than ever. Further, if we are wise adults, we know that we need Christlikeness and maturity far more than we need relief from pain. However, the world is full of foolish adults who want nothing more than pain relief. Is it any wonder then that most kids think this way too?

God tells us these beliefs lead to disaster: "The rod of correction imparts wisdom, but a child left to himself disgraces his mother" (Proverbs 29:15). Teens left to themselves will gravitate toward the view that trusting themselves and pursuing pain relief is a workable plan for their lives. The disgraceful results of such foolish beliefs are legion: drugs, dropping out of school, family conflict, and so on.

Some may wonder why teens take such foolish and destructive notions as their basic beliefs about life. If humans were essentially rational creatures, it would make sense to wonder. But the Bible portrays immature human nature as anything but rational. It is essential that we understand this: *Kids have an active disposition to choose foolish beliefs; it's the way they're built.* Proverbs 22:15 says, "Folly [or foolishness] is bound up in the heart of a child." Foolishness is deeply imbedded in teens' thought processes. Dr. Dan Allender compares foolishness to the barnacles cemented to the hull of a sea vessel. Barnacles intractably wed themselves to a ship's hull to the point where they change the shape of the hull and hinder the ship's ability to steer. Like barnacles, foolishness is firmly cemented to a child's heart and cannot be easily dislodged through the parents' strategies of discipline. These barnacles do not simply cling to a child's outer behavior; they are attached to the inner person, the heart, which steers the child's emotions and choices.

---

4. Why won't good education alone fix a kid's foolishness?

Children begin to form foolish beliefs before adolescence, but the shift from concrete to abstract thinking and the other disruptions of adolescence, seem to cement these beliefs in place. Once they form in a teen's heart, they are *very, very resistant to change!*

While my mom and I were still at the hospital, I made a decision that affected my life well into adulthood: "If my own mom can wreck my whole life like this and hurt me this much," I reasoned, "I'm not ever going to be close to her or anybody else. I will never let anyone hurt me like this again." A hook was now set in my heart, unknown to anyone, and not even fully known to me. My disappointment left me emotionally exposed. I felt justified in trusting only myself because my disappointment was deep and needed immediate relief. In reality, my father too failed my mother, but I needed someone to blame for my pain to somehow cope with life. A foolish foundation was laid in my thinking and relating that began to show visibly, above the waterline, in my relationships.

Guiding Strategies

All of us allow our basic beliefs about the world to form our "guiding strategies" for getting what we want out of life and other people. These strategies determine the behavior we will use to meet our goals, so they explain a lot about teens' unpredictable behavior. Adolescent strategies are the unique ways in which kids try to make life work out in a disappointing, often hostile, relational world. Some examples of teen strategies are:

- *The good kid,* who tries to earn love and significance from others
- *The defiant kid,* who uses power, intimidation, and anger to control parents
- *The manipulative kid,* who is extremely personable, charming, and seductive
- *The enmeshed kid,* who gives up on his or her own sense of self and looks to a parent to manage his or her life
- *The promiscuous kid,* who uses sex to disgust, shock, and hurt parents
- *The beautiful kid,* who uses exceptional beauty or strength to gain approval

5. What strategies do your kids use to make life work for them?

Because teens long for unfailing love, significance, and security, and because they believe they can meet their own needs independently of God or others, they tend to come up with guiding strategies that will earn them love and acceptance based on their own efforts. Their strategies enable them to meet other people's expectations in order to get those people to fill their emotional gas tanks. In many cases, strategies involve yielding to peer pressure to be accepted by other kids or using attention-getting behavior to get love from parents. In some cases, kids use distancing strategies to avoid being hurt by others.

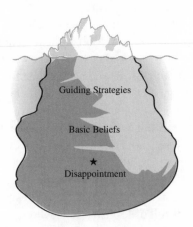

I decided that I had to avoid pain at all cost, and it was up to me and me alone to earn love and acceptance. I developed a guiding strategy that I would do what was necessary to meet others' expectations of me and gain the acceptance I longed for, but only as long as there was little threat of being hurt. This strategy led me to dress and act like my peers (to gain acceptance) and to distance myself emotionally from my mother (to avoid pain). As I met and began dating Cathy in college, and later married her, I was afraid to become emotionally close to her because she might hurt me as my mom had. This distancing strategy plagued my relationships throughout my adolescence and early adulthood.

Relational disappointment does not result only from dramatic family failures like mine. Kids can become disappointed over time because of multiple and sustained little wounds as well. A teen who feels habitually ignored by her parents, one who receives confusing feedback from parents about her efforts, or even one who comes to believe that her choices make no positive difference to others can experience disappointment just as profound as that from a more traumatic single wound to her heart.

The baffling behaviors that teens demonstrate are not nonsensical. They are purposeful actions designed to achieve love, significance, and security. They are guided by strategies born of a foolish basic belief that a teen can meet her own needs with no help from God or others.

---

6. Why is it so important to help kids connect their behaviors to the purposes that lie behind the behaviors? Why isn't it enough just to make rules about their behavior?

7. How does defiance serve this foolish belief: I can come up with ways to gain love and acceptance all by myself.

8. How does compulsive goodness serve this foolish belief?

So their strategies won't work; they will be even more disappointed than ever.

There's good news, however! It's when kids are dealing with the consequences of their failed strategies that parents have the most influence with them. Wise parents look for ways to bring on the collapse of these strategies, for then God begins to look attractive to kids. We'll learn more about this in a later chapter.

Remember

The sometimes baffling behavior of our teens is only the tip of the iceberg. Wise parents know that outward behavior, however strange, is always purposeful, and they learn what forces are operating under the waterline. Those unavoidable forces are disappointment, foolish basic beliefs, and guiding strategies. Fortunately, parents have an opportunity to have influence with their kids if they understand what's going on.

A working definition for adolescent foolishness is the belief that "I can come up with ways to gain love and acceptance all by myself."

Reflection

1. When you did last session's Action Lab, what one or two things did you discover about how others saw you as an adolescent?

The Good News and the Bad News

Teens will face some unfortunate consequences as they act upon the belief that they can succeed on their own. The truth is, all paths apart from God lead to disappointment.

A wise parent will want to develop "hunches" about what's happening below the waterline with his or her teen. Pick one of your kids and think about what might be going on with him or her.

2. *Disappointment.* What kinds of disappointment might your teen be experiencing?

3. *Basic belief.* Put into words how your teen would complete this phrase: "Life works for me when . . ."

4. *Guiding strategies.* What kinds of guiding strategies or behavior patterns do you see in your adolescent's life?

Action Lab

As you observe your teen this week, jot down several observable behaviors that seem to reflect basic beliefs about how life works for him or her. Bring your notes to share with the group next week.

NOTES
1. Kevin Huggins, *Parenting Adolescents* (Colorado Springs, CO: NavPress, 1989), pp. 41–45.
2. Huggins, pp. 62–68.

Five

Drifting Apart

IT was summer at a rustic lake cabin. My grandpa and I rose early in the morning. With a steaming cup of coffee in his hand, Grandpa surveyed the lake and did a double take.

"Where is it? Where's my beautiful blue fishing boat?! It's gone!"

Grandpa was beside himself with anxiety over the loss of his boat. He paced up and down on the dock. Finally he said, "David, did you do anything to my boat yesterday?"

I assured him, "No Grandpa, I wasn't even on the dock yesterday. But Susie was there playing with a friend."

Grandpa went into the cabin and found my sister, Susie, then nine. She looked away from Grandpa's eyes as he asked her the same question about his boat. "Grandpa, I think I left the boat untied. We were playing with it, and I just forgot about tying it back to the dock! I'm sorry. I'm sorry!" she blubbered.

Grandpa stormed out of the cabin. He ran to the edge of the lake, frantically scanning it for his boat. Nearly a half-mile away he could see a little blue dot ebbing away from the

cabin, bobbing up and down on the choppy lake. He had found his boat but had no idea what to do next.

My sister learned a hard lesson that day: there are currents below the waterline that will make a boat drift away unless it is securely tied up.

Just as waves will inevitably cause a boat to drift away from the dock unless the boat is tied securely, so the upheavals of adolescence can cause our kids to drift away from us unless we actively work to slow the rate of drift. Many parents never notice that their kids are drifting away until they, like the little boat in our story, are just specks on the horizon.

King David was such a parent. Recall from session 2 that David had a terrible problem of distance in his relationship with his son Absalom. Absalom had been in exile for more than three years after having his brother Amnon murdered. Yet David loved Absalom: "And the spirit of the king longed to go to Absalom, for he was consoled concerning Amnon's death"

(2 Samuel 13:39). David felt a continual longing to connect with his son. Yet his actions took him in the opposite direction toward continued emotional distance and a refusal to reconcile. David's emotions and actions weren't adding up.

Eventually, David allowed Absalom to return home, but with this condition: "He must go to his own house; he must not see my face" (2 Samuel 14:24). David and Absalom had drifted apart to the point that David would no longer set eyes on his son, even though he longed to see him. Absalom continued to drift further away from David over the next two years. In desperation, Absalom used "juvenile delinquent" behaviors to force the issue of David's avoidance—he had his men burn General Joab's field (2 Samuel 14:30). Absalom was frantically trying to use whatever persons or resources he could to get his father's attention. But David continued to relate to his son in ways that maintained emotional distance.[1]

What made David respond in this way? He was unaware of his own heart and the forces driving his decisions. His unstated relational goal with his son was to maintain distance by using three defenses: continuing to justify his anger, ignoring his own past failures, and building a self-protective layer around himself so he wouldn't feel his sorrow and loss. David was like a boy standing inside a stack of tires and saying to the world, "Now you can't hurt me. I'm safe."

---

1. When have you felt or acted out defensiveness toward your teen in ways that maintained an unhealthy distance?

OBJECTIVE: In this session, you will learn how teens drift out of relationship with their parents unless parents take active steps to keep them close.

Five Stages of Drifting

Why do parents and kids drift apart? There are several stages of drifting in the parent-teen relationship.

1. Changes in Kids

We learned in session 2 that as children reach adolescence, they experience physical, emotional, intellectual, and spiritual changes. At times, parents can hardly recognize the people their kids have become. These changes, although perfectly natural and necessary, alarm parents.

For example, Jay was a big, awkward, quiet, and powerful twelve-year-old. When he was in the sixth grade, his parents began to be concerned at how he bullied younger kids and even threatened teachers in class when he was angry with them.

2. Fear

As parents observe the changes in their kids, fear starts to grow within them. Parents realize their kids could make life miserable for them, perhaps by failing school or doing drugs or becoming sexually active. Any of these things could expose parents as failures, a fate that threatens all parents (whether they know it or not!).

Jay's mother began to panic when she thought about her son continuing to perform poorly in class. She repeatedly had to go to school to take Jay home because he would just sit in class to pass time. He ignored the teachers, often smiling and folding his hands behind his neck.

3. Strategy

Once a parent has been hit by these growing fears, he begins to develop a strategy to feel that he's back in control. We call this response "knee-jerk" parenting: a parent doesn't reflect; he just reacts. Knee-jerk strategies usually take the form of rules for behavior: what boys a daughter is allowed to date, how early a kid must be home at night, or how much time a teen must devote to homework.

Jay's dad, the enforcer, became angrier and tried to demand that his son study for school. Jay's dad threatened withdrawal of his fatherly relationship and took away all of Jay's privileges, even grounding his son to his bedroom most of the day.

4. Hardening Response

Most of the time, teens greet their parents' control strategies with a hardened resolve that no one, especially their parents, is going to control their lives. Adolescents are very intolerant of control and will react with defiance of some sort.

Jay continued to defy his mom's pleading and his dad's yelling to force him to do his schoolwork. By age fourteen he was tardy most school mornings, moody, and increasingly disrespectful to teachers.

5. Power Struggle

The final stage of drifting in the parent-teen relationship is a cycle of power struggles in which the incompatible goals of the teen and his parents clash outwardly, followed by periods of "cold war" in which there is no outward conflict but tremendous emotional distance. This cycle of power struggle, cold war, power struggle, cold war will continue indefinitely. At this stage, the teen is just a speck on the parent's horizon because the kid and parent are growing apart.

Jay continued his pattern of passive noncompliance toward his parents and teachers. He half-heartedly went to school, conveniently "lost" assignments, missed classes, and failed most courses. His mom and dad were furious and terrified. How could their fourteen-year-old fail school? What had they done wrong? Dad continued to yell, and Mom pleaded for Jay to "just stay in school." Jay smiled, enjoying his parents' pleadings while he did nothing.

---

2. How have you responded to the changes in your teens? Do you notice any signs of power struggles in your responses to them?

It's Easy to Create Distance

Jay's parents had no idea they had done anything to create distance between Jay and them. That's true for many parents. There are all kinds of ways in which parents can distance themselves in order to avoid feeling out of control. Let's look at some of these strategies. Even if you don't see yourself in any of them, these examples may help you to think of ways in which you create distance.

Trivialize or Ignore Kids' Struggles

Parents who are afraid to get involved with the painful side of their kids will refuse to take seriously problems with boyfriends, the swim team, or the "in" group at school.

An extreme example of ignoring struggles is the parent who is taken completely by surprise when a child attempts suicide. "Sure, he mentioned that Betsy had broken up with him and that he couldn't live without her, but I never dreamed that he was *this* upset!"

Develop Parallel Lifestyles

Some families look great on the outside, but inside there is a tremendous emotional gap between parents and kids. These families are very busy: Mom and Dad play tennis three times a week, and the kids are involved in numerous after-school activities. They simply don't spend any time together. Their lives are on separate tracks.

Avoid Emotional Interaction

Some parents do not interpret any of the nonverbal signals their kids are broadcasting through body language and other means. Also, they don't interact nonverbally with their kids. Touching, sitting close, and especially *eye contact* are the primary means of nonverbal communication. It's not unusual to find parents who will talk at their kids but never look them in the eye.

Sam and Mary had all teenage boys in their family. Yet whenever any of the kids voiced a disagreement with Sam, he would avoid eye contact and raise his voice. This strategy used power to silence the kids. "What do you mean, I never listen to you! You're so wrong, as usual." Sam never dealt with the boys' emotions.

Take No Initiative in Confronting Obstacles to Unity

Many parents have the vague feeling that there are problems with their kids, but they avoid the pain of dealing with those problems. For instance, parents who are called to the school office because their daughter has cut class three times in two weeks might get through the meeting with the counselor, extract a promise from their daughter never to cut school again, and go on their way. They're content as long as the bad behavior stops, but they don't investigate to see whether there are underlying problems that caused the behavior in the first place.

Criticize or Attack Small Offenses

Parents who are deathly afraid their kids might turn out badly often drive their kids away with an exaggerated discipline style.

Withdraw and Pout

That's easy enough. If your kids aren't turning into the people you'd like them to become, just back away. Don't forget to pout; it lets your kids know how unhappy they're making you!

Marge had four children. The oldest two teenagers were "good kids," usually eager to please her. But sometimes when Marge wanted them to do extra chores or run to the store for her, Tim and Deanna would complain. She would usually sigh, lower her head in mock despair, and faintly say, "Oh well, I guess I'll just have to do for you all by going myself." Then she left the room until the kids responded by giving in. The kids were made to feel guilty for not responding quickly to mom's subtle demands.

Delegate "Care and Feeding" to Someone Else

Many parents feel that someone else has a responsibility to take care of their kids' emotional needs, or can do it better than they ever could. Countless parents fall into this trap, from single moms who beg friends to act as "male role models" to a busy couple who expect the school counselor or youth pastor to handle any emotional problems their kids might face.

Keep Them Helpless or Dependent

On the surface these parents seem to be doing everything for their kids. But really, they're just attempting to bring about closeness with their teens by making the kids incapable of functioning on their own. Unfortunately, this strategy usually backfires.

3. Which, if any, of these strategies do you use with your kids?

Disappointment causes distance. Distance destroys relationships. It is essential that parents recognize these warning signals of distancing within themselves and take active steps to combat it.

Warning Signs in Kids

It's equally essential that parents pay attention to signals from their kids that they're drifting away. Warning signs in teens include:

Role Reversal

The teen accepts responsibility for the drift he feels in his relationship with his parents and blames himself. This causes him to become the pursuer in the parent-teen relationship. Over time, such a teen becomes emotionally exhausted.

Unmanageable Levels of Anger, Confusion, or Depression

When their yearning for unfailing love from their parents meets with distance, kids find themselves on an emotional path that begins with discouragement, moves on to frustration, escalates to anger (sometimes extreme or violent anger), and ends in depression, which is simply anger turned inward.

Premature or Abnormal Sexual Activity

Kids who don't find love at home will look for it elsewhere, and many are deceived into thinking they can find it in sexual relationships.

Deliberate Violation of Boundaries Established by Parents

This can take the obvious form of disobeying curfews, or it can be more sneaky, such as cranking the stereo to an unbearable level in response to being grounded.

Increasing Expressions of Indirect Anger

Kids often express their emotions in ways that seem totally unrelated to the cause. For example, an angry, discouraged kid who has been unable to get his parents' attention in any other way might let his grades drop in order to get a reaction.

In the story above, Jay was trying to get his dad's involvement by failing school and provoking his dad to anger. Some emotional involvement from parents, even negative emotion, is better than no involvement.

My Kid's Drifting Away! What Do I Do Now?

In the story at the beginning of this session, my grandfather had to take action once he realized his fishing boat had drifted away from the dock. Fortunately, parents have some options when their kids start to drift. The following is a list of general ideas for fighting distance in parent-teen relationships. (We'll get into specific ideas in a later session.)

Priority

Make it your top priority to develop a relationship with your teen. It will take a huge commitment of time, energy, and skill.

Goals and Behaviors

Practice recognizing the goals and behaviors of your own distancing strategies. For example, before Sam can improve his relationship with his sons, he will need to look at his attempts to control them by silencing their complaints. Control and avoidance of pain are common goals of nonreflective parents. You will learn more about how to identify the goals that dictate your behavior in session 8.

Purposes and Plans
Behind all of your distancing strategies are purposes and plans deep within your heart. Begin to look at those. For example, fear is often at the base, and your plan is to do whatever it takes to keep the most fearful issues away. Session 8 will address parental plans in depth.

Acknowledging Distance
When you sense distance in your family, bring it up for discussion.

For example, Jay's dad could reflect upon the tension between him and his son, instead of yelling. "Jay, I know I feel angry with you, but that's my issue that I need to work on. I do feel the tension, but I really don't want it between you and me. I want something good between us."

Permitting Distance
You can't force your kid to be close to you. Permit distance to exist between you and your teen, but *only when it's his choice.* Express regret that you're not closer ("I wish we could be closer."), but not despair ("How can you treat me like this?!"). Always remain available if he decides to move back into the relationship.

Communicating Acceptance
Make deliberate attempts to let your teen know that you accept her, especially when conflict, discipline, or disappointment is present in your relationship.

Remember
Unless parents take action to prevent it, kids will drift away during adolescence. Parents are often guilty of under-the-waterline strate-

gies that distance them from their teens. There are warning signals that indicate distance is creeping into the relationship, and there are deliberate steps parents can take to fight the distancing process.

Reflection
1. When you did the Action Lab in session 4, what basic beliefs did you conclude your teen lives by?

2. Recall how drifting was handled in your own family when you were growing up as an adolescent.

3. What did your parents do to combat or contribute to the drifting?

4. What do you do to deal with the drifting in your relationship with your teens?

Action Lab
Have a chat with your teen about your relationship. Explore how he or she might feel separated or distant from you. Discuss possible ways the two of you could be closer.

NOTES
1. Adapted from Kevin Huggins, *Parenting Adolescents* (Colorado Springs, CO: NavPress, 1989), pp. 95–110.

Six

How the Home Affects Kids

FOURTEEN-year-old John had just returned from riding his new 100 cc Suzuki motocross cycle. John and his cycle were a greasy mess. As usual, he ignored his dad's safety rules and was cleaning his cycle engine with gasoline while smoking a cigarette. Suddenly, a burning ash fell on the engine, and the whole cycle erupted in flames. John panicked and kicked the flaming bike into his parents' backyard swimming pool!

Mom and Dad drove up just as the cycle did the "deep six" into the pool. Although John was flustered and embarrassed, he was already planning how he could replace his bike. He knew he could count on his mom to take care of things when he messed up. He also knew his dad was too absorbed in work to interfere with the way his wife dealt with their son.

A few days later, John's mother, Lilly, went to visit Allen, John's school counselor. She went to discuss John's failing grades, but the conversation got around to the motorcycle incident:

Allen: Wow, Lilly! This motorcycle fiasco of John's is unbelievable. What have you decided to do about it?

Lilly: Well, I think we need to put it all behind us. John is so sorry, and it was an accident. Things like this happen to teenagers—you know that. Anyway, I think some good has come out of it. He promised he'd work harder in school if I would help him out with his bike.

Allen: Help him out? John has repeatedly ignored teachers' efforts to help him with his homework. And surely you don't mean fixing that burned-up Suzuki?

Lilly: Oh, no. It couldn't be fixed. I called every motorcycle shop in town and they all said they couldn't help. So I decided to surprise him! I bought him a brand-new Suzuki. He was so excited! It was only $1,800. I used the insurance money from his old bike, plus part of the money I'd been saving for vacation.

Allen: Lilly, are you sure that was the best thing to do? John caused the fire! Shouldn't he have to pay something to replace it?

Lilly: You're too hard on him. John just needs a little encouragement. . . .

1. What do you think Lilly was trying to accomplish by getting a new motorcycle for her son?

2. How do you think John saw his mother in light of the way she parented him in this typical example?

John made a costly error by violating the safety rules of motorcycle maintenance. But the error didn't cost *him* a thing. It did cost Lilly something. And the cost was more than just the money—it was something far more valuable.

OBJECTIVE: In this session, you will learn about how the home environment shapes teens' foolishness.

Home Environments

By their actions and reactions, parents shape the home environment that affects their teens. The home environment can be on "firm footing," where kids feel secure, or on "quicksand," where they don't know their boundaries or what they can count on from their parents. A home environment on firm footing weakens teens' foolish thinking.

Sometimes, actions that on the surface seem loving and helpful are doomed to strengthen a kid's foolishness. For example, Lilly made things much easier on John (and herself!) by buying John a new motorcycle with no cost to him. Yet this was a destructive parenting move because it fueled John's foolishness. We'll look more at this later in the session.

Taste and See

We have two choices when adolescent foolishness develops in our kids (and it *will* develop sooner or later). We can either unknowingly strengthen their foolish thinking, or we can consciously work to weaken it. A maturing parent actively takes steps to thwart foolishness, or built-in arrogance, in the heart of his or her teen.

The Bible offers some insight into how we can best encourage our teens to forsake foolish paths in life.

> Therefore, rid yourselves of all malice and all deceit, hypocrisy, envy, and slander of every kind. Like newborn babies, crave pure spiritual milk, so that by it you may grow up in your salvation, now that you have *tasted* that the Lord is good. (1 Peter 2:1-3, emphasis added)

Do parents really use deceit, hypocrisy, and even malice with their adolescents? Perhaps more than we think. Yet teens need to taste relationships with their parents that are flavored with the love and grace that stimulate repentance in kids' hearts. Parents can't force involvement with adolescents, yet teens are drawn to parents who give them a taste of God's goodness.

foolishness = built-in arrogance

Two Forces That Shape the Home Environment

God demonstrates both justice and grace toward His children. The following passage from Jeremiah reflects God's passionate heart as a father. God expresses His redemptive love through justice and grace *at the same time.*

> "Is not Ephraim my dear son,
> the child in whom I delight?
> Though I often speak against him,
> I still remember him.
> Therefore my heart yearns for him;
> I have great compassion for him,"
>   declares the LORD. (Jeremiah 31:20)

In loving us, God never ignores our sin. Yet at the same moment, in disciplining us, His heart is always good toward us. God's love ("delight") and justice ("speak against him") operate simultaneously toward His children. Even as imperfect parents, we are to model this kind of love and justice to weaken foolishness and promote wisdom in our kids.

3. How would you evaluate yourself in terms of relating to your teen with love and justice operating together?

In our opening story, Lilly's reactions to John were motivated by her *feeling* of love for her son. This feeling was so strong, it caused her to completely ignore John's *actions,* his foolishness. However, if we want to challenge a teen's foolishness and promote maturity, we need to deal with both feelings and actions. The forces that shape the home environment are the parents' feelings and actions, as well as their responses to the feelings and actions of the kids. Let's look at these forces in more detail.

Uncompromising Responsiveness [1]

Uncompromising responsiveness is one dimension of a maturing parent's feelings and actions. When a parent's reaction to her teen's actions manifests a willingness to do whatever it takes to help her teen see how his actions affect God, others, and himself, the parent is demonstrating justice. We are to attach the same significance to our teen's heart and choices that God attaches to ours.

When we are uncompromising in our response to our teens' actions, we can look like the "bad guys" to them, and at times it will engage us in conflict with them. But this *just* response is essential if we are to weaken their foolishness and guide them to maturity.

An uncompromisingly responsive parent always asks himself: *Do my own purposes seek to weaken and confront my adolescent's foolishness, even when it hurts our relationship at times?* A wise parent never ignores a teen's foolishness.

Deep inside herself, a teen will ask this question: *Am I free to do whatever I want?* Obviously, no adolescent can do whatever she wants, regardless of relational consequences, without a wise parent confronting such choices.

The real question teens are often asking by their actions is, *What kind of person do I have to be to accomplish something of lasting significance?* Basically, teens want to know that adults and others stand up and take notice of what they think and do in the world.

When he was thirteen, Seth approached me after we played a game of basketball. He had beaten me badly, and I was catching my breath. Seemingly out of nowhere, he said, "Dad, I want to be not just okay in basketball, but I want to be incredible, like Michael Jordan. Is that wrong?" I knew his question was important. I could have rebuked him as unspiritual or tried to convince him that he lacked the raw athletic talent to protect him from the pain of later disappointment. But what he really wanted to know from me was, "Do you and other adults really take notice of me and see my contributions as significant?" A wise parent's response will show his kid how he is having an impact on others, whether positive or negative.

That kind of responsiveness often requires a parent to set aside feelings (anxiety about damaging the relationship, yearning to protect the child from pain, rage at being challenged) and act in the best interests of the teen. However, uncompromising responsiveness is not cold. Parents need to demonstrate the same kind of passionate concern for their teens' maturity that God does.

Unconditional Involvement[2]

Unconditional involvement includes both feelings and actions. Unconditional involvement is unconditional love, or what the Bible calls grace. God loves us regardless of who we are or what we've done. Below the waterline, teens are asking, *What kind of person do I have to be to get someone to want and love me?* The wise parent's answer is, "You don't have to be anyone but yourself to be loved and valued." The parent's attitude is, *I love you because my heart is good toward you.* This attitude bubbles up from warm feelings of affection even though it sometimes coexists with hurt and anger.

My parents' divorce while I was in high school plunged me into personal chaos. I felt confused, betrayed, and alone except for one family member, my grandmother Ruth. She became a parent figure to me. Her home became the only refuge I knew during those lonely high school years. She frequently invited me over for dinner, spent hours chatting with me, and sought ways to help me meet financial and school needs. One scene stands out poignantly. On a Tuesday evening she opened the door and greeted me with a spreading smile. Putting both hands upon my face, she pulled me close to her face, and gently whispered my favorite words, "Oh, David, it's so good to see you again." Her hands lingered on my face, her eyes locked on mine in full enjoyment of just seeing me. In those moments at her door, I knew she deeply delighted in me. I didn't need to prove anything, for Grandma tangibly expressed to me the reality of unconditional involvement. Those warm greetings made me feel alive and secure in my turbulent world.

My grandmother did not have to blind herself to my many character flaws in order to feel that way about me. No doubt it's sometimes hard for us to be so enthusiastic about seeing our kids' faces, especially when foolishness has been driving their behavior. Yet it's possible to respond with justice to teens' behavior while cultivating the kind of compassionate, generous, affectionate heart that God has toward us.

---

4. In what ways would your teen say he or she feels deeply loved by you? How do you show that love?

An attitude of unconditional involvement tends to pull kids toward the home and ultimately toward God. It gives them a taste of God's grace, which is attractive to them. Like sharing a sweet, juicy watermelon on a hot summer day, parents offer relationship that "tastes good" and draws their kids' hearts.

The Four Basic Home Environments

Our home environment is shaped by our particular combination of responsiveness and involvement. The chart on the next page maps out the four basic home environments. Note that the horizontal axis represents the level of uncompromising responsiveness, while the vertical axis represents the level of unconditional involvement, from low to high. The gray area in the center is a balance of those forces that maturing parents strive for over time. This area represents a home environment on firm footing. Outside that area are home environments built on quicksand that fail to adequately incorporate both justice and grace.

The two axes create four quadrants, or four home environments shaped by the balance of responsiveness and involvement. Each environment tends to create a type of parent and a type of kid. Those types are listed in the quadrants along with characteristics that might serve as clues as you try to find yourself and your teen in the chart.[3]

We won't examine each home environment in detail; the chart is easy to follow. What we will do is look at John and his parents to see where they fit in the chart and why. Then you'll be able to consider where your family fits and identify areas that God may want you to look at in your own home.

John is a bright, personable, social kid. He's well liked by peers and adults. He is popular, yet constantly performs below his abilities at school and at home. John's parents see him as a manipulator, even a con artist. Looking at the lists of characteristics on the Home Environments chart, John shapes up as a Controlling/Manipulative kid. That makes sense when we see that a Controlling/Manipulative kid lives in a home that is high on the involvement (love) scale, yet low on the responsiveness (discipline) scale. Remember, Lilly was willing to overlook John's setting a motorcycle on fire because she

didn't want to be "hard on him." Her husband, Rick, was relationally detached from John—low on both involvement and responsiveness. His influence in the home was almost zero, so Lilly's approach set the tone.

John came to have an under-the-waterline basic belief that "life depends on controlling others." His parents played right into his hands. His father was under control just by staying out of the way, so John focused his efforts on his mother. John worked hard to get his mom to lower her expectations for him because it made his life much easier. Lilly feared that conflict with her son could destroy her relationship with him, so she appeased him in every potential area of conflict. This parental strategy is called "silencing kids by giving in." Yet Lilly was unknowingly losing influence over John.

When I asked John to express in one word how he felt about his mother, his quick response was, "That's easy. The word is *gullible*. I can get whatever I want out of my mom." He loved her, but he knew she could be controlled. Here was a fourteen-year-old who clearly understood the below-the-waterline relationship with his mom *better* than she did. He used it to manipulate his mom for foolish purposes that she failed to challenge.

Remember

Both uncompromising responsiveness and unconditional involvement create a home environment that shapes teens' basic beliefs toward maturity. On the other hand, if parents ignore either of these responsibilities, teens will head toward deepened foolishness.

The Four Basic Home Environments

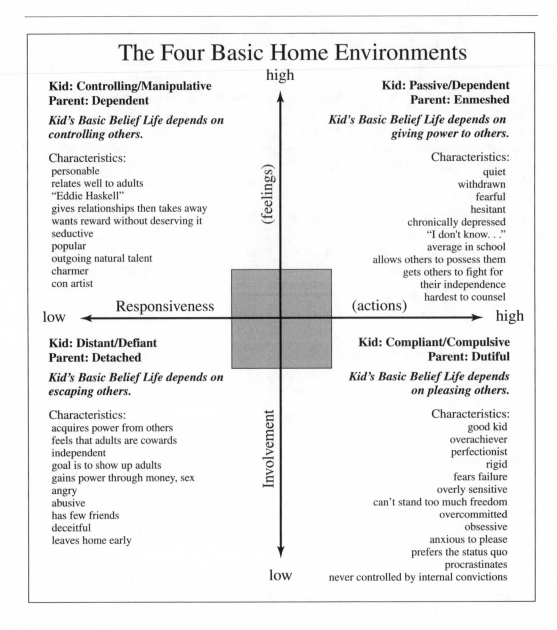

high

Kid: Controlling/Manipulative
Parent: Dependent

Kid's Basic Belief Life depends on
controlling others.

Characteristics:
personable
relates well to adults
"Eddie Haskell"
gives relationships then takes away
wants reward without deserving it
seductive
popular
outgoing natural talent
charmer
con artist

Kid: Passive/Dependent
Parent: Enmeshed

Kid's Basic Belief Life depends on
giving power to others.

Characteristics:
quiet
withdrawn
fearful
hesitant
chronically depressed
"I don't know. . ."
average in school
allows others to possess them
gets others to fight for
their independence
hardest to counsel

(feelings)

low ←——— Responsiveness   (actions) ———→ high

Involvement

Kid: Distant/Defiant
Parent: Detached

Kid's Basic Belief Life depends on
escaping others.

Characteristics:
acquires power from others
feels that adults are cowards
independent
goal is to show up adults
gains power through money, sex
angry
abusive
has few friends
deceitful
leaves home early

Kid: Compliant/Compulsive
Parent: Dutiful

Kid's Basic Belief Life depends
on pleasing others.

Characteristics:
good kid
overachiever
perfectionist
rigid
fears failure
overly sensitive
can't stand too much freedom
overcommitted
obsessive
anxious to please
prefers the status quo
procrastinates
never controlled by internal convictions

low

Reflection

1. From last week's Action Lab, what one or two things did you talk about with your teen that will help you become closer to each other?

2. Look together at the Home Environments chart. Determine where your kids fall by looking at the Characteristics section of the chart. Explain why you see your kids that way.

3. What style of parenting do you see in your own life? What kinds of foolish thinking does it reflect?

Action Lab

Look hard at your teen's behavior this week. What does your kid's behavior confirm or deny about the hunches you had concerning his or her foolish thinking? What do you learn about yourself when you see your teen's behaviors?

Bring back your observations next week to discuss with the group.

4. What style of relating do you see in your adolescent's life? What foolish thinking does it reflect?

NOTES
1. Kevin Huggins, *Parenting Adolescents* (Colorado Springs, CO: NavPress, 1989), pp. 130–132.
2. Huggins, pp. 129–132.
3. Huggins, pp. 132–140. The chart entitled "The Four Basic Home Environments" is adapted from Huggins, p. 132.

Seven

Influencing Our Teens

ROBBY is a family man in his mid-forties. He has a great job, is well respected by his peers, and has a loving, involved wife. Robby and Mary have four adolescent kids, ranging in age from fourteen to nineteen. All the kids are doing well socially and at school. Every area of this dad's life is "wired down" tightly and doing well. Every area except for fourteen-year-old Cal.

Cal is Robby's "problem child." It seems that Robby and Cal are always locked in a power struggle, always at each other's throat. Cal is so defiant and distant that Robby has decided that the best way to deal with him is simply to wait until he's eighteen and leaves home. Mary is caught in the middle, trying to play referee. Robby describes her goal as "emotional détente with my son," just an easing of tensions in the home so that father and son don't destroy each other. Because every attempt Robby has made to control Cal's behavior has resulted in failure and rejection, Robby has stopped trying to be involved. Who can blame him?

OBJECTIVE: In this session, you will learn to maximize your influence through increased relationship with your teens.

A Dad Who Yearned for Relationship

Most people have heard the story of the prodigal son (Luke 15:11-32). This young man demanded his inheritance early, went off into the wide world and blew it all, found himself poor, hungry, and ashamed, and decided to head for home again. Even though his father had every right to tell his son to get lost or at least say, "I told you so," he didn't. He welcomed his wayward son home with open arms. Here's what happened when the boy "came to his senses" (Luke 15:17).

At the end of his burned-out partying days, the son was reduced to the most degrading work. When he could stand it no longer, he decided to return home to his father. "But while he was still a long way off, his father saw him and was filled with compassion for him; he ran to his son, threw his arms around him and kissed him" (Luke 15:20).

In our modern society, we miss the aspect of this story that would have shocked Jesus' audience. In Jesus' day, no self-respecting father would ever have treated a rebellious son the way Jesus described in this story. The returning son would have had to grovel on his hands and knees in front of the father, pleading to return home. The father could have harshly received the son into servitude or sent him away, but he could *never* do what this father did.

This father did something reckless. He was passionately moved and he responded to his son's needs without regard for what others might think or say. Do we do that with our kids? This father's heart was deeply moved by his son's desperate situation ("filled with compassion for him"), and he took the initiative to rebuild their relationship ("ran to his son"). A Jewish father in Jesus' day would have had to hike up his long outer garment, tie it to his waist, and run to meet his wayward child. Only a man heading into battle would run like that; no "good" Jewish father would dare to do it. This father also chose to get emotionally involved with his son again ("threw his arms around him and kissed him"). This kind of relationship building is a model for us as we seek to have relationships with our own kids.

---

1. When your kids mess up and seek forgiveness, how do you respond to their efforts to return to relationship with you?

It's a Dirty Job, But Somebody's Gotta Do It!

It's easy to understand why Robby wouldn't want to pursue a relationship with Cal. Dealing with Cal is painful and usually feels as though it will do absolutely no good. However, the only way for parents to influence their kids is by building relationships with them that can stand up to the testing of adolescence. As the saying goes, "It's a dirty job, but somebody's gotta do it!" And that somebody is the parents; they are the ones vested with the responsibility for guiding their kids into adulthood.

As parents become increasingly involved with their teens, they'll notice some uncomfortable side effects: the potential for relational pain increases, and the need to expend more and more energy in the relationship also increases. On the plus side, they'll become filled with compassion for their teens as they see the world through their kids' eyes, and their level of influence with their kids will increase.

The Consumer Parent[1]

Robby didn't want to bother working on a relationship with Cal anymore because the only thing he ever got out of it was pain. There's a disturbing passage in the Bible that speaks of this dilemma:

> You were called to freedom. . . . If you keep on biting and devouring each other, watch out or you will be destroyed [consumed] by each other. (Galatians 5:13,15)

This passage describes relationships in which people frantically pull and grasp at each other to get what they want until they end up consuming or destroying each other. It is a horrifying fact that even parents can devour their kids—to greater or lesser degrees—in order to meet selfish desires. Whenever they fail to minister to their kids' needs because they are more concerned with their own needs, parents are acting as consumers.

Isn't this what Robby was doing? He tried to manipulate Cal into giving him the respect and love he needed. When that failed, he withdrew from the relationship because it wasn't doing anything positive for him. Robby had become a consumer parent who wanted only relationships that made him feel good. His relations with Cal were focused solely on changing his son into an acceptable person. He was siphoning the fuel from his son's emotional gas tank in order to keep his own tank full.

The consumer model of parenting is ineffective in developing influence. In this model, parents "consume" or use the teen for their own purposes. One dad told me that his life-long motto toward his teen was, "I'm outta here!" The internal "motto" of the consumer parent often is little more than *"Nothing can be gained by staying in a painful relationship if it doesn't benefit me."*

The Ministry Parent:

It is possible to build a strong relationship with an adolescent. And it's vitally necessary that parents do this in order to influence their kids. One definition of parental influence is this: "Influence is a parent's active involvement in his or her teen's world in order to produce positive effects by intangible or indirect means."

The parent becomes emotionally "alive" to the teen and so has greater ability to stimulate the teen's thinking toward maturity. There's no way that can happen without a strong relationship. And it's hard work!

We called the parenting model that focuses on the parent's needs a *consumer* model of parenting. An alternate model, in which the parent takes emotional risks in order to address the teen's deepest needs, is a *ministry* model. Some parents may be astonished to learn that God calls them to minister to their children. They would like to leave youth ministry to the professionals. But real parenting is a ministry, requiring the same commitment and offering the same eternal results that any pastoral ministry requires.

A teen's deepest need is to become a mature human being, intimate with God and other people. In order to serve this need, a parent must practice both uncompromising responsiveness and unconditional involvement. We will explore how to put responsiveness into practice in sessions 12 through 15. In sessions 7 through 10, we will focus on involvement.

Five Levels of Deepening Influence[2]

Involvement is the key to deepening our influence with our teens. A parent's involvement must start on the lowest level and slowly work up. Think of the levels of involvement as a series of concentric circles, each circle repre-

The Consumer Model of Parenting

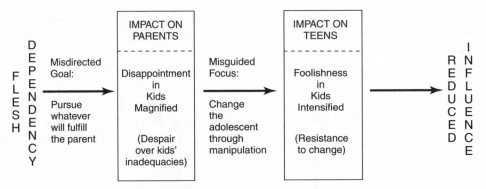

From Kevin Huggins, *Parenting Adolescents*, p. 148.

Levels of Parent-Teen Involvement

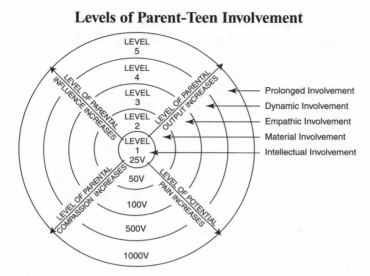

From Kevin Huggins, *Parenting Adolescents*, p. 177.

senting a "voltage" of risk. A parent can, in this model, withstand up to one thousand volts without being destroyed.

Level 1: Intellectual Involvement

Intellectual involvement is an awareness and appreciation of the nuts and bolts of a kid's life. What's going on at school? Who is his girl-friend? What music does he like? What do he and his friends do after school? It's important for this involvement to be a healthy curiosity about the details of the kid's life and not incessant nosi-ness that simply pushes the kid further away.

When Robby decided to abandon his role as a Consumer Parent and to begin his active pursuit of a relationship with Cal, he had to start by being involved on the lowest level—intellectual involvement. Robby became *curious* about Cal's life and discovered, through observation and by asking questions, that Cal's primary interest was video games. After school, Cal spent time with friends in arcades. He subscribed to *Game Players* magazine. (There actually is such a thing!) All of this was in addition to the hours he spent in front of the television at home playing Nintendo. Robby learned the names of Cal's favorite games and a little about each one.

Cal was taken aback by his dad's sudden interest and rejected it at first. But Robby gently persisted, bringing up casual questions when he could. Over the course of many weeks, he gradually learned more and more about his son's world. Up until then, he'd had little awareness of his son's interests, friends, music, or hobbies because he wasn't involved at even low levels of relationship.

2. What do you know about your teen's world? What does he like? What are her interests?

Level 2: Material Involvement

Material involvement requires deliberate acts of kindness toward others in order to com-municate they are loved and valued. The two main avenues of material involvement with our kids are doing something fun (like play-ing video games) or something productive (like teaching the teen to read poetry or bake pastries). Material involvement is something we are used to doing with our adult friends. For instance, sending a friend flowers and a card in response to the death of a family member is material involvement.

It's absolutely essential that you have gone through the intellectual involvement stage before you attempt material involvement. In the example above, a sympathy card and flowers might not be appropriate if our friend's mother abused our friend as a child and they hadn't spoken in years. We have to know what's going on in a person's life (and this can take weeks and months!) before we try to get materially involved.

After learning more about Cal's passion for video games, Robby decided to take the next step into material involvement with his son. Robby started to play Nintendo at home and went with Cal to the video arcade to play games. This took a lot of effort on Robby's part because, like many adults, he couldn't stand video games! (Warning: To avoid his teen's resistance, a parent must first involve himself in his kid's world, not force the kid into his world.) Although Cal rolled his eyes and shrugged the first few times his dad suggested they play Street Fighter, eventually they started going to the arcade together every Saturday morning to play. Robby was starting to look at his son's passions and desires, and he wanted to begin to meet his son's needs.

3. Try to explain material involvement in your own words.

4. In what ways are you materially involved with your teen?

Level 3: Empathetic Involvement

Empathy is allowing yourself to feel the emotions and thoughts of others. Empathetic involvement with a kid is coming to understand the very personal forces (the unmet desires and foolish plans) that motivate her to act the way she does and to be the person she is. Many parents never get to this level of relationship because it requires increased effort, deeper self-reflection, and desire. Once a parent understands his teen's desires and plans, he must respond with gentleness and empathy, lest his kid withdraw once more.

It's just about impossible for a parent to have this level of involvement until his kid feels comfortable and safe enough to let down her defenses and allow the parent to have a glimpse into her feelings.

As the months went by and Robby continued his weekly trips to the video arcade with Cal, there were a handful of occasions when Cal let Robby know how he felt. Robby was surprised to learn that Cal had always viewed him as hostile and that Cal had backed away from him to avoid being hurt by his harsh words.

5. How do your teens see you exhibit empathy toward them?

Level 4: Dynamic Involvement

Dynamic involvement with a teen is the result of months of prayerfully waiting and working on intellectual, material, and empathetic involvement. Parents moving into this level need greater levels of trust in the Lord in order to continue to pursue the hearts of their kids. At this level, parents are finally able to help their kids make the inner shifts necessary to change the kind of persons they are becoming. This is the level where parents have deep influence. Furthermore, parents can challenge a teen's foolish thinking at this stage with a higher degree of openness and dialogue.

One night, Robby looked in on Cal right after he went to bed. He caught Cal fully dressed, climbing out the window. Robby grabbed Cal, and after a scuffle Cal gave up. He was just going out to be with his friends, he explained. "You know you're not allowed to go out late at night like this," said Robby. "What keeps you from responding to me? It must be in part some way I am relating to you. Why do you feel like you have to fight me on things all the time?"

"You're mean! You never want me to be with my friends! You don't care about me," screamed Cal.

In the midst of this painful conflict, Robby and Cal got into some issues that were at the bottom of Cal's distance and defiance. They even discussed some possible solutions to some of those issues. Had Robby not been working hard at increasing his level of involvement with Cal at every opportunity, this might have been just another miserable fight with a "rotten kid." Instead it became an opportunity for Cal to discuss some important issues with his dad. Robby's heart had begun to change and soften toward his son. And Cal, who had learned over the months that his dad sincerely desired relationship with him, was willing to listen and respond to his dad's involvement.

Level 5: Prolonged Involvement

Now, here's the bad news: Once you've worked and worked your way up the staircase to the highest level of involvement, it's not over. Parents must continue to stay involved with their teen at each of the first four levels until the teen is actually mature enough to do the same for others. Prolonged involvement takes place over months and years of influence.

What If It Doesn't Work?

As you read this chapter, you might be thinking, *This stuff's okay for most kids, but there's no way it's going to work on my kid!* It's true that many teens are resistant to parental involvement in their lives. If we have failed to get involved before their teen years, it's likely we'll encounter resistance when we try to get involved later on. Here are some things to keep in mind if your teen is resistant to your attempts at involvement:

- Even an unwilling adolescent can't totally block parents' involvement at all levels. Personal contact within the home breeds influence at some level with our kids. Something is getting through to them.
- Keep trying. There's almost always a crack in an adolescent's armor because deep on the inside your teen wants to be loved and respected.
- You cannot force involvement or else you will get more resistance. You must respect a teen's decision to resist your involvement.
- Express regret, but not anger or despair, when your teen resists involvement. For example, Robby might say, "I'm here for you if you want to talk," rather than, "Cal, how can you ignore your mother and me?"

- Never retreat. Never stop asking for involvement.
- Use your teen's reluctance and discomfort as a mirror to look at your own relational style. This part is the tough stuff for a parent to continue to do.

Remember

A ministry model of parenting calls you to put your teen's need for maturity ahead of your desire for a smooth, pain-free life. To minister effectively you need to build influence by deepening your involvement with your teen. Your involvement must start at the lowest level and work slowly up to higher levels. You will move back and forth in these levels with your kids as you attempt, then fail when they frustrate you, and finally begin again to seek to increase your involvement. Developing influence with your teen is not a quick fix but a long-term process to see him or her move toward maturity.

Reflection

Using the chart below, evaluate how well you offer involvement to each of your teens at each level. Place a score in each box: + (good), S (satisfactory), - (poor).

	Level 1 Intellectual	Level 2 Material	Level 3 Empathetic	Level 4 Dynamic	Level 5 Prolonged
Name:					
Name:					
Name:					

Action Lab

Take another look at your responses to your teen. Use the chart below (the same one you used in the Reflection section) to evaluate your relational involvement this week. Compare the two charts, and bring both to the next group discussion.

	Level 1 Intellectual	Level 2 Material	Level 3 Empathetic	Level 4 Dynamic	Level 5 Prolonged
Name:					
Name:					
Name:					

NOTES
1. Kevin Huggins, *Parenting Adolescents* (Colorado Springs, CO: NavPress, 1989), pp. 146–150.
2. Huggins, pp. 176–186.

Eight

Building Bridges, Not Walls

IN the song "Carpenter Story," David Wilcox tells of two neighboring farmers. Even though they were neighbors, they hadn't talked to one another for years. They'd had a falling out over a stray cat, of all things. The cat went over to one farmer's porch for awhile, and that farmer thought it was his. Then the cat meandered across the field to the other farmer's porch. Whenever the farmers talked about whose cat it was, they argued. They finally stopped talking.

A traveler came to the second farmer's land one day, looking for work. He was a carpenter. The farmer bitterly told the carpenter his neighbor had plowed the land, changing the direction of a creek that crossed their property lines. He felt betrayed by his neighbor for dividing the creek. The farmer said, "Well, if he's going to divide us with that thing, I'd just as soon finish the job. I want a fence all the way across. I don't want to look at him." The carpenter said he could do it but he asked the farmer to go into town for more lumber for such a large job.

When the farmer returned, driving his old truck up his rutted road, he gazed out onto his field where the fence should have been. Instead of a fence, the carpenter had built a bridge across the creek! The farmer was dumbfounded. Just then his neighbor walked across the bridge onto his land, hand outstretched, a big dumb smile spreading across his face. The neighbor told the first farmer he was a brave man; the neighbor had feared the first farmer never wanted to hear his voice again. The neighbor earnestly asked the first farmer to forgive him. The farmer in the truck said sheepishly that he knew the cat belonged to his neighbor.

As the farmer in the old truck was talking to his friend, he spied the carpenter getting set to leave and asked him to stay on to do some more work. The carpenter smiled at both men and turned to leave. He said the two of them would be just fine; he was now needed elsewhere. There were other bridges to build.

Have you ever found yourself facing off with your adolescent over something dumb like the cat in this story? Did you notice a wall slowly being built in your communication? The carpenter in Wilcox's song is a picture of Jesus trying to free two old friends locked in a destructive silence by constructing a "bridge of forgiveness" between their hearts.

Like the wise carpenter, it takes brave parents who are willing to build bridges, not walls, with their kids. Tim and Judy are examples of parents who learned bravery in a parents' group. Although their friends had always regarded them as great parents, they were at their wits' end over Janice, their sixteen-year-old.

> "Janice has always been a good daughter," Tim told the group. "But recently, she's gotten very serious with this boy that Judy and I don't know much about. She never brings him home, and she's started to violate our rules about curfew times. She's always pushing us for more and more freedom to see this guy, and I won't stand for it!"
>
> Tim continued, "Not only is she not to see this new boyfriend at all during the school week, we're only allowing her to go out with him once each weekend. Double dates only. That seems reasonable to me for a sixteen-year-old, and she's never had a problem with our rules before. But now she's screaming bloody murder! She claims we're being unfair. She says I don't listen to her. Can you believe that kid?
>
> "We need you folks to give us advice on how to regain a sense of stability and control over this situation. I'll admit that I'm mad. Judy is losing sleep over it. What can we do to get back to normal again with Janice?"

OBJECTIVE: In this session, you will explore your own goals as a parent and begin to work on developing realistic ministry goals.

Proverbs 18:1-2 talks about goals:

> An unfriendly man pursues selfish ends;
> he defies all sound judgment.
> A fool finds no pleasure in understanding,
> but delights in airing his own opinions.

These proverbs call it poor judgment and foolishness to pursue selfish ends and to take no interest in understanding others. Yet it's easy for us to get caught up in pursuing selfish ends and to resist understanding our teens. We do this without realizing it, partly because we're preoccupied with our own needs and partly because understanding our kids can be painful. However, the result is usually the building of walls that separate us from our teens instead of building bridges that bring us together. In this session, we'll take a look at our desires and how they affect our goals. We'll look at styles of parenting that build walls and styles of parenting that build bridges. And we'll consider how to shift from the selfish goals of a consumer parent to the generous goals of a ministry-minded parent.

Unmet Desires, Foolish Goals, and Consumer Parents

When unmet desires and foolish goals control our behavior, they handicap us from helping our kids. That's why it's important to look inside ourselves to identify our true desires and goals. Here are two principles:

1. Unmet desires fuel parents' foolish goals.
2. The primary characteristic of a foolish goal is that it is easily blocked by your teen.

A parental *goal* is something a parent can achieve or express without the teen's direct participation. The goal depends only upon the parent to accomplish it as he trusts God to love his kids. A parental *desire* is a strong feeling of something a parent longs for or wants from a teen, but it takes the teen's cooperation to accomplish it.

Feelings of anger and frustration are often symptoms of a blocked goal. Tim's anger and

Judy's sleepless nights indicated they had powerful desires stirring within them, as well as personal goals that Janice was managing to thwart. Much of what Tim and Judy desired from their daughter was legitimate: respect for them and honor for their request to maintain a certain level of dating. They were legitimately concerned about her boyfriend and her decisions to keep him away from them. Likewise, their desires to protect Janice from being hurt and from becoming prematurely sexually active were also healthy.

However, Janice could thwart these desires because Tim and Judy needed her cooperation for most of what they were asking her to do. Tim and Judy's unstated parental goal was to make sure Janice obeyed them without complaint, as she had done as a dutiful child, so that the family could look good to others and feel good to them. Both parents were pillars in their church and were known for having a model family. Until now, Janice had always complied with the rules. Because Janice was slowly drifting away from their control, fear and anger were now driving both parents' decisions. For example, could they really prevent her from seeing the boy at school during the week? Not likely, because her actions at school were beyond their direct control. Janice could easily see her boyfriend at school and not tell her parents, if she so chose.

While their desires were legitimate, it was foolish for Tim and Judy to treat those desires as goals. Because Janice's obedience depended on her choices, not on Tim and Judy's, they were setting themselves up for frustration by making her obedience their goal.

What would have been a wise parental goal for Tim and Judy? For instance, Tim may have desired emotional closeness with Janice. Yet his *goal* would have been a decision to move closer to her, regardless of her angry silence. Because Janice often said her dad never listened or expressed what he felt, he could have

decided to do those things. He could have decided to tell her he loved her. Opening up to Janice in this way would have been a legitimate goal, for Tim could accomplish it without Janice's cooperation.

For a parent to want a teen to say "I love you" in return is a *desire,* not a goal, because it requires the teen's participation, which the teen may or may not give. To want her to respond lovingly is a good desire, but to *require* a kid to say "I love you" when she is obviously feeling distant is a foolish goal. Tim was provoked to great anger when Janice refused to cooperate. "How can you ignore my words! Just forget it!" he raged. She had blocked his goal. A wise goal for Tim would have been a decision to increase his involvement. If Janice rejected his verbal love, he could honestly express sadness without expressing rage or despair: "I know you don't want to talk to me now, and it hurts. But I want more for you and me as soon as you are ready."

Wise goals will keep us moving forward with our kids, however slowly, rather than fostering attack or withdrawal. Our goals as parents should be: (1) to examine our emotions and our kids' reactions so that we can see ways in which we need to change in order to minister to our kids more effectively, and (2) to make those changes in ourselves, regardless of what our kids do.

To understand the choices we make in relation to our kids, we need to look closely at our true desires. Dr. Larry Crabb explains that all human beings (including parents) bring into relationships three central longings, or desires, that we often don't recognize or deal with.[1] The first category is *casual desire.* A casual desire is usually expressed as a *preference*—for example, a parent wants something to occur (or to not occur) with his teen. When a parent's casual longings aren't satisfied, he experiences it as *manageable discomfort.* Tim experienced some discomfort when Janice wore certain clothes and listened to certain music, but it didn't threaten him in his relationship with her.

The second category, *critical desire,* includes desires parents experience that are vital to the well-being of their kids.[2] Parents' healthy critical desires are usually expressed as clear directives. Tim and Judy wanted Janice to attend school, do her homework, see appropriate movies, relate with positive friends, and attend church. These are normal desires. Parents will experience a sense of legitimate pain and temporary immobilization when kids fail to make good decisions in these areas. But parents will pick up and go on relating well with them.

Crucial desire, the third category, is entirely different: Parents experience *crucial* desires when something they believe to be vital to their own well-being is at stake. When parents believe the fulfillment of these desires actually depends on their children, most everything that happens to their kids becomes a crucial concern for them—almost a matter of emotional life and death. Parents who come to depend on their kids for this level of satisfaction end up fearing their own children far more than they fear God.[3]

Notice that with critical desires, our kids' well-being is at stake. With crucial desires, *our* well-being is at stake. We'd like to think that our kids' needs come ahead of our own, but that's true only when we're rational. Unacknowledged crucial desires aren't rational; they are deeply passionate and usually consume us. The problem with misplaced crucial desires is this: Only God can meet our crucial desires. Our kids never can.

---

1. Think about the difference between critical and crucial desires. In your own words, how would you describe critical desires?

2. What critical desires do you have for your kids?

3. What area might you be experiencing as a crucial desire for your teen?

A crucial desire is the same thing as an unacknowledged, illegitimate goal. In order for parents to mature beyond being immobilized by anger or fear toward their kids, parents must address an illegitimate goal consciously and honestly.

Tim and Judy exhibited crucial desires, or illegitimate goals, in their parenting group. Their primary crucial desire was making sure Janice completely obeyed them, without any complaint. Her choices with the new boyfriend, including her increased anger, made them feel powerless, unable to maintain control in their world. They desperately wanted stability and control. Their felt loss of control severely threatened both their reputations and how they saw themselves. As a result, ongoing power struggles felt like emotional life-and-death issues. They foolishly believed they could manipulate Janice with threats and more control to silence her anger and force her to stop challenging them.

Deep down, they knew they couldn't stop her from seeing her boyfriend during the school week. The more they talked about Janice, the more apparent it was that both of them were emotionally "frozen." Did they still love her? Of course; she was their daughter. But their crucial desires were now controlling their decisions. They were acting primarily out of fear, without reflective thinking. Their fear of "losing Janice to her boyfriend" was controlling their decisions, even though they had not acknowledged their fear even to themselves. One moment they were yelling at Janice, the next moment they were fearfully avoiding her and her anger. Both parents felt they might not survive emotionally if they continued to challenge Janice.

Tim and Judy would continue to be consumer parents until they chose a new goal. That goal would have to concern their choices, not Janice's, or it would be foolish. It would have to focus on her growth into adulthood, not on their reputation, or it would be selfish. In order to be ministers rather than consumers, Tim and Judy would need to put Janice's deepest need ahead of their desires for control and comfort.

---

4. Does a crucial desire control your interaction with your teen in ways you don't like? If so, what evidence do you see in your emotions and actions that you are being controlled by a crucial desire?

Take a look at the chart below and see if you are working toward a foolish goal your child is blocking. The left column lists behaviors you might observe in your teen. The right column lists some feelings and reactions you may experience in response to those behaviors.

Any of the experiences in the parent's column indicates that you may be operating with a foolish or selfish goal. Inappropriate goals often fuel irritating behaviors in kids. Their behaviors influence parents to have these feelings and reactions. This destructive looping

Kid's Behavior	Parent's Feelings
goody-goody	annoyed
excess charm	irritated
bright remarks	bugged
clowning	nagging
endless questions	coaxing
bashfulness	talking
laziness	angered
arguing	defeated
breaking rules	threatened
tantrums	forcing
stubbornness	punishing
dawdling	giving in
"forgetting"	hurt
mean remarks	humiliated
destroying property	rejected
physical attacks	getting even
running away	punishing harshly
promiscuity	hurting back
drug abuse	despair
excessive absence	giving up
unattempted jobs	discouraged
playing "dumb"	no action because
hypochondria	there's no hope
non-participation	
"I can't do it"	

cycle continues until parents deal with their own goals. That's why parents' feelings are such good indicators of potentially blocked goals.

Notice that the solution to the cycle is *not* finding a way to change your teen's behavior. The solution is to address any elements of foolishness in your goals first. Jesus told His disciples that when they saw a speck in someone else's eye, it was essential to first remove the plank from their own eye before even attempting to tackle the speck in the other's eye (see Matthew 7:3-5). This is the principle parents need to apply with respect to their goals.

Tim and Judy didn't know they were pursuing a selfish and foolish goal. But their goal was far more than just protecting Janice from a possibly harmful boyfriend. Their goal was complete control of her behaviors and attitudes so she would continue to be the model "good kid" they had always enjoyed. Their goal was to keep her from threatening their stability. Yet Janice was driving them crazy by blocking that goal. They wanted things to be "back to normal" with Janice. That was a perfectly reasonable *desire,* but as a *goal* it was bound to fail. Tim and Judy wanted Janice to obey the family rules completely and to curtail her dating. Janice wanted more freedom to make her own decisions. The result was a power struggle with no winners.

Ministry Parenting: Choosing a New Goal

In session 7 we talked about the consumer model of parenting. Tim and Judy were operating on the consumer model. Their consumer parenting led them to behave in ways that drove Janice to block their goal. In the end, they had even less influence on her than ever, and they felt miserable and unfulfilled. Wise parents know they can't control a teen's

impulses; they can control only their own responses to them. Wise parents also avoid depending on their kids for fulfillment in life, especially in the area of crucial desires that only God can meet.

If the consumer model of parenting always backfires, then what is a parent supposed to do? The opposite of the consumer model is the ministry model. The ministry model requires parents to shift their dependence from *earthly* things (like well-behaved, good kids) to *spiritual* things (a relationship with God). They must shift their focus from serving their own needs to serving their kids' deepest needs: maturity and intimacy with God. Finally, they must shift their energies from trying to change their *kids* to trying to change *themselves.* When kids see evidence in their parents of genuine sadness over the parents' own failings, they often paradoxically begin to open up to their parents. In this way, parents can begin to have growing influence in their kids' lives.

Below is a chart of the ministry model. It highlights the process of increasing our influence by focusing on redirecting our goals.

If Tim and Judy shifted from depending on themselves to depending on God, they would be free to pursue new goals that would allow them to function as biblical parents. While things might never be exactly "back to normal"

THE MINISTRY MODEL OF PARENTING

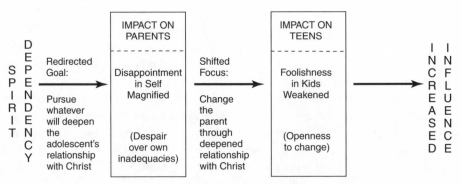

From Kevin Huggins, *Parenting Adolescents*, p. 152.

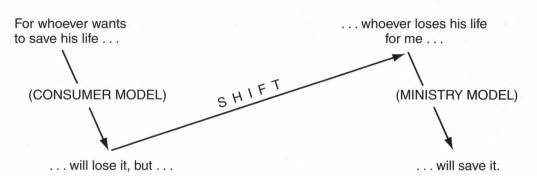

For whoever wants to save his life . . .

(CONSUMER MODEL)

. . . will lose it, but . . .

S H I F T

. . . whoever loses his life for me . . .

(MINISTRY MODEL)

. . . will save it.

From Kevin Huggins, *Parenting Adolescents*, p. 155.

with Janice, they would have influence in her life. This shift wouldn't be easy for Tim and Judy, nor for any of us. It involves a lot of risk, and trust in God.

Our guideline for how to shift to a more effective model of parenting comes from the words of Jesus:

> For whoever wants to save his life will lose it, but whoever loses his life for me will save it. (Luke 9:24)

In order to shift models, we have to "lose" our lives. In other words, we have to stop relentlessly pursuing the things that seem to give us life. In Tim and Judy's case, those things were control, stability, and their reputation as model parents. Letting go of crucial desires like those feels like sacrificing our very lives. But we will remain consumers until we do it.

Losing our lives means ceasing to depend on others—including our kids—for our deepest desires and joy. We must risk the pain of being involved with our kids and expect no reward. This really isn't possible unless we can learn to depend utterly upon God to provide strength and relationship if our kids abandon us, as Janice abandoned Tim and Judy.

Shifting our goals and adopting the ministry model of parenting involves two very difficult avenues for parents: self-denial and self-sacrifice.

Self-Denial

Self-denial is the parents' decision to allow their desires to be unmet by others. It is a decision that works only when they choose to trust Christ to meet their desires. Parents who practice self-denial stop demanding that others (especially their kids) meet their desires. Tim and Judy, for instance, had desires they believed only Janice could fulfill for them. For Tim and Judy to practice self-denial, a first step would be to stop pressuring Janice to be the "good daughter." Tim began to see his rage toward Janice as nothing more than trying to use his daughter to make him look good by powering up and getting her in line. He chose a new goal: to listen attentively to his daughter's desires without demanding she agree with him on everything. Over time, Tim began to soften in his anger as he chose to listen to his daughter's heart. Janice began to respond warmly to her dad, letting go of the icy contempt she felt for him previously.

5. Describe self-denial in your own words.

6. What might self-denial look like in your relationship with your kid(s)?

8. In what ways does your teen see you as a self-sacrificing parent?

9. Can you describe those areas in which you could grow in self-sacrifice on behalf of your teen's true needs?

Self-Sacrifice

Self-sacrifice goes even further than self-denial. It is *"the decision to take whatever personal risks are necessary to help another* [in this case an adolescent] *enter into a trust relationship with Jesus."*[4] It is a decision to continually pursue whatever will promote in others a deeper relationship with Christ, regardless of how painful that self-sacrifice may be. In dealing with a teenager, the greater the risk of pain a parent is willing to take, the greater the level of influence she will have with her kid. Judy risked talking honestly with Janice, over time, about how much she loved her. Judy didn't allow her fear to control her in dealing with Janice's bad choices with boyfriends. Judy had the courage to say that she thought Janice was acting as though she needed her boyfriend for security, yet she didn't need God in this area. Judy chose a new goal of ministry to Janice that started to develop relational influence.

7. What's the difference between the kind of self-sacrifice described above and a false self-sacrifice that just does whatever will make a kid happy?

A Motto for Ministry-Model Parents

A parent who follows the ministry model of parenting will set as his goal to pursue whatever it takes to deepen his kid's relationship with Christ (not increase the parent's personal comfort). His motto will be: *I will move toward my teen regardless of the pain it might cause me personally. My focus as a parent will be to change myself first, not to manipulate my kid into external obedience. I will pursue the heart of my child above all else, to see him or her passionately know God.*

Remember

It's important to uncover our unmet desires and foolish goals and to replace them with goals based on a ministry model of parenting. Unfortunately, this shift is not without pain and personal risk. Deepening dependence upon Christ lived out through self-denial and self-sacrifice is the biblical route to influence with our kids.

Reflection

1. What did you learn from last session's Action Lab when you examined the level of involvement you have with each of your kids?

2. What goals do you see yourself pursuing with each of your teens?

3. Are your goals representative of ministry or consumer parenting?

4. In what ways can you become more involved in demonstrating ministry parenting toward your kids?

Action Lab

Keep a log of some situations that come up with your teen this week. List your kid's behavior, how it made you feel, and how you responded to him or her. Bring your log back next week to discuss in the group.

NOTES
1. Larry Crabb, *Inside Out* (Colorado Springs, CO: NavPress, 1988), pp. 82–85.
2. Kevin Huggins, *Parenting Adolescents* (Colorado Springs, CO: NavPress, 1989), p. 73.
3. Huggins, p. 74.
4. Huggins, p. 157.

Nine

Asking Questions That Open Kids' Hearts

HAVE you ever asked your adolescent why she did a certain thing and been met with that blank stare and shrug of the shoulders that say, "I don't know"? Perhaps you have felt she's telling the truth: she *doesn't* know! It's possible, because teens usually don't know what motivates them at deep levels because they lack the maturity to know their hearts' purposes well. The parents' job is to help kids understand their motivations "below the waterline." Here is a typical scene:

Renae is fifteen years old. She has just arrived home two hours late for dinner.

Dad: Where have you been for the last two hours? You've totally blown off dinner!

Renae: Oh, sorry I didn't call. I was talking to Penny after school.

Mom: You know you should have called us. We've talked about this before. You can't just waltz in here any time—dinner is at six and you need to be here at six!

Renae: Mom, it was really important. I was at Penny's house.

Dad: We worry about you. We need to know where you are at all times. So where were you?

Renae: Okay, OKAY! I was at Penny's house. She had some personal problems she wanted to talk about, and we lost track of the time.

Mom: Honey, you need to be more considerate and let us know where you are. We just couldn't forgive ourselves if something ever happened to you.

Renae: Give me a break! I was fine! I was at Penny's! She needed me! She really needed to talk to me; I had to be there for her.

Dad: Don't you raise your voice at your mother, young lady! I don't like this disrespectful attitude. I won't stand for it!

Renae: I don't know why I ever try to talk to you. I hate this stuff! (She runs to her room and slams the door.)

Parents frequently ask their kids questions that cause them to shut down. The only way to have effective communication with an adolescent is for the teen to recognize her parents' sincere interest in her life. This way she'll feel secure enough to share what's on her heart. Without this communication, parents cannot have effective influence in the lives of their kids.

OBJECTIVE: In this session, you will learn to ask questions that will open up your teen's heart.

Words of Wisdom

The Bible reminds us that we must actively seek out information from our kids:

> He who answers before listening—
> that is his folly and his shame. . . .
> The heart of the discerning [seeks out]
>   knowledge;
> the ears of the wise seek it out. . . .
> The first to present his case seems right,
> till another comes forward and questions
>   him. (Proverbs 18:13,15,17)

This passage makes a couple of important points. First, it is desirable to listen before responding. In fact, we're foolish if we answer others before we earnestly try to listen to their words and the motives of their hearts.

The driving theme of our study is courage. The word *courage* comes from the Latin word *cor,* which means *heart.* Our kids' hearts are more than merely the place of their emotions. The heart is the focal point, or control center, of their entire being—the center of their thinking, feelings, passions, and decisions. Therefore, it takes courage—strength of heart—for parents to pursue the hearts of their teens to get to the control center of their lives.

Any parenting strategy that fails to move toward a teen's control center is an inadequate parenting strategy. Listening with understanding is vital if we want to know more intimately the deep waters of our kids' lives and build influence with them.

Second, listening must be active. We must seek out knowledge with our ears and minds fully engaged. Renae's dad didn't seek out what his daughter was *really* saying at the dinner table. He just heard Renae's words, which conflicted with his agenda of having his daughter home on time. He missed the underlying meaning of her words. If kids sense that parents are seeking only *agreement* from them ("You are late for dinner—admit it!") and not honestly trying to *understand* them ("Could you help me understand why you are late?"), kids will progressively withdraw and close off their hearts.

The Art of Listening to a Kid's Heart

Jesus talked about the centrality of the heart as it relates to loving God and others. An expert in the religious law asked Jesus what he must do to inherit eternal life. Jesus and the man had this dialogue about the heart:

> "What is written in the Law?" [Jesus] replied. "How do you read it?"
> He answered: " 'Love the Lord your God with *all your heart* and with all your soul and with all your strength and with all your mind'; and, 'Love your neighbor as yourself.' "
> "You have answered correctly," Jesus replied. "Do this and you shall live." (Luke 10:26-28, emphasis added)

The heart described here is not merely some organ in a person's chest, pumping blood, but a picture of pulsating life. "Since the heart is regarded as the center or focus of man's personal life, the spring of all his desires, motives, and moral choices—indeed, all his behavioral trends—it is not surprising to note that in both Testaments the divine appeal is addressed to the heart of man."[1] Jesus commended the legal expert's understanding about loving God and others from the heart.

Further, the heart is the source of motives, the seat of passions, the center of thought processes, and the spring of conscience: "Above all else, guard your heart, for it is the wellspring of life" (Proverbs 4:23). The heart is a "wellspring" that needs to be guarded zealously so it stays unpolluted by tainted motives, thoughts, and desires.

A number of years ago a friend and I stumbled upon an artesian spring while backpacking in the mountains of eastern Washington. The water came out pure and icy. It came bubbling, gushing, even playfully cascading over itself as it flowed down the mountain. It was energizing just to touch it and see it move, seemingly with a life of its own. My friend and I were in awe. As the water rivulets branched off in different directions on the hard ground, life was evident. A thin ribbon of green plants snaked its way down the mountain wherever the water trickled. The rest of the area was lifeless and barren. Where the water flowed, there was life.

The image of the artesian well challenges us to think of our kids' hearts as a wellspring flowing from within them.

> The inner life, the story of the heart, is the life of deep places within us, our passions and dreams, our fears, and our deepest wounds. It is the unseen life, the mystery within. . . . It cannot be managed like a corporation. The heart does not respond to principles or programs; it seeks not efficiency, but passion. Art, poetry, beauty, mystery, ecstasy: these are what rouse the heart. Indeed, they are the *languages that must be spoken* if one wishes to communicate with the heart."[2]

This is why Jesus so often taught and related to people by telling stories and asking questions. His desire was not just to engage their intellects, but to capture their hearts. Listening carefully to the language of our kids' hearts and responding wisely is one of the keys to godly influence.

Teens need to feel that their parents are sincerely interested in their lives. They will tend to feel this when their parents are really listening to them. The best way to listen is to ask thoughtful, probing questions that get to the truth in kids' hearts.

When asking probing questions, it's important to do two things. First, *listen to the implicit meaning of the teen's words.* In other words, listen for hidden meanings that express what's going on below the waterline. Listen for "pregnant" words or phrases that help you get a handle on deeper meanings:

"I hate this stuff."
"I'm sick of you."
"You are deaf when I talk."
"These rules suck."
"Your reason is so lame."
"You're so unfair."

One parent imagined a yellow highlighting marker when her son talked to her. She would mentally highlight his words and their potential implicit meaning so that she could later reflect with him and clarify his intent. This strategy equipped her to speak into his heart.

1. Describe the idea of "implicit meaning" in your own words.

2. What words or phrases do you hear from your teen that indicate implicit meaning? What might these words mean?

The second thing to do with probing questions is to *help kids clarify their words in order to make their feelings explicit, or out in the open.* When a teen makes his implicit meanings explicit, both parent and teen understand more about what is going on in the teen's heart.

Asking questions that get at kids' underlying purposes and plans takes a lot of practice! For instance, Renae's dad could have asked, "Honey, you obviously are two hours late for dinner and you sound frustrated, but I'm curious as to why you didn't call. Could you help me understand?" This question gives Renae an opportunity to explain her reasons and examine her feelings in an emotionally safe environment.

---

3. What questions could you ask to help your teen get his or her desires safely out in the open?

"Okay," you're saying. "I need to ask questions to open the door to what's going on in my teen's heart. But how? I'm no mind reader. I don't have a crystal ball."

You don't have to be a mind reader to communicate with your kids. You just need to remember there are three characteristics of questions that open doors to communication:[3]

1. They are nondefensive.
2. They are open-ended.
3. They are biblically perceptive.

All three characteristics require practice. Here is more information about each one.

Nondefensive Questions

When Renae told her parents, "Oh, sorry I didn't call. I was talking to Penny after school," her parents had an opportunity to clarify what was going on. Instead, they focused only on the fact that she was late for dinner. The conversation was a disaster. Her mom's comment, "You know you should have called us," was accusing and angry. Renae started to close herself off from her parents at that point.

A nondefensive question to clarify Renae's late arrival might have been, "Renae, could you help us understand the reason for your lateness? It would help us because we're confused right now." This remark is open and contains no subtle putdowns.

Parents need to work hard to get at the heart-level truth. Often parents don't want to because they know it will be painful. For instance, they might find out that their teens feel betrayed by them or feel more loved by other people. Parents who don't want to deal with such feelings often take a defensive stance. This keeps the parent comfortable, but it also keeps the truth from coming out. Here are some examples of *defensive questions:*

"Why do you always make unkind remarks about me? What's with you?"

"Who do you think you are, acting like you have the right to do anything, no matter who it hurts?"

"When did I ever say or do anything to make you think I don't love you?"

"Why do you think you can question the fairness of our rules?"

Defensive questions usually challenge a person to rationalize or defend his foolish position, rather than reflect on it and get to the truth. Defensive questions shut the door to communication because they encourage teens to say less about their problems and concerns when parents need to know more. "Why" questions, in particular, tend to cause kids to rationalize—to give likely reasons but not real reasons for their behavior.

4. Do you think your kids usually see your questions as nondefensive or defensive? Why?

Open-Ended Questions

Open-ended questions encourage adolescents to open up and talk freely about the purposes of their actions and the things that concern them. Open-ended questions don't invite one-word answers, but instead encourage reflection and sharing.

My friend Ray remarried a number of years ago. One day he called his adolescent daughter about a summer visit. She lived in another state with her mom, and he was checking on her coming to spend the summer with him and his wife. The next words were surprisingly hard for both Ray and his daughter: "Daddy, I don't think I want to come out there to visit you next summer. I have never spent a summer here, and I want to know what it's like."

Ray felt as though someone had ripped his heart out of him. He felt like telling his daughter he was just fine with her decision and didn't want her to come for a summer visit ever again. The phone call was tense for both dad and daughter. Fortunately, he didn't tell her any of his feelings, but instead said he would call her back after he thought about her request. Ray knew it would be months before he could see her again, and he wanted to be thoughtful about how he responded.

The next Saturday he called her with his response. "It's sad for me not to have you come out to see me," he said. "I bet you thought about this decision for a long time before you told me, because you knew it would be hard on me. You knew I would miss you. I'm very proud of you; I'm proud you took the risk to make a decision that would affect me. I'm glad you told me what you wanted to do—that took great courage on your part. What was that like for you to tell me you didn't want to come?"

What came next was more than Ray hoped for: "Oh, Daddy, I can tell you anything and you will listen to me!"

Ray was able to connect with his daughter by addressing an open-ended question to his daughter's fearful heart. He heard her relief and the sense of freedom she felt with him. His question was well thought out and directed toward his daughter's needs, not his own. She experienced him ministering to her at deep levels. Then she touched his heart by her joyful, free response.

5. Can you give an example of an open-ended question you have used to draw out your kid's heart?

Biblically Perceptive Questions

Parents who have a biblical understanding of what makes people tick know that their kids, like all of us in this fallen world, experience heartfelt disappointment. Teens have a desire for unfailing love that is impossible to satisfy without God. Kids make foolish plans to get

A question like Ray's promotes more discussion. The following chart contains a number of parent-teen situations, with both closed and open-ended responses from the parent:

Kid's Remark	Closed Question	Open Question
I'm never going to hang out with her again!	Why do you continue complaining about her?	You sound upset at her. What are you feeling?
I hate algebra.	Why would you say that when you know you have to take the class?	What is it that makes this class so hard that you feel you can't do it?
I wish I could go on the ski trip. Everyone else is going!	Since the answer is "no," why do you insist on bringing this question up?	It sounds like you feel I'm being unfair. What is it that makes you feel this way?
Look at my new shoes! Aren't they cool?	Okay, I see them. So what do you want me to say about them?	I can tell you like the way they look. What is it about them that you think is cool?
I don't want to go to school. Nick will be waiting for me in the parking lot.	Since you have to go to school because it's the law, what is your problem here with Nick?	Sounds like you're afraid of Nick. What's that like for you when he says he'll "be waiting for you"?

that desire met. Biblically perceptive questions talk about those desires and plans.

Seth came into our bedroom one night and lay down, looking up at the ceiling and saying nothing. He appeared bored and sullen for several minutes. Initially, I felt irritation that he was interrupting my sacred reading time. (I think I was reading a book on parenting!) But my wife asked a perceptive question: "So here you are, kind of quiet. What's up with you as you're lying there?" Initially he said, "Nothing," in a less-than-convincing way. She reframed the question: "You lay down so quietly. I wonder what's on your mind?" Cathy went to the heart of the issue by speaking to Seth's desires, even though we had no idea what they were. He slowly began to talk about how he was feeling neglected by us both because of our busy schedules during the past week. He just wanted to talk to

us, unhurriedly and without an agenda, because he felt angry and lonely. Parents who are trying to move toward their kids' hearts will attend to the desires and plans of the heart. Here are sample questions that move toward kids' hearts.

Questions designed to get teens talking about their desires:

1. What do you hope to get out of youth group this year?
2. What kinds of things make school a scary or difficult place for you?
3. If you had the power to change anything about you, what would it be?
4. If you could try to make one thing better between you and me this year, what would that look like?

Questions designed to get teens talking about their plans:

1. If you could accomplish anything you wanted this year at school, what would it be?
2. What kinds of things do you want to see changed in your relationship with your friends this year?
3. If you were standing in front of a magic mirror and could change anything about yourself, what would you change?

Remember

It's critical that we ask questions to open our kids' hearts, rather than focus just on changing their external behaviors. We need to be committed to learning to speak the language of their hearts. We need to listen wisely and ask questions that draw out the below-the-waterline meaning of our kids' words. Our questions should be nondefensive, open-ended, and biblically perceptive. Questions like these help kids experience deep emotional security with us, and that security helps them talk richly about the desires and plans of their hearts.

Reflection

As a group, look at the following remarks a teen might make. Fill in possible *closed* questions to be avoided and *open* questions a parent could use in response:

Action Lab

As you relate to your teen this week, actively look for emotionally pregnant words your adolescent uses to describe concerns or disappointments. Determine to ask one nondefensive, open-ended question that invites your teen to share more about his or her disappointments. Bring back your experience next week to share with the group.

NOTES
1. "Heart," in *The Evangelical Dictionary of Theology,* edited by Walter Elwell (Grand Rapids, MI: Baker, 1984), p. 499.
2. Brent Curtis and John Eldredge, *The Sacred Romance: Drawing Closer to the Heart of God* (Nashville, TN: Thomas Nelson, 1997), p. 6.
3. Kevin Huggins, *Parenting Adolescents* (Colorado Springs, CO: NavPress, 1989), pp. 202–205.

Kid's Remark	Closed Question	Open Question
I can't stand the food around here. I'm not eating this stuff!		
My gym teacher is such a jerk.		
I shouldn't have to be home at 5:30 for dinner. It's stupid.		
I'm not wearing those dress pants. Nobody wears pants like those.		
I don't want to go to Grandma's. It's boring.		

Ten

Speaking "Life Words" to Your Teen

I stumbled upon the following conflict when I went to pick up a young man at his home to attend a wilderness camp. It was an early experience in youth ministry that left a painful image in my mind about the power of words.

Dad (angrily): Lee, I told you to pick up your room and mow the lawn before you go to this camp. You didn't even have the brains in your head to get the garbage out. You are just so stupid! And you're so damned lazy as well. Your ten-year-old brother has more smarts than you. The way you do things, you better plan on working at McDonald's flipping burgers the rest of your life.

Lee: I worked it out with Tim to do the lawn. We're switching chores this week. It's taken care of, so just back off me, will you?

Dad (sarcastic): "It's taken care of." You must think I'm dumb as a brick like you! Nothing you do is ever "taken care of." Get out of here! (Throws sleeping bag at Lee.) You and I are going to talk when you get back. This conversation is not done.

Lee: It's done for me! You're always on my case, hassling me! You said I could go, now you say this crap to me. I'm out of here!

I felt as though I had just watched an emotional auto collision, with mutilated body parts all over the living room. When Lee got into the van next to me, I watched the tears well up in his eyes as he gazed out the window. I knew he didn't want to make eye contact, lest he cry and look weak. I enjoyed this boy — he became a friend to our family over time. Yet this scene still haunts me about the awesome power of parents' words.

Later, Lee's mom met me in a restaurant to talk about her husband and son. I can still see the tears streaming down her face as she shook her head and said, "There is such hatred in my family." Lee's heart had been pierced by his dad's words.

Reckless words pierce like a sword, but the tongue of the wise brings healing. (Proverbs 12:18)

This father's words brought no healing to his son. The father's words were thrust into Lee's heart with bloody results. On the contrary, he shamed his son in order to force Lee into complying with his requests. Negative words, spoken in anger or vengeance, kill the parent-teen relationship. Lee experienced words we will call *death words*: "stupid," "lazy," and "dumb as a brick." He couldn't help feeling deeply wounded and wanting to withdraw from his dad. He experienced his father as unsafe.

---

1. What do you think will be the long-term effects upon Lee if his dad continues down this path with him?

One might think this is an extreme, rare example. But all parents use words in less-than-healing ways. Most of us have caught ourselves speaking death words to our kids in moments of anger. How can parents make the shift to communicating life to their kids?

OBJECTIVE: In this session, you will learn to speak life words to your teen's heart, words that capture what a kid thinks and feels to help him make sense of his world.

What we say communicates life and death to others:

> The tongue of the wise commends knowledge, but the mouth of the fool gushes folly. . . .
> The tongue that brings healing is a tree of life, but a deceitful tongue crushes the spirit. . . .
> The tongue has the power of life and death, and those who love it will eat its fruit.
>   (Proverbs 15:2,4; 18:21)

The writer of Proverbs said our words can be used either to crush the spirit or to bring healing. Our objective must be to bring life-giving healing to our kids. To do that, we must first understand what it means to speak to someone's heart. Second, we must learn to recognize the difference between life words and death words. In this way, we can increasingly find creative ways to speak life to our kids.

Seeing Our Kids' Hearts As Stories to Be Entered

Sometimes parents say useless words when they try to promote life in their kids. Have you ever had someone try to encourage you, but you only felt more defeated and alone when they were done?

A friend told me about a man who came to "encourage" him and four other men as they were chatting together after a worship service. This man grabbed two of the men by their shoulders and shouted, "Man, I just *love* you guys. Let me give you all a big bear hug!" The men were not encouraged! My friend wanted to flee, to escape from the man mauling him. This loud person honestly cared about the five men, but somehow his words were useless for promoting life. Words like these resemble copper BBs shot at an eight-inch armor-plated tank. They bounce off because they have no power and find no entrance through people's emotional body armor to encourage the heart.

The apostle Paul described speaking into the heart, or the "story," of people's lives. He likens people to living letters:

> You yourselves are our letter, written on our hearts, known and read by everybody. You show that you are a letter from Christ, the result of our ministry, written not with ink but with the Spirit of the living God, not on tablets of stone but on tablets of human hearts. (2 Corinthians 3:2-3)

Paul said people are like living letters others can know and read. He speaks of the heart, the control center of a person's being. He describes people not as flat ("tablets of stone"), scripted, and two-dimensional like a cartoon character, but rather as vibrant and living—an ongoing story the Spirit of God is continuing to write as the director of a great drama "on tablets of human hearts."

Dr. Daniel Taylor expands this theme that each person, including our kids, is a living story:

> You are your stories. You are the product of all the stories you have heard and lived—and of many that you have never heard. . . . Our greatest desire [and our kids' greatest desire], greater even than the desire for happiness, is that our lives mean something. This desire for meaning is the originating impulse of story. We tell stories because we hope to find or create significant connections between things. . . .
>
> Our stories teach us that there is a place for us, that we fit. They suggest to us that our lives can have a plot. Stories turn mere chronology, one thing after another, into the purposeful action of plot, and thereby into meaning. . . .
>
> It is crucial, therefore, that we surround children, and ourselves, with healthy stories. These stories should be filled with mentors, models, heroes who do the kinds of things, physically and spiritually, that we ourselves wish to do. If I cannot imagine myself doing something, I am unlikely even to attempt it. Stories multiply our possibilities.[1]

Lee's personal life story had no plot, no purpose within his family. By calling him degrading names like "stupid" and "lazy," his father actually created a sense that Lee's life had no meaning and no possibilities for love. Lee didn't fit anywhere in his family. Not fitting, or having a meaningless story, is a form of emotional death.

Taylor further states that it's critical for us to understand a person's story if we want to talk powerfully into the deepest parts of him or her. If we want to go beyond the kind of generalized reasoning parents often use with kids, we need to connect with their unique stories. Perhaps you remember the story of Smokey the Bear. Which of these do you think had the most influence on reducing forest fires: the story of the cute little bear wearing the fire hat, telling us to be careful of fires, or environmentalists with their lists and graphs? The story of Smokey the Bear affected people more because it was specific and concrete, a story they could get their minds and hearts wrapped around to produce change.

> We certainly profit from the perception of generalized truths, but it is the conviction of story—and all art—that they can best be understood as they are embodied in the messy particulars. In the case of story, those are the particulars of time, person, place and action. Story transfuses the pale abstractions of disembodied reason with the blood and bone of the senses and presents them for inspection by the whole person—rational, emotional, spiritual, sensual. . . . *No matter how much our heads know, if our hearts are not persuaded, we are not truly convinced, certainly not enough to act.*[2]

Parents need to engage kids' hearts convincingly. Speaking to their heads alone will not produce the positive changes we desire. Parents who use life words to speak to kids' stories engage kids fully, much more than with reason alone.

We are not to throw words at our kids randomly, like BBs bouncing off their armor. We are to purposefully speak life to them.

---

2. What do you think it means to speak purposefully into your kid's story?

Life Words and Death Words

If speaking life to the heart is so important, how can we tell the difference between life words and death words? *Life words* are words, phrases, and questions that encourage teens to share about their inner worlds. Life words help kids to understand their own behavior. Life words communicate unfailing love and acceptance.

3. How would you define "life words"? Can you give personal examples?

Death words are negative words that kill the parent-teen relationship. Usually spoken in anger, death words leave kids feeling discouraged and confused. Like Lee, kids usually feel confused, hurt, hesitant, and often angry when they hear death words. Parents always forfeit influence whenever they speak death words.

Here are three benefits of speaking life words to your teens:[3]

Life Words Help Kids Make Sense of Their Own Behavior.

When parents use the opportunity to put into words what they see going on in their kids' lives, it helps teens make sense of their world. Life words communicate that there really are logical reasons for what teens think and feel. Many teens feel they're "going crazy" or are at least confused because they think they're the only ones who feel and react the way they

do. Life words help them realize they're not crazy, and this news is a great relief to them.

When I was in graduate school in Denver, Seth went to a new public school that he didn't like. One evening, Cathy and I had a disastrous conversation in which we tried to convince him why we had relocated to Denver. The more I tried to persuade him of my logic, the greater his anguish. Seth ended with the following words: "Dad, you don't know what it's like at school, when even my new friends won't give me the time of day! I hate riding the school bus—kids just hassle me. I hate recess. It feels like things are falling apart. I miss my friends back home. You're not listening to me. I hate this school!"

Seth was obviously in pain, but we weren't sure of all the reasons. Cathy and I felt we were stumbling badly in our attempts to speak to his heart. Ironically, life is often like a merry-go-round. God has a way of allowing parents to circle around, revisiting their past mistakes and struggles to learn from them. Several months later, Cathy and I had another opportunity. I chose to speak life words to Seth, trying to put my finger on what he was going through: "It sounds like your relationships with your friends are causing you a lot of pain. When they don't give you the time of day, you probably feel awful, maybe even scared. I bet you're feeling terribly lonely. I know you're hurting a bunch. My guess is you're angry at me as well. I'm really interested in what you're thinking. Could you help me understand what you're feeling now?"

4. How do you think Seth felt when I responded to him in this way?

When parents accurately capture the emotional content (the below-the-waterline sources) of their kids' behavior, kids feel understood and accepted. Parents can then help their teens understand the logical reasons for what they think and feel. This is done *tentatively* ("You *probably* feel awful, *maybe* even scared"), *graciously* ("I bet you're feeling terribly lonely"), and *compassionately* ("Could you help me understand what you're feeling now?"). It is not said boldly, like the thrust of a sword. Notice I did not say, "I know just what your problem is, son. You've got low self-esteem." Parents who make bold assertions like this are perceived as "psychological vultures" who feed off their kids, trying to tell them what they think and feel. That is not a life-giving way to relate. Instead, Cathy and I expressed tentative hunches about what we thought might be going on with Seth. His heart began to open to talk more about his confusion and pain.

Our kids are desperately trying to find love and significance and to make sense of their world. At first, I was trying to help Seth logically understand my reason for our move to Denver. Unfortunately, our son needed much more than solid, logical thinking from me. He needed passionate involvement as he was dealing with the terror of living alone in a strange city. He felt like a freakish alien unfairly rejected at school. My ineffective words of logic alone didn't speak to his heart.

> It is important to realize that no amount of reasoning or persuading is powerful enough to make us change our course of action. At our deepest level, in the decisions that count the most, we have moved beyond the reach of pressure. *We have become more passionate than reasonable* . . . passionate involvement is needed if passionate people are to really change.[4]

Seth needed the passionate hearts of his mom and dad as he struggled with deep con-fusion. Sadly, kids are usually doing this in the midst of selfish people. A parent who helps kids make sense of things is an attractive parent, one to whom kids will be more likely to turn. Parents who speak life-giving words breathe life into the parent-teen relationship.

Life Words Let Teens Confirm or Dismiss Parents' Conclusions About Their Behavior.

It is life-giving for parents to try to put their kids' purposes into words, but it's also difficult. Unless we are mind readers, we will occasionally draw conclusions about our kids' behavior that are off base. That's not the end of the world; we just need to explore other alternatives with our teens to get to the real purposes they are pursuing. By using life words, we give them the chance to let us know if we are out of tune so that we can redirect our words more effectively.

For instance, when I suggested to Seth that he was frightened because his friends were treating him badly, Seth could either confirm or dismiss that hunch (if he felt I was open to hearing him honestly). He might completely *dismiss* my hunch by saying, "No, I didn't mean that at all." Or he might *modify* my hunch by saying, "No, I don't really feel scared by my new friends. But I am lonely here. And I am angry at you because you don't listen to me, even when I told you I didn't want to come to Denver."

Even when a teen dismisses or modifies a hunch, life words can still give a wise parent important data to better understand his kid.

Life Words Communicate Unconditional Involvement to a Teen.

Many of us don't really want to be deeply involved with our kids because we want to avoid their pain. When we communicate this lack of desire for involvement, our relationship with them suffers. More importantly, we can seem emotionally dead to our kids. We don't seem to be people with whom they can have relationship. So they look elsewhere for love and acceptance, and often make illegitimate or immoral choices. These are the results of death words.

On the other hand, life words that communicate interest and involvement make a parent seem alive to a teen. The teen will actually seek relationship with a parent who does not seem put off by the pain, fear, anger, or shame the teen is experiencing.

For instance, after our painful discussion in Denver, Cathy was later able to speak more life words with a real message of hope. Seth was confused and hurt, and Cathy was not leaving him to get through it on his own. She made it clear that she wanted to be involved in whatever was going on with him. She did not pull away from Seth's pain and confusion, but actively looked for ways to enter his inner world in a follow-up conversation: "Seth, it sounds like your relationship with your friends is hurting you. I see you hang your head every morning as you leave for school looking anxious. I just want you to know my heart is for you as you struggle to be in a school not of your choosing. It takes a lot of courage to deal with these kids' hurtful words day after day. I'm so proud of you for sticking with school when you really want to quit and go back home. I'm curious. How are you feeling about Dad and me now?"

---

5. How might Seth have experienced hope from his dialogue with his mom?

6. How would your kids experience hope if you spoke life words to them?

Cathy was willing to enter Seth's emotional struggle with honesty ("It takes a lot of courage to deal with those kids' hurtful words day after day"). She was also willing to explore his immediate feelings about the strained relationship with her and me ("How are you feeling about Dad and me now?"). It was still a long struggle, yet our growing desire was to move toward his heart in the midst of his anger and confusion.

Parents who communicate a willingness to be involved seem more emotionally alive to their kids. Then, when a teen's foolish strategies fail and his world crumbles, those parents can attract the teen into relationship with them and with God. Such parents are very different from "dead" parents, who get involved with their teens only to have their own needs met.

Parents who seem dead to their kids will remain distant and unattractive. Kids know when parents are committed to serving their own self-interests before their kids' interests. But when parents become alive to their teens, an awareness and hunger for Christ begins to surface and grow.

Remember

Parents must learn to find purposeful ways to speak into the heart story of their teens by speaking life words. Life words accurately capture what kids are thinking and feeling about themselves and their world. Life words need to be spoken tentatively, graciously, and compassionately. These words communicate unfailing love and acceptance. Life words also stimulate greater connection to parents and movement of kids' hearts toward God. Death words leave kids feeling discouraged and confused.

Reflection

As a group exercise, construct a life-word response to each of the situations below:

Action Lab

Identify a potential area of conflict with your teen, and make an effort to speak a life word to him or her this week. Bring back your responses to discuss next week in group.

NOTES
1. Daniel Taylor, *The Healing Power of Stories* (New York, NY: Doubleday, 1996), pp. 1-2, 28.
2. Taylor, pp. 30, 35.
3. Kevin Huggins, *Parenting Adolescents* (Colorado Springs, CO: NavPress, 1989), pp. 208-209.
4. Larry Crabb, *Who We Are and How We Relate* (Colorado Springs, CO: NavPress, 1992), p. 25.

Family Situation	Life-word response
Your daughter appears sullen and quiet about low grades on her report card.	Sue, you seem pretty discouraged about your grades right now. Are you worried about what others will think about you?
Your son comes home, looking dejected after being cut from an important position on the basketball team.	
Your daughter is in tears because other girls at school made fun of her latest haircut.	
Your son is angry after learning he was not invited to a party at his best friend's parents' lake cabin.	
Your daughter comes in at 1:00 A.M., two hours after her weekend curfew.	
Your son walks into the family room, head hung low, after his first solo drive in your car. He hit another friend's car while showing off at the Burger King parking lot.	

Eleven

What Lies Behind Kids' Emotions

JOHN was having a great time at the video arcade with his three sons: Keith, eighteen, and the fourteen-year-old twins, Aaron and Josh. Suddenly, Keith interrupted their fun for one of his "habits" that his dad struggled with.

Keith: Dad, I need to run down to Safeway for a pack of cigarettes. I'll be back in about fifteen minutes, okay?

John: Hold on a minute. The whole point of us going out together as a family is for us to stay together. Your cigarettes can wait until later.

Keith: It's important to me! And it's a stupid rule that I can't just run over to the store when we're so close. I'll be back in a few minutes. (turns to leave)

John : *(gently grabs Keith's elbow)* Whoa, pal! I guess you didn't hear me. I said you could go out for cigarettes later. Right now, you stay with us—

Keith : *(explosively)* Don't tell me what to do! Get your hand off me! I'm sick of all your idiotic rules and I'm sick of all this stupid family stuff. I'm leaving! (runs out of the arcade)

John : *(incredulously)* What on earth was that all about?

Keith has just given us a case study in powerful *negative emotions*—in this case, anger. Most of us can relate to his father, John; our teens also have episodes of negative emotion that leave us scratching our heads. These emotions confuse and scare us. Often, we want to shut down or minimize negative emotions because they feel uncomfortable to us and our kids. Yet negative emotions provide vital data about our teens. We can use this data to better discern their heart directions and thus to minister more effectively.

OBJECTIVE: In this session, you will learn to trace teens' negative emotions to their disappointed goals and strategies. These goals and strategies (below the waterline) explain a lot about kids' observable behaviors (above the waterline).

1. How do you typically respond when your teen expresses strong anger or fear?

The Primary Negative Emotions

There are many negative emotions, but for our discussion they can be boiled down to three primary ones: *anger, fear,* and *shame.* Like the three primary colors that can be blended in different combinations to form every different shade, these three emotions are the basic palette for negative feelings. Furthermore, they tell us much about what is occurring in our kids' hearts. We'll look at each of these emotions in some detail, but first, let's look at what the Bible says about them.

All three negative emotions turn up just a few pages into the biblical story. As soon as Adam and Eve sin, they start relating to God and each other defensively:

> Then the man and his wife heard the sound of the Lord God as he was walking in the garden in the cool of the day. And they *hid from the lord God* [shame] among the trees of the garden. But the Lord God called to the man, "Where are you?"
>
> He answered, "I heard you in the garden, and *I was afraid* [fear] because I was naked, so I *hid* [defensive strategy]." (Genesis 3:8-10, emphasis added)

A couple of verses later, Adam continues to respond angrily to God:

> The man said, "The woman *you put here with me* [anger]—she gave me some fruit from the tree, and I ate it." (Genesis 3:12, emphasis added)

Before this event, Adam and Eve felt complete freedom with God and each other. They felt neither shame nor fear, even though they were naked (Genesis 2:25). Most people cringe at the thought of others looking at their bodies unclothed. Yet these two were able to enjoy God and each other fully in their innocent nakedness of body and soul. They had nothing to hide from God or each other. "They were at ease with each other, without fear of exploitation for evil. This integrity was shattered by the fall. . . . [T]heir nakedness was literal, but it also signified something far more."[1] Adam and Eve's innocent nakedness became shameful nakedness when they sinned. Something profound had occurred.

Then, God came for intimate communion with them "in the cool of the day." The cool of the day was the most intimate time for conversation. After visiting France, a friend of mine told me about people drinking coffee in the outdoor cafés. They would lounge around for hours during certain times of the day, unhurriedly enjoying each other. In a similar way, God was approaching His children for unhurried, open dialogue, But like John in our opening story, God was terribly disappointed.

Adam was ashamed, afraid, and angry because he had gotten himself into deep trouble with God. Teens have the same reactions. At times, so do parents. Negative emotions are worth thinking through carefully: "The reason for looking inside is not to effect direct change of negative emotions to positive emotions. Instead, we are to listen to and ponder what we feel in order to be moved to the far deeper issue of what our hearts are doing with God and others."[2] We need to ponder what our teens feel in order to understand what's going on in their hearts. At the same time, we need to ponder what *we* feel in order to understand what's going on in our hearts.

2. What do you do when you feel negative emotions toward your teen?

3. How do you react to the idea of listening to and pondering these emotions in order to better understand your heart? (Does that seem like a good idea, a waste of time, too hard...?)

Negative emotions generally have to do with a person's goals. In session 8, we saw how important it is for parents to be aware of their own goals and to choose wise ones. We observed that parents get angry when kids block their goals. The same is true for teens. Like us, teens get angry when their goals are blocked, afraid when they think their goals might be blocked, and ashamed when they blame themselves for failing to reach a goal. Just as we need to see the connection between our own emotions and goals, we need to see the connection between our kids' emotions and goals. This session will focus on that link. However, as we look at each emotion, we'll also keep our own feelings in mind.

Why did we talk about parents' goals back in session 8 and are only now getting to kids' goals? We talked about parents first because it's essential for us to look at our own hearts before venturing into our teens' hearts. As important as it is to figure our kids out, they will experience us as amateur psychologists trying to control them unless we address our own goals first. All of the skills you will learn in the second half of this course need to be practiced with the commitment to get your own heart right before addressing your teen's heart.

Anger: A Blocked Goal

To make the connection between emotions and goals, let's look first at anger. In our opening story, Keith wanted to go out for cigarettes; John wouldn't let him, and Keith blew up. John was stunned. What happened?

Keith experienced a *blocked goal.* He was unable to get what he wanted because something or someone (Dad) stood in his way. Resistance, defiance, and anger are classic responses when parents say no to their kids, blocking their goals.

Adults have these reactions as well. When you're late for work and get behind someone driving only half the legal speed limit, don't you feel angry? Your goal of getting to work on time is being blocked, and frustration builds. I once was late for an important meeting because two cars side by side slowed to 20 mph in a 35mph zone. My simmering frustration ("What is wrong with these people?") began to heat up after a few minutes ("Get out of my way! Who do you think you are?"). Frustration rose to boiling anger when I realized they knew each other and were carrying on a conversation out their open windows while blocking both lanes!

This simple blocked goal revealed something of my heart. I wanted satisfaction *now.*

We want satisfaction—the resolution of our tension and emptiness—but we can't obtain relief because satisfaction of our deepest desires is in the hands of those we can't control. We feel irritated when others do not comply with our desires, but our anger seems utterly justified when our desires are not satisfied because of injustice. . . . Unrighteous anger is a dark energy that demands for the self a more tolerable world *now,* instead of waiting for God's redemption according to divine design and timing.[3]

We live in a world where justice isn't available the way we want it to be.

My irritation crossed the line into unrighteous anger when I demanded the two drivers *get out of my way now!* (I had fleeting visions of playing bumper cars with them from behind. Fortunately, I didn't act on those angry passions!) The book of James describes the process by which blocked desires move to destructive anger:

> What causes fights and quarrels among you? Don't they come from your desires that *battle within you*? *You want something but don't get it.* You *kill* and *covet,* but you cannot have what you want. You quarrel and fight. You do not have, because you do not ask God. When you ask, you do not receive, because you ask with wrong motives, that you may spend what you get on your pleasures. (James 4:1-3, emphasis added)

4. What do you think James means by the terms "kill" and "covet" in this passage?

5. How might this process work itself out between you and your teen?

Anger turns unholy when our desires are blocked. The results are ugly: We "kill" (seek revenge) and "covet" (demand that others give us what we want) in our relationships.

Once we notice anger and realize our teen is experiencing a blocked goal, we have an opportunity to *reflect on what that anger and blocked goal might mean.* This reflection works in two stages. First, we look at our *own* feelings. If John reflects on his own anger toward Keith, he will more easily respond later in a thoughtful, nondestructive way. John might say to himself, "I'm feeling angry at having been blasted by my son. What's going on in me now?" Such reflection is hard and requires an ongoing commitment to seek God. The second stage of reflection deals with the teen's feelings. If John also reflects on what might be behind Keith's anger, he will be in a position to help Keith significantly in the days ahead.

In Keith's case, his blocked goal may have to do with bigger issues than just a pack of cigarettes. John might say to himself, "Boy, this cigarette thing is really important to Keith. I seem to be standing in his way. I wonder if there are other things that Keith isn't telling me? His quick rise in anger makes me think there's a major blocked goal I need to explore further with him. Something just set Keith off that was disproportionate to my request that he stay. Something else is going on with him."

The data of the conflict can become useful as father and son dialogue later about Keith's explosion. If John were to reflect in this way, he would be in a much better position to help Keith make some sense of his feelings and behaviors.

Many parents fear their own anger as well as their kids'. However, some anger can be good. Jesus displayed redemptive anger when He drove the moneychangers out of the temple, rebuking them for making the temple "a den of robbers" (see Mark 11:15-17). The Lord expressed His anger as a warning to the people to change their ways. We too must deal with and express our anger, even imperfectly, in redemptive ways with our kids.

> We have learned to distance ourselves from anger, irrespective of whether it is righteous or unrighteous. And when is righteous anger not stained by unrighteous motivation? Never. . . . If our anger must wait for perfect purity to be honored and expressed, then we are better off as frozen, unfeeling automatons. Our human anger may sometimes need to be silenced, but at other times it may need to be spoken. Our hope must be that our anger will grow more righteous as we are shaped to the contours of God's anger. If we allow ourselves to join God's fury and then focus on what we are to hate—evil, sin, ugliness—our hearts may discover a new dimension of the character of God.[4]

It's easy for parents to make the mistake of either ignoring their kids' anger or responding with an unthinking demand or discipline. Unfortunately, these responses have weak effects on teens' thinking and choices. A better response is to view anger as evidence of a blocked goal. Anger provides important information about what's going on inside a teen or a parent. This critical data can help us shape consequences that address not mere surface disobedience but the deep foolishness of the heart. (We will discuss discipline and consequences in sessions 14 and 15.)

Fear: An Uncertain Goal

When a teen has a goal and doesn't know if he's going to be able to achieve it, he experiences some level of *fear. Webster's Dictionary* defines fear as "an unpleasant often strong emotion caused by anticipation or awareness of danger." All people are affected by fear at some level.

> Different people fear different things with different levels of intensity, but all of us fear what we cannot control. Fear is our response to uncertainty about our resources in the face of danger, when we are assaulted by a force that overwhelms us and compels us to face that we are helpless and out of control. Fear is provoked when the threat of danger (physical or relational) exposes our inability to preserve what we most deeply cherish.[5]

6. What do you fear in regard to your kids?

7. What fears do you believe your teen may be operating from?

One area of life in which adolescents strongly want to preserve a sense of control is acceptance by the opposite sex. Many boys have told me their private fear is first-time dating, specifically when they want to ask a girl to a school dance. When I was a sophomore, I was anxious about asking a particular girl to a mixer. Problem was, I didn't know how to dance. I remember begging my younger sister to show me how to dance in the basement of our home. After a couple of minutes of coaching, she said with exasperation, "You are pathetic. It's going to take forever for you to get this." I remember thinking, *What if I can't do this? I hate feeling so helpless!* I was scared.

Eventually, all kids experience fear like this. For instance, Sean's mom can't understand why Sean hasn't asked Andrea to the prom yet. He's been talking for weeks about how cute and nice she is. He said he wanted to take her to the prom. But the day is approaching, and now he's not sure he's going to ask her. He's not even sure he wants to go to the prom at all. His mom is bewildered, but if she were to reflect on Sean's actions and statements, she would see clearly what's going on.

Sean really wants to take Andrea to the prom, but he is uncertain that she will agree to go with him. What if she already has a date? What if she has some other guy she really wants to go with and is going to hold out and hope he asks her? What if she doesn't even like Sean and spreads it all over school that "Sean, the geek, had the nerve to ask me to the prom! Can you imagine it? Sean and me! He's nuts!"

If Sean's mom ponders the way he talks about the prom, she will remember that every time she has asked him who he's going to invite, his voice gets tight and his words seem anxious. She can state a tentative hunch about his feelings to help him put his struggle in the open for discussion: "Sean, every time I ask you about the prom, you seem to avoid my question about who you're going to ask. Your voice gets tight, your eyes widen, and your words trail off as we talk. I'm guessing you're fearful of asking this girl, Andrea, because you don't know what she will do with your request. Is that close to what you're feeling?"

Sean's mother is now using the data about Sean to help him deal openly with his feelings and thoughts. Parents need to look at their kids' fearful responses to help them make sense of their world.

Shame: An Unreached Goal

One of the most powerful emotions, yet the least easy to admit, is shame. We may have no problem expressing our anger, but who wants to admit he's ashamed? Yet when kids (or adults) fail to reach a goal, they often feel shame. *Webster's Dictionary* defines shame as "a painful sense of having done something wrong, improper, or immodest."

Allender and Longman describe the trauma of shame:

> Shame is *the traumatic exposure of nakedness*—for example, when a person does something harmful (has an affair), commits a blunder (forgets a wallet), or is caught in some flaw of appearance (smudged mascara). This exposure occurs when we feel the lance of a gaze (either someone else's or our own) tearing open the various cultural, relational, or religious covering we put on. What is revealed, we feel, is an inner ugliness.[6]

Yet we must delve deeper to understand the spiritual significance of shame:

> It is more biblically accurate to affirm that we feel shame when people treat us badly—or even when they treat us well—because *shame is rooted in our inherent preference to trust false gods rather than depend on God for each and every moment of our existence.*[7]

In the garden, Adam defensively told God, "I was naked, so I hid" (Genesis 3:10). Adam had begun trusting himself for his existence and worthiness, rather than trusting God. So he felt ashamed when he realized that to see him exposed was to see his deficiencies. Back when he was depending on God, his deficiencies didn't bother him. In the same way, our kids will struggle with shame in their relationships because they are depending on themselves to win the acceptance they need.

8. Shame, at its core, is an "inherent preference to trust false gods rather than depend on God." It is not just a sense of personal deficiency. Can you put into your own words what this means?

Our kids' budding sexuality is one of the most powerful areas where shame strikes. Many parents avoid dealing with their teens' sexuality. However, when parents don't deal with it, kids can feel confused and anxious.

One father told me of strongly moving into his thirteen-year-old son's heart in the midst of the boy's anguish. Fortunately for his son, the dad was growing in his ability to listen and respond to the data of his son's heart.

Tim stumbled into his dad's hobby room early on a Saturday morning, crying and unable to look his father in the face. "Dad, I can't believe what happened to me last night. It's horrible!" Dad was confused and asked Tim what he meant. Tim looked down. He quietly said, "I have semen in my underwear, and I don't know how it got there. I feel sick." Tim felt he had done something horribly wrong.

Dad knew his next words were critical for his ashamed son. "Tim, you had what most boys your age have. You had a wet dream. It's called a nocturnal emission, when semen comes from a buildup in your testicles through your penis while you are sleeping. It's a normal process for boys your age. To be honest, I had the same thing when I was a kid. I felt bad, as you are obviously feeling now. But I want you to know you are okay, truly. It's nothing to feel dirty or unspiritual or sick about. It's the way God made you as you grow into manhood." Tim fell into his dad's arms.

By the time this dad finished telling me his story, we were both weeping. He had offered Tim grace instead of further shaming him. This father had used his son's shame and moved toward it in a way that was healing. Tim saw that his dad had the courage and wisdom to move into the heart of his shame. His father took what easily could have been a disastrous event and turned it into something lifegiving. We can be fairly sure that when kids fail to make eye contact and want to emotionally or physically flee, they are probably feeling shame. These are pieces of data we can use to minister to them.

Tracing Negative Emotions to Foolish Goals

We've learned to recognize the primary negative emotions and how they indicate unmet goals. In this section, we'll learn to identify those goals specifically. There are two basic steps in this process:

1. Observe your teen's emotions and behavior.
2. Reflect on your own reactions to and feelings about your kid's behavior.

The chart titled "The Goals of Misbehavior" will help you identify your teen's goals in general terms. These goals will show up again and again. Our job is to trace our kids' emotions down to their likely foolish goals below the waterline.

The next chart goes into more detail about a vicious cycle between kids' behaviors, parental feelings about those behaviors, parental responses, and kids' responses. To use this chart, first identify the feelings you are having about your teen. Then notice in the chart the behaviors that typically go with those feelings. Are you doing what the chart describes? Then note what kids typically do when parents respond in that way. See how the parents' feelings and kids' behaviors are a vicious cycle. Your feelings end up causing your kid to act in a certain way, which causes you to feel a certain way, which causes them to react in destructive ways. Often the cycle continues until parents reflect upon their kids' negative emotions and choose a course of ministry.

THE GOALS OF MISBEHAVIOR

Child's Faulty Belief	Child's Goal*	Parent's Feeling and Reaction	Child's Response to Parent's Attempts at Correction	Alternatives for Parents
I belong *only* when I am being noticed or served.	**Attention**	Feeling: Annoyed Reaction: Tendency to remind and coax	Temporarily stops misbehavior. Later resumes same behavior or disturbs in another way.	Ignore misbehavior when possible. Give attention for positive behavior when child is not making a bid for it. Avoid undue service. Realize that reminding, punishing, rewarding, coaxing, and service are undue attention.
I belong *only* when I am in control or am boss, or when I am proving no one can boss me!	**Power**	Feeling: Angry; provoked; as if one's authority is threatened Reaction: Tendency to fight or to give in	Active- or passive-agressive behavior is intensified, or child submits with "defiant compliance."	Withdraw from conflict. Help child see how to use power constructively by appealing for child's help and enlisting cooperation. Realize that fighting or giving in only increases child's desire for power.
I belong *only* by hurting others as I feel hurt. I cannot be loved.	**Revenge**	Feeling: Deeply hurt Reaction: Tendency to retaliate and get even	Seeks further revenge by intensifying misbehavior or choosing another weapon.	Avoid feeling hurt. Avoid punishment and retaliation. Build trusting relationship; convince child that she or he is loved.
I belong *only* by convincing others not to expect anything from me. I am unable; I am helpless.	**Display of Inadequacy**	Feeling: Despair; hopelessness; "I give up" Reaction: Tendency to agree with child that nothing can be done.	Passively responds or fails to respond to whatever is done. Shows no improvement.	Stop all criticism. Encourage any positive attempt, no matter how small; focus on assets. Above all, don't be hooked into pity, and don't give up.

*To determine your child's goal, you must check your feelings *and* the child's response to your attempts to correct him or her. Goal identification is simplified by observing:
    a. Your own feelings and reaction to the child's misbehavior.
    b. The child's response to your attempts at correction.
By considering your situation in terms of the chart, you will be able to identify the goal of the misbehavior.

Systematic Training for Effective Parenting (STEP): The Parent's Handbook by Don Dinkmeyer and Gary D. McKay. © 1989 by American Guidance Services, Inc., 4201 Woodland Road, Circle Pines, MN, 55014-1796. p. 14. Reproduced with permission. All rights reserved.

PARENTS' EXPERIENCES AND KIDS' RESPONSES

Parents' experiences	Kids' responses
annoyed by kid irritated bugged coaxing talking to get things accomplished	goody-goody kid charmer bright, uncalled-for remarks clowning around (I was just kidding!) endless questions to parents (why? how come?) laziness in tasks bashfulness
angered defeated emotionally threatened forcing kid to comply punishing kid giving up because kid is too tough	nonstop arguing with parent breaks family rules (you can't make me!) tantrums: kid screams and carries on to get parent to comply purposeful "forgetting" stubbornness

hurt
humiliated by kid
feeling rejected by teen
parent feels like getting even
how could they do/say that!?
	mean remarks (designed to hurt parent: "You're
	  stupid" "You don't care")
	deliberately destroys property (breaks household
	  goods, trashes rooms)
	running away ("I'm leaving this crummy place")
	promiscuity ("I am going out with him/her, and I
	  won't be back 'til tomorrow)
	drug abuse
	physical attack on parent

despair
giving up
discouraged with kid(s)
no action taken due to
hopelessness of situation
	unattempted jobs ("I might go to school if I feel
	  like it")
	excessive absences ("I just can't handle going to
	  school")
	playing dumb ("You know I can't do that")
	hypochondria
	non-participation ("I can't do it, so don't ask me")

9. In the chart above, find the main feeling you have toward your teen. Are you caught in the cycle the chart depicts? How is your teen responding to you?

Remember

Observing negative emotions in our teens as well as ourselves will give us valuable data to ponder so that we can respond wisely to our kids. Identifying our feelings allows us to move into the deeper issues of what our hearts, and our kids' hearts, are doing with God and each other. The three negative emotions indicate unmet goals in our kids' hearts. Noticing anger, fear, and shame enables us to trace our kids' unmet, foolish goals and then minister to our kids.

Reflection

Below are some sample situations with teens. Your group assignment is to determine what specific foolish goal each kid and parent is likely pursuing. Explain the reasoning for your choice.

1. Thirteen-year-old Darien is late again for dinner. Dad is annoyed because Darien is always late. Dad yells at Darien. Darien runs to his room and slams the door, yelling that Dad never listens to him.

   Kid's Actions   **Parent's Feelings/Response**   **Kid's Response**   **Kid's Goal**

2. Kara is seventeen and has just come home at midnight with alcohol on her breath. When she is questioned she says she wasn't drinking. She and her boyfriend just went to a movie and came right home. Mom and Dad remind her that drinking is against the family rules. When Dad stops Kara on the steps to continue talking to her, she glares at him, mutters a hostile comment, and walks back out of the house. Dad is stunned.

   Kid's Actions   **Parent's Feelings/Response**   **Kid's Response**   **Kid's Goal**

3. Fifteen-year-old Marc is playing Nintendo in the family room when Dad comes home and sees his son's report card. Marc is failing in four subjects. When Marc sees Dad red-faced and entering the family room, he hangs his head and tries to leave. Dad starts yelling. Marc turns sarcastic: "What do you care about my grades? All you care about is church!" Dad is furious and continues yelling at Marc. Marc tells him he can't wait to turn eighteen and leave home. Dad storms out of the room.

   Kid's Actions   **Parent's Feelings/Response**   **Kid's Response**   **Kid's Goal**

Action Lab

During the next time of conflict with your teen this week, stop to:

1. examine your feelings and reactions
2. examine your kid's responses to your correction

By looking at your teen's negative emotions, try to determine what foolish goal he or she is pursuing. Bring your observations to the group next week for discussion.

NOTES

1. Allen P. Ross, *Creation and Blessing: A Guide to Study and Exposition of the Book of Genesis* (Grand Rapids, MI: Baker, 1988), p. 127.
2. Dan Allender and Tremper Longman III, *The Cry of the Soul: How Our Emotions Reveal Our Deepest Questions About God* (Colorado Springs, CO: NavPress, 1994), p. 15.
3. Allender and Longman, pp. 56, 58.
4. Allender and Longman, p. 70.
5. Allender and Longman, p. 51.
6. Allender and Longman, p. 195.
7. Allender and Longman, p. 196.

Twelve

Conflict: Surviving the Tsunami

A tsunami is a tidal wave caused by an underwater earthquake or volcanic eruption. A July 1998 headline, "Tidal Wave Kills Hundreds in Papua New Guinea," captured the devastation of a tsunami that leveled coastal areas of the small Pacific island nation. A massive tidal wave powered by an underwater earthquake destroyed at least ten villages. One village on a spit of land was wiped away, leaving only "clean sand" according to an eyewitness. A surviving resident said the twenty-foot waves swept another village away like a broom. Three waves crashed with little warning.

Tsunami is a Japanese word used as the scientific term for a seismic sea wave. An undersea wave can travel hundreds of miles and reach speeds up to 500 mph. Yet the wave is only one to two feet high in the open ocean. As the unremarkable wave reaches the shore, however, it becomes a towering wall of water fifty feet high or more. Without the ability to detect and use early warning data, people along the coastline are vulnerable to this unforeseen destruction.

Teens can have the same emotional effect on parents. If parents don't notice the warning signs, they can be knocked flat by a conflict with their kids. Parents say adolescent tsunamis make them feel that their kids have them spinning out of control. They are caught in a violent wave and unable to gasp for breath before the next one hits.

One Tuesday evening after dinner, fifteen-year-old tsunami Darcy crashed into her parents, seemingly without warning.

Darcy: I'm going out tonight to see my friends. I don't want to spend any more time on studies. I am sick of school and the housework you give me. I just want to do as I want tonight. Don't plan on telling me I can't go either. I just can't handle the pressure I feel from you both. I want out tonight!

Phil: What do you mean you're going out with friends? What friends? You didn't ask us or tell us until now, and you have other things you need to do around here. You always ignore your responsibilities. You just want to hang out with your girlfriends. Not tonight, young lady.

Marge : *(pleading)* Darcy, you know your father and I told you about your responsibilities at school and around home. Your grades are suffering; you need to study, and you haven't this semester. You promise, but you aren't doing your work. Your friends can wait until the weekend. Come on, honey. Just do what your dad and I ask you to do tonight, okay?

Darcy : *(angrily)* Dad, you are always on my case about something. I told you I need to go now. I don't want to be around you! I'm getting my stuff to stay at a friend's tonight. (runs to her room, hastily packs her overnight bag, and walks to the front door)

Phil : *(tensely pacing)* Darcy, I said you were forbidden to leave! You will do as your mother and I have said. Now unpack your clothes and get back to your studies!

Darcy : *(screaming)* To hell with you! I hate you! You try to control me, and I won't do it! You and your rules can all go straight to hell. I hate you! I HATE YOU! And I'm not coming back to this house again!

Phil : *(pushing her out the door)* I'm sick of you as well! You're so disrespectful and ungrateful. Here's your stupid bag! (He throws it at her.) Go make it on your own. Just don't plan on ever using me again!

---

1. Have you ever experienced conflict like this with your teen? If so, how have you dealt with this kind of conflict?

Phil and Marge had just experienced the full power of an adolescent tsunami. Both parents truly loved their daughter. Yet now Phil was beside himself with rage and confusion. Marge was weeping hysterically.

Phil tried to talk with Marge, but his words just felt like blowing leaves going anywhere and nowhere. He knew he had messed up, but what should he have done? He had felt helpless to change his daughter's thinking or her feelings toward Marge and him. The tsunami had struck violently and seemingly without warning. Where could Phil and Marge go from here?

OBJECTIVE: In this session, you will learn to develop the kind of relationship with your teens that will enable you to deal with conflict in a positive way.

Three Ways to Handle Conflict

Darcy was the teenage equivalent of a tsunami. Obviously, some kind of underwater earthquake had caused her outburst. Yet Phil and Marge weren't aware of it. They never saw the tsunami coming because they didn't have any way to read the emotional seismic activity in their daughter in the months before the wave hit them.

Did any good come out of this disastrous Tuesday evening? Possibly. As we think about it and the conflicts that go on in our own homes, it's helpful to look at the facts about conflict. The chart below shows that parents like Phil and Marge are demonstrating relational immaturity in the way they handle conflict. This immaturity ensures that tsunami-sized conflict will repeat itself endlessly if not honestly addressed by both parents.

Kevin Huggins describes three general responses parents exhibit when dealing with conflict with their kids:

1. Regard the conflict as the real threat to their relationship with their kids
2. Use the conflict to maintain distance in the relationship

3. Wisely use conflict to identify and address the weaknesses it exposes in the parents' and teens' character[1]

The chart at the bottom of the page highlights the ways parents choose to deal with adolescent conflicts.

---

2. Consider the three general ways to handle conflict. Which of these ways do you typically use with your kids?

Marge regarded conflict itself as the *real threat* to relationship with Darcy. If we look closely at Marge, we find that she tried to *avoid conflict* with Darcy. Darcy was powerful, popular, and manipulative. She was attractive and easily got adults to give her what she wanted. Marge found it easier to give in to her daughter's demanding ways. She took Darcy to the mall for new clothes, even though she knew Darcy liked mom's attention but still wasn't truly grateful. Marge tried to give Darcy whatever she wanted. Her efforts were never enough.

Marge was at a point where she defended Darcy in front of Phil, knowing that she wasn't helping Darcy to deal with her lack of respect and gratitude. Marge was a relationally immature mom whose real goal was to avoid conflict.

Phil was at the opposite end of the scale: He *created conflict* with Darcy to the point that the only relationship the two had was fighting. He often used conflict *to maintain distance* from Darcy. He viewed Darcy's manipulation and anger as a personal affront to his authority. He had a close relationship with Darcy when she was young, often holding his little girl in his big chair. Yet his relationship with her grew distant as she became an adolescent. Phil believed that Darcy needed to be raised by a firm hand to compensate for Marge's weakness. Yet he was guilt-stricken by his angry words and the way he had pushed his daughter out into the night. Even though he was in counseling and had begun to look at his heart, Darcy's fury was more than he could handle. His aim had been to use conflict to avoid the painful truth that he often felt like a failure as a father and had a daughter he did not understand or love very well.

If conflict got Marge and Phil into so much trouble, how could it possibly be positive?

---

3. Are you like Marge or Phil in any way? If so, how?

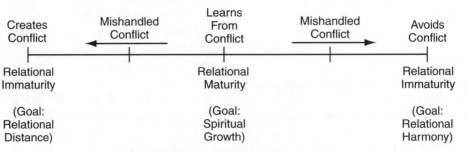

From Kevin Huggins, *Parenting Adolescents*, p. 166.

A Secure Fortress

The biblical idea of parental maturity in the midst of conflict is vital to weathering conflict well with teens:

> He who fears the LORD has a secure fortress,
> and for his children it will be a refuge.
> (Proverbs 14:26)

If we deepen our relationships with God, we will be able to give our kids a feeling of safety and refuge in a painful world. This sense of safety allows us to pursue increased involvement with them. This involvement, in turn, allows us to stand firm in times of conflict, offering both love and justice rather than retreating or lashing out.

Three Myths About Relational Conflict

Many of us have mistaken ideas about conflict. Let's look at some of the myths we may believe and what the reality is.

Myth #1: Conflict Should Be Avoided

Marge grew up in a "peaceful" family. Her parents almost never argued, at least not in front of the kids. Whenever Marge witnessed conflict in her friends' homes, she felt frightened and confused. When she became a mother, her goal was to keep the peace. She retreated from conflict and nervously anticipated it.

Unfortunately for Marge, Darcy was not like that. Darcy used her words and charm to manipulate. She was unafraid to get mad. She found she could manipulate her mom with her demands and complaining. Marge's insistence on avoiding conflict with Darcy actually caused greater problems in the long run!

Myth #2: Conflict Can Destroy a Relationship

Marge fervently believed that conflict could destroy her relationship with Darcy. That's why she tried to avoid it at all cost. What Marge didn't realize was that *parents' relational immaturity can destroy a relationship with a teen, but conflict alone cannot.* Many of the difficulties Marge ran into with Darcy were the result of Marge's fear of conflict. She refused to look at this important information about herself, and that decision motivated her refusal to deal honestly with Darcy.

In order to mature, Marge had to realize that conflict was sometimes necessary because it helped her to understand and change the weaknesses in her parenting style. For example, she needed to stop taking Darcy shopping or out to eat every time Darcy asked. When Darcy pouted or complained, Marge had to talk honestly about the pouting or demanding. She had to decide not to avoid the conflict. By making this decision, Marge inevitably encountered more conflict with her daughter. Yet over time, Darcy gained respect for her mother.

Warning: If parents avoid conflict because they want only respect and love from their teen, ultimately they will have neither.

Myth #3: Conflict Means You Are Doing Something Wrong

In reality, a mature parent may be doing something very right when he enables conflict to surface. *Good conflict management is not simply peaceful coexistence with teens under the same roof.*

I use the term "relational détente" to describe a stance parents may unwisely adopt. Détente was a political strategy the United States used in the 1970s and 1980s to contain Soviet communism. It meant finding ways to ease tensions so two powerful forces could coexist without destroying each other.

If a parent tries to use a strategy of "relational détente" (whatever works to ease tension), conflict may be avoided without any maturity taking place in the parent-teen relationship. By contrast, wise parents see conflict as a way to deepen involvement with their kids.

---

4. Which myths about conflict are operating in your family? How do you see them at work?

The Value of Conflict in a Relationship

As we've seen, conflict is not necessarily all bad. In fact, conflict can actually be helpful. In the long run, there is potentially great value in conflict with teens.

Conflict Engages People in an Emotional Level of Communication.

We learned earlier that Marge grew up in a home where everyone avoided conflict. Although her home may have been peaceful, it was not emotionally rich or attractive to her or her siblings. It was a sterile home—peaceful, yet passionless.

John was a forty-year-old dad with a rebellious fifteen-year-old son named Ken. I was seeing them for counseling. One Sunday after church, John got upset at Ken about suspected pot usage. He grabbed Ken's wrist out in the church parking lot in order to make him come home in the car. Ken bolted down the street, with John pursuing and yelling for him to stop. (It was quite a sight in the neighborhood after a worship service!) Eventually, John was able to help Ken see his disappointment and fear about Ken's choice of friends and that he feared they were hurting Ken spiritually and personally. Ken

was able to open up slowly to his father because John entered the conflict honestly. John said, "It was wrong for me to hurt you by grabbing your wrist. But I want the truth in our relationship. I am fearful about the friends you are hanging out with. Are you experimenting with pot?" I remember John's courageous and open spirit that drew Ken's heart toward his father over the weeks in counseling.

Each conflict with a teen has the potential to open a window to his heart. It confuses teens when their parents don't retreat from conflict but actually enter it as John did. Kids usually find this strangely attractive and start to be drawn to their parents, allowing them to develop influence with them.

Conflict Opens a Window for Past Wounds and Offenses to Be Explored.

Seth attends a school with a hair policy—kids are not allowed to dye their hair in weird, bright shades. Early on, Cathy and I did not know about this policy. At the end of summer vacation several years ago, Seth and some friends dyed their hair, hoping the principal would not notice the bleached blond look. No such luck. I got a call from the principal asking me to have our son redye his hair back to his original brown color or risk a short-term suspension.

I felt frustrated. What was Seth thinking? I didn't handle the incident as well as I wanted. Instead of stopping to reflect on my heart, I reacted automatically. I started barking orders at him like a drill sergeant, overwhelming him without allowing him to explain how he was going to deal with the problem. "Seth, you knew the school rules about the dye policy, and the principal called me today, telling me you have no options. Today is Friday. You have until Monday to redye it. Just do it."

"I don't want to dye my hair back to brown," Seth retorted. "No way! It will damage my hair if I do it so soon. I'll find a way to wash it out, okay? I hate it when you blast me and don't let me talk when you're upset. You did this last month about my staying at a friend's home when you didn't know the whole story and after mom and I already worked it out. I hate it when you just start talking at me like I'm some little kid you can order around."

We had an unresolved conflict, and both of us were feeling tense. Yet this kind of conflict can set the stage for parents to grow in their capacity to love if they use the opportunity to look at their conflicts honestly.

Conflict Allows Family Members to Grow in Their Capacity to Love.

As we experience conflict with our kids, we will often be reminded of how poorly we love them. If we are wise parents, this reminder helps us to move to a deeper level of love. We do this by *focusing on our own actions* rather than exclusively on what our kids do.

That Sunday, I asked Seth to go driving with me. I was still feeling anxious and frustrated at my anger, yet I wanted to address his choices with his hair before Monday's classes. I said, "I'm still upset at your choices about your hair. I feel like you ignored Mom and me, just blew us off. But I realize I got too angry and said some harsh words. It was wrong of me. And you're right about last month. I really didn't listen well to you about staying at your friend's house. I was angry and harsh. However, you still have to deal with your hair and the principal tomorrow."

Seth said, "Yeah, I know. I tried to redye it yesterday. It didn't work. So I've decided to go to Super-Cuts to cut out the blond color by going short. I'm sorry about how angry I was toward you and Mom last night. I was just having a really bad day."

Seth and I were able to reconnect after a hard weekend of conflict. Yet the deeper issue was my struggle to look at my condemning heart first, allowing God to take me to a better place in my thinking and relating with my son.

5. Can you describe, in your own words, the process that encouraged Seth to move back toward me?

6. What areas might need to be addressed in your family so that you can use conflict in a healing way?

God cares more about a repentant heart than about what we can do to fix situations. Often the things we value most are beyond our ability to correct on our own without God. King David wrote,

> You do not delight in sacrifice, or I would
>   bring it;
> you do not take pleasure in burnt offerings.
> The sacrifices of God are a broken spirit.
> A broken and contrite heart,
> O God, you will not despise. (Psalm 51:16-17)

Instead of concentrating on our kids' rotten behavior or how we're going to deal with it, we need to concentrate on ourselves ("contrite heart") and how we might be failing to love our kids. Conflict gives us ample opportunity to ponder our hearts. We need to know how to have healthy conflict and to build relationships that can withstand conflict.

Handling Conflict in a Positive Way[2]

The book of Nehemiah is about the governor of a hurt, discouraged, angry people. Nehemiah virtually parented his people into a functioning nation. At one point, the wealthier citizens were oppressing the poorer ones. They were even selling their countrymen's children into slavery to pay debts. Nehemiah got involved to promote change and maturity. The guiding principles he used can help us move positively into conflict with our kids.

Nehemiah Encouraged Emotional Vulnerability When His People Were Hurt and Angry.

> When I heard their outcry and these charges, I was very angry. (Nehemiah 5:6)

Nehemiah fully experienced his anger at the horrible situation. Allender and Longman make this bold statement:

> Christians are never angry enough. . . . [R]ighteous anger warns, invites, and wounds for the greater work of redemption. It is full of a strength that is neither defensive nor vindictive, and it is permeated by a sadness that is rich in desire and hope. Most importantly, righteous anger allows the offense to be seen as an issue between the offender and God.[3]

Nehemiah allowed himself to feel his people's pain and sadness. It is never easy for any parent to listen to pain or complaining from a teen. Usually we feel threatened when kids vent their pain and anger toward us. Our kids' anger fuels our sense of inadequacy. It is so easy for us to respond automatically; who needs the discomfort that comes from truly hearing and feeling their pain? Parents have a choice: to pursue *comfort* (by not bringing up the tough issues) or *truth*.

Nehemiah allowed his people to freely surface whatever complaints were on their hearts. Kids also need to sense an openness on the part of their parents to deal with pain and anger.

Nehemiah did another important thing. As he listened to his people's story, he actively clarified what the complaints were about. He wanted to understand. He encouraged emotional vulnerability by listening nondefensively. He put their interest before his personal comfort. When parents relate to their kids with honest vulnerability, kids intuitively sense they are safe to discuss further the deeper issues of their troubled hearts. Such safety and deep sharing are essential to the healing process.

7. Do you allow yourself to be emotionally vulnerable when you hear the complaints of your teen's heart? If so, how do you do that? If not, what do you do instead?

Nehemiah Allowed Personal Impact in His Own Heart.

Nehemiah did not simply listen to and clarify his people's complaints.

> I pondered them in my mind. . . . (Nehemiah 5:7)

He actively allowed his brothers' woes to affect him. Instead of brushing off their emotions, he allowed them to stir his mind and heart to passionate involvement as he reflected upon what course of action he would pursue to help them. Healthy parents allow their kids to fully affect them emotionally. At the same time, they carefully evaluate the choices they can make in their responses.

A parent who allows personal impact allows the possibility that the parent may have contributed, perhaps unknowingly, to the teen's pain, or perhaps failed to lessen that pain. "Conflict in the parent-teen relationship can give parents the same opportunity Nehemiah had—not only to hear about what troubles their kids, but to feel it with them and to understand what role they as parents might have had in causing it."[4]

It's natural to want to put a lid on our complaining adolescents, or to minimize their anger. Marge always tried to appease Darcy by giving her whatever she wanted. Phil tried to quiet his angry daughter with hard words. Neither of these approaches resolves conflict. Kids' anger will simply go underground and come back again and again to haunt us.

Wise parents understand that in the midst of conflict, some of their teens' most important hurts and disappointments will surface. And we want them to surface! Imagine if Phil had stepped back and pondered Darcy's pain without letting his own anger get in the way. Phil would have begun to have compassion rather than anger.

Nehemiah Found Ways to Relieve Suffering.

When kids get up the nerve to cry for help, they will watch us closely to see what action we will take to help them. They want to know we will get involved. Here's what Nehemiah did when his people desperately asked for his help:

> I pondered them in my mind [allowed personal impact], and then accused the nobles and officials. I told them, "You are exacting usury from your own countrymen!" So I called together a large meeting to deal with them [took steps to relieve their suffering]. . . . (Nehemiah 5:7)

Nehemiah was sensitive to his people's needs and demonstrated by his actions that they could depend on him to relieve whatever stress he could. Do you look for opportunities to relieve your teen's pain, no matter what the personal cost? Or does that seem too fearful and painful?

When parents act as ministers rather than consumers, kids' hearts begin to soften. The consumer parent asks, "What should I do in light of the distress I feel?" This is a selfish approach. A ministry parent asks, "What do I do for my teen in light of the distress *he* feels?"

Remember

All of us will face conflict with our kids from time to time. The conflict may come like a crashing tsunami that leaves us feeling disoriented. There are three myths about conflict that we need to reject in order to move into conflict wisely. Creative use of conflict allows us to engage our kids on an emotional level, encourages past wounds to surface, and most importantly, allows family members to grow in their capacity to love. The biblical character Nehemiah gives us wise guidelines in dealing with conflict: encourage emotional vulnerability with our kids, allow kids to have personal impact on us, and find creative ways to relieve our kids' suffering when we can.

Reflection

1. Remember the last conflict you had with your teen. Did you find yourself pulled toward avoiding the conflict or toward creating more conflict to avoid dealing with the situation? What happened?

2. Do you see conflict as something to be avoided with your teen? What concerns or fears does conflict stir up in you as you approach your son or daughter?

Action Lab

Brainstorm several ways you might take positive action to relieve some problem areas your teen is experiencing. Attempt to help your teen in one area this week. Bring your experiences back to the group for discussion.

NOTES
1. Kevin Huggins, *Parenting Adolescents* (Colorado Springs, CO, NavPress, 1989), p. 165.
2. Huggins, p. 164–165.
3. Allender and Longman, pp. 66, 70.
4. Huggins, p. 169.

3. In what areas of your teen's life can you get involved to relieve some of his or her pain? What might prevent you from doing so?

Thirteen

Rebel with a Cause

IN session 12, we witnessed an explosive family scene between Darcy and her parents. A week later, Phil and Marge were in a counselor's office, trying to figure out what happened on that Tuesday evening.

Counselor: What do you think caused Darcy to get so furious?

Phil : *(anguished and strained)* I know she feels huge disappointment with me. She sees me trying to control her, tell her what to do. In some ways she's right. In my anger, I try to "fix" things between us. Like I tell her to get her homework done. But I know that isn't the real problem. She hates the sight of me now.

Marge: I know Phil loves Darcy. I keep trying to put them together, and when that doesn't work, I try to defend Darcy in front of Phil, which only makes the situation worse. I'm so afraid of Phil's anger and Darcy's hatefulness. I've never felt more fear that she might not want to come home. She's with her friends for now, but we have to work on our relationship or we might lose her. We all walk on eggshells.

Counselor: Being real and getting to the below-the-waterline truth is hard in any angry family situation. Darcy sounds like a tough kid who needs you each to relate differently to get to her heart. Phil, you need to offer her more grace and let her see how she not only angers you but also hurts you. Then she'll see her full impact on you. Marge, you need to speak honestly and let Darcy feel your anger when she manipulates you. What I'm describing is a very challenging avenue, but it's necessary in order for God to have freedom to help each of you to forgive Darcy and move to better places as parents.

Phil : *(thoughtfully)* I want Darcy back, but not if we have to keep walking on eggshells. I want to have truth and love in our home. I know it needs to start with me first, even as much as I want to blame her and stay angry. But if I camp on my anger, I'll have no heart for Darcy, and she's smart enough to see through any new strategy I come up with. I'm scared, but my daughter won't change until she sees something different from me and Marge.

You remember or have heard of the classic 1950s James Dean movie *Rebel Without a Cause*. Dean played an angry young man rebelling against all adult authority. In real life, Dean lived fast and died young in a high-speed auto wreck. But unlike Dean's angry young rebel, our kids have purposes *with* causes, and we need to open our minds and hearts to see them.

Phil and Marge were confused and in pain. They were struggling with why their attempts to love and discipline Darcy always ended in disaster. They were forgetting that *no adolescent behavior is without a purpose*. No matter how bizarre the behavior, whether it be compliance, distance, or in Darcy's case, open rebellion, kids have reasons for their actions (even if they aren't fully aware of them). Our adolescent rebels, like Darcy, do indeed have a cause.

---

1. What do you think Phil and Marge were feeling in the counselor's office? Have you ever felt like this? How so?

OBJECTIVE: In this session, you will begin to understand the reasons for your teen's rebellion and find better ways to move into his or her despair.

Despair Is the Culprit

In session 4, we learned about a number of forces that act on kids below the waterline and cause them to do what they do. At the core of those forces is disappointment (Proverbs 20:6).

In a fallen world, we all experience disappointment when people don't fulfill our deep desires for security, significance, and unfailing love. Yet all kids are on a search for unfailing love.

When the adolescent becomes disillusioned with the relationships he experiences at home, he'll often begin to regard relationships he finds outside the home (especially with peers) as the answer to the love he feels he has lost. However, by midadolescence the teen experiences enough betrayal by his friends to create an even greater disillusionment toward relationships outside the home than inside. This constitutes another real crisis for the adolescent: he must find the love he longs for while stranded in a sea of relationships that offer more disappointment, rejection, and heartache.[1]

When Darcy walked off into the night, she believed that her friends could give her what she desperately desired. However, no one but God can do that. All of us live in a world east of Eden, where such unfailing relationships are no longer available. All of us face disappointment. But during adolescence, when many emotions intensify, teens' disappointment can turn to despair. That's what happened to Darcy. Her relationship with Phil had grown tense. The little girl sitting on her daddy's lap had changed into a budding young woman. She wore the latest fashions, had cool friends, and developed an attitude about adults. She learned she could use charm to manipulate others.

Darcy began to see her father as a controlling man who didn't understand her heart, and she saw discipline as punishment. She increasingly wanted her freedom to do as she pleased—to be with friends and later with boyfriends. She saw Phil and Marge as adversaries. Whenever either parent questioned her, she became belligerent, demanding, and sullen. She saw both parents, but especially Phil, as responsible for her unhappiness.

She continued to feel angry, isolated, and needy in relationships. Her boyfriends helped for awhile, but even boys could not meet her need for unfailing love. She despaired. She couldn't find security, impact, or unfailing love anywhere. Her world was primed for disaster.

How Kids Respond to Despair

Webster's defines despair as "utter loss of hope; a cause of hopelessness." Hopelessness can be terrifying. When an adolescent encounters despair, he makes assumptions about life that shape his actions.

> Since every teen has foolish intentions to make life work apart from God, *his basic assumptions about the events of life are always designed to maintain his illusion of self-sufficiency.* This enables him to avoid facing two painful realities: the unpredictable and hostile nature of his world and the helpless and dependent nature of himself. No adolescent wants to accept the fact that the world will never be the kind of place that can deeply satisfy him, or that he will never be the kind of person who can find satisfaction in it on his own.[2]

All teens have the foolish intention to make life work without help from God or anyone else. But self-sufficiency always backfires.

I worked with a bright sixteen-year-old nicknamed "Winner" who struggled deeply with despair. On the surface he was pleasant, handsome, and relational. However, he had grown up in a musical family but lacked the family gift. His father saw him as a disappointment, unmotivated, and without initiative. Winner's mom saw him as needy and tried to meet his needs by making life easier for him. He was living in a group home because of ongoing family conflict. I was asked to visit him and try to build a relationship.

I asked about his name, Winner. He laughed, saying he was anything but a winner. "Loser" was closer to his real life. His thoughts of suicide deepened. He felt alone, helpless, and hopeless. One day he risked what he really felt and said with tears, "I feel totally without hope in this world. I planned to jump off the highest bridge, but I didn't even have the guts to do it. My parents see me as a complete loser. Even the kids in this group home keep their distance from me. School is awful—I just get made fun of. I've tried to act like a winner, but it's a show. Life sucks. I don't want to live if my life is like this."

2. How would you define despair in your own words?

3. Based on your observations, how would you say despair affects kids?

Allender and Longman write,

> As with other emotions, the manifestations of despair spread across a spectrum of intensity: regret . . . sadness . . . depression . . . despair. . . . The bottom floor of this progression is despair: the utter absence of any sense of hope, accompanied by a feeling of powerlessness. Despair leads to resignation and possibly to suicide. If you attended college in the sixties and seventies, you may recall the popularity of French existentialism. Some advocates of this philosophy suggested that suicide is the only logical response to the despair evoked by a meaningless world.

Despair looks at the world and notes its emptiness—the lack of true relational intimacy, the utter blackness of death. It concludes that life is not worth it. This is the core of all forms of destructive despair: abandonment, loss, the desire of death, and the subsequent refusal to hope.[3]

Both Darcy and Winner were trying to create a self-sufficient world that could not sustain itself. Both teens were building a house of cards where the slightest wind of relational loss could destroy the illusion. Why did they work so hard at a fragile illusion? It helped them avoid two painful realities:

The World Is Unpredictable and Hostile.

It will never satisfy a kid's deepest desires for love and significance. Darcy was trying to create order in her chaotic world by using manipulation first to get her parents and then her friends to come through for her. Her strategy began to collapse upon itself.

We Are Helpless and Dependent on Others.

Kids will never be able to find satisfaction on their own, no matter how hard they try to change themselves. Teens often try to earn love and significance by their own resources, independent of others. The internal message of the teen is "I can do it all on my own! I will find a way." Darcy became more frantic in her manipulating, with decreasing effectiveness.

Teens make two assumptions about life when they're in despair:

Assumption 1: I'm a failure. Something's wrong with me.

Despairing teens look around and see they're not getting what they want from the world, but everybody else seems to be doing fine. They figure the reason they're not doing well is that they're the wrong kind of person. The key to life, then, is to change into the kind of person the world will desire.

The teen's thinking process goes something like this: *Since I'm a failure, it's up to me to fix my deficiencies in order to be desirable to others. I will find a way to make myself desirable, no matter what.* Kids decide to pull themselves up by their own bootstraps, only to have their boots fall apart with the laces shredded in their hands.

Assumption 2: God is even more intolerant than the world. He wouldn't want to have anything to do with a mess like me.

James Dean isn't the only angry adolescent role model influencing young people today. Shock rock star Marilyn Manson identifies with disenfranchised youth. He looks like he could win a lead role in someone's worst nightmare. Dark makeup sets his eyes strangely into his head. His belly is covered with scars of self-mutilation. His music is angry, frantic, driving, and chaotic. Sadly, he grew up in a Christian home and school, both weak on grace and strong on shame. In a school play, he was cast as Jesus. During a crucifixion scene he went backstage with a loincloth costume. Older boys ripped it off, whipped him with it, and chased him naked down the hall in front of other kids. Manson came to view God as intolerant.

> Manson says, "I always wanted to become what adults feared most." . . . He has bought into Nietzsche's idea that God is dead, and openly stated that his band's role is to awaken a "collective disbelief in Christianity." Believing that Christianity makes people weak, Manson says that "your only salvation is yourself."[4]

Extreme, obviously. Yet many young people today have subtly come to believe that God is intolerant of them as well, and they too have to find their own salvation. Because a relationship with God seems so unreachable, many kids decide to avoid the whole subject. They prefer to believe that God doesn't exist, or at least is indifferent, so they don't have to deal with failing to meet His high expectations.

God's desire is to do for us what we can't do for ourselves: correct our deficiencies and satisfy the longings of our souls through a personal relationship. But kids, by maintaining their image of self-sufficiency (in Darcy's case, by angrily pushing people away), will experience little need for a personal relationship with God.

A Sick Heart

The Bible talks about despair and how it affects us:

> Hope deferred makes the heart sick,
> but a longing [desire] fulfilled is a tree of life.
> (Proverbs 13:12)

The image of the loss of hope as "heart sickness" vividly depicts despair. This heart-sickness can feel like nausea.

---

4. How would you define hope?

5. Have you seen this kind of heartsickness in your own teen? If so, how have you dealt with it?

Have you ever experienced food poisoning? I was introduced to it through a tainted hamburger. I remember feeling so awful I curled up in a fetal position on the cool bathroom floor and tried to stop my world from spinning and my stomach from retching. I wanted to stop living by the end of that long night of misery. Nothing else mattered more than to stop the pain. This agony is akin to the sickness produced in the teen's heart.

> Inevitably, naive and human-centered hope leads to profound disappointment. And when hope is shattered, it is usually too painful to hope again. . . . We desire fulfillment, but disappointment robs us of stability, sending us reeling under the sickness of despair. Over time, the often-repeated cycle of desire aroused, hope disappointed, and the soul deadened through despair leads to a hatred of desire.[5]

One woman described hating hope so much that if she could find it in her heart, she would "cut it out with a knife." She would not have to feel hope again because it was just too agonizing to have it go unsatisfied. When kids' longing to be the kind of people the world will love and value is not satisfied, they too become heartsick.

> Even in laughter the heart may ache,
> and joy may end in grief. (Proverbs 14:13)

Kids can appear on the surface to have their act together, but below the waterline they may be in despair. Winner sought to end his life because he couldn't stand to have hope deferred any longer by failed relationships. He acted upbeat and cheerful, but in the private recesses of his heart, his pain felt overwhelming. He just wanted life to be over.

Darcy's outward rebellion made it easy to see she was in pain, but many other kids try to turn themselves into people the world will value by being incredibly "good kids." It's important to know that those kids may be in despair as well, and when "being good" doesn't do the trick (remember, only God can satisfy the longings of the heart), they may begin down a path of self-destructive behavior.

Five Common Errors in Dealing with Adolescent Despair

When we know that our kids are in pain or despair, our impulse is to help them out. We want to make them feel better without confronting the deeper issues of their hearts. Unfortunately, many of us forget that our only hope of really helping them is to draw our kids toward God. It's tempting to outwardly rearrange our kids' lives in the belief that they can be happy without dealing with the inner heart issues that only God can satisfy.

Below are five common strategies parents use to deal with their kids' despair. These strategies, if used alone without calling teens to something higher, often promote a quick fix without any lasting change in the way teens think or relate.

Self-Improvement

Parents can try to help their kids look better, relate better, or think better, in the hope they'll be more accepted by the world. Weight loss, tennis lessons, modeling lessons, bodybuilding—there's an endless list of things to try. But getting rid of pain without moving to the real cause is, at best, a short-term solution.

Self-Assertion

Naturally, teens need to speak the truth in their relationships. But some parents go overboard when they suggest that their son or daughter get a handle on peer relationships by asserting his or her "right" to be respected and loved. ("Don't let them pick on you. Tell your teacher how he has hurt your feelings. Get in his face and let him know how you feel!") While no kid should be an emotional doormat for others to walk on, self-assertion as an answer to pain and despair is only a superficial solution if parents neglect to help teens discover the inner purposes of their behaviors.

Self-Indulgence

It's tempting to reduce or eliminate our kids' pain by giving them things to make them feel better. Again, this might have a superficial effect, but the underlying pain can't be healed with more things. Darcy's mom found that shopping trips and new clothing eased tensions, but Darcy's despair was still lurking below the waterline.

Self-Seclusion

A common solution is for parents to encourage teens to avoid those people who are causing them pain. Transferring into a different math class to avoid a mean teacher might make sense occasionally. Yet if parents model to their kids that they can avoid hassles by avoiding relationships, they again offer only temporary solutions. We need to equip our kids to deal with pain. Learning to deal with painful relationships in the midst of disappointment is the wiser path.

Self-Delusion

Many parents address their adolescents' pain with a well-intentioned pep talk. Just "buck up," because things aren't all that bad. Advice like this, which minimizes a teen's pain or suggests it isn't real, is dangerous. When sixteen-year-old Tom voiced complaints, his mother said, "You have it great compared to when I was a kid, so just be happy." Yet Tom's life was anything but happy. This strategy teaches kids not to face a disappointing world head-on, but to be self-deceptive in order to feel better quickly.

6. Why is this last error called "self-delusion"?

_____

_____

_____

_____

_____

_____

If parents pursue these strategies, they will rarely touch the despair in their teens' hearts. If kids don't understand their hurt and the reasons behind it, and experience their parents' strong support, they will simply avoid dealing with it honestly. These erroneous strategies only create more despair, as short-term relief is replaced by pain again and again. Controlling the circumstances that hurt teens is like treating symptoms of a cancer without trying to get rid of the cancer itself. The long-term result? More disillusionment, withdrawal, and anger toward their parents, themselves, and God.

A Biblical Approach to Dealing with Adolescent Despair

So what are parents supposed to do? How can they deal with the foolish intentions and false assumptions kids have about the world? Huggins suggests three paths parents can pursue: to enter kids' pain, to invite them to reflect, and to model the fear of God. It's important to understand that the seeds that destroy kids do not lie in the *teens' circumstances,* they lie in the *teens' own hearts.* When parents understand this, they increasingly shift to the ministry model of parenting discussed in session 8.

Enter a Teen's Pain.

The best way for parents to encourage their kids is to actively enter their pain. To do this, they must work to develop an emotional climate that communicates acceptance *no matter what feelings the teens express.* More and

more, parents must invite their kids to share the pain they're experiencing.

To succeed, this has to be done in a non-judgmental way and should strive to touch on crucial or critical desires as often as possible. If kids can talk honestly with their parents about the deeper desires of their hearts—freely and without fear of criticism or revenge—they will start to catch a glimpse of incarnated love. Our teens will *experience our love personally,* not abstractly.

7. What do you think it means to enter kids' pain?

_____

_____

_____

8. Would your teens say you do this? If so, how?

_____

_____

_____

_____

_____

_____

_____

Parents are called to risk loving their teens in tangible ways they will understand and receive. Even honestly struggling with our kids in conversation is better than telling them nothing about how we feel. Proverbs captures the reality of speaking love to others, including to our kids:

Better is open rebuke
than hidden love. (Proverbs 27:5)

Obviously, parents cannot enter their teens' pain overnight, especially with someone like Darcy who has effectively shut down all communication. But as parents boldly work to do it, they will become more and more alive and attractive to their kids.

Invite the Teen to Reflect.

Situations in which adolescents demonstrate despair are a great chance for parents to talk to them about unfulfilled desires, plans that fail, and distorted assumptions about life.

> Parents should encourage their teen to reflect on all these things. While being careful not to assume a tone of rebuke or condemnation, they should challenge their teen's assumption or expectations that the world can be manipulated to respect or love her in the way she most desires. Parents who talk openly at this point about some of their own despair and wrong assumptions can produce a climate that says, "We can relax because there's something broken about all of us. None of us will ever be good enough to get the world to give us what we most desire.[6]

Over time, Phil and Marge had to move toward helping Darcy make the connection between her failing desires and plans and her false assumptions about life. An effective way to encourage kids like Darcy is for parents to share openly with them about some of their own despair and wrong assumptions as adults.

Model the Fear of God.

In session 12 we looked at Proverbs 14:26:

> He who fears the LORD has a secure fortress, and for his children it will be a refuge.

As Phil and Marge reflected on their inability to fix their daughter or to take away her pain, they began to trust the Lord more and more to calm their deepest fears of Darcy abandoning the family. As this happened and they talked openly about it, God could become attractive to Darcy as a refuge.

We know it won't work with a teen like Darcy to simply give her a how-to list for living that includes belief in God. But as parents talk honestly about their own failures and how God helps them, God will become more attractive. It's like one thirsty person telling another where he can find water.

With Phil's permission, I include here a letter he sent to his daughter a week after the tsunami, as she was still furious and living at a friend's home. The letter shows him moving courageously into her despair to model God. It oozes an honest hope.

Darcy,

I have been thinking about writing this letter ever since you left a week ago last Tuesday night. I had hoped that by now we would have had a chance to sit down and at least talk about what happened. I know that you are incredibly angry at me and not without cause. I guess the main reason I haven't written before now is that I have been pretty angry with you as well for the terrible ways that you spoke to me and the awful things you screamed as you went down the steps and into the night. I won't ever forget it! It was one of the most terrible experiences of my life and I am incredibly sad that it ever happened. I wish there was some way that I could go back and replay that scene. I am deeply sorry that I ever laid a hand on you. I honestly do not remember what I said, but I am sure that it was something awful. Like you, I tend to say some pretty terrible things when I get angry. Anger is no excuse. What I did is wrong and I hope someday you will be able to forgive me.

The unfortunate thing about that incident is that it destroyed all that I had shared with you only minutes earlier. I was sincere when I told you that there is nothing in the world I want more than a close relationship with my one and only daughter. I was speaking from my heart when I said how sad it makes me feel when I think of all that both of us are missing. There is a very special relationship that God intended for fathers and daughters.

Neither one of us is experiencing that. This is perhaps only the second time in my life that I have had the courage to tell you how I really feel about you. You may recall the first time. I made reference to how painful it was for me to watch *Father of the Bride* because I was afraid that you and I would never experience anything like the relationship portrayed by the characters in the movie. You may remember that I was crying at the time. Those were tears of regret and sadness, not unlike the tears that I have shed since you left, not unlike the tears that I have shed when you refuse to even speak to me on the phone or come by so we can talk. I am not telling you this to try and make you feel guilty, but I do want you to know how you impact me. For some strange reason, it is awfully hard for me to tell you how I really feel about you.

As awful as it has been not knowing where you are or whether you are safe, the past ten days has given me a lot of time to think about you and me. I have thought a lot about how we have gotten to this point. It is obvious that you and I have hurt each other deeply — not deliberately even though it probably seems that way to both of us at times. Nonetheless, we have both been hurt and we find ourselves somewhat content to be apart because it is too painful to be together. It's like we both have a wound that just won't heal. No matter how hard we try not to, we seem to always find a way to break the scab off and expose the other's raw, open wound. You know what comes next — we just avoid one another, trying to steer clear of each other long enough for the scab to again cover the wound. The trouble is, the wound just never seems to heal and neither one of us knows what to do about it.

Darcy, I am at the point where I want more than anything to have the wound healed for both of us. I don't know how to do that but I do know one thing: it isn't going to happen without your involvement. I can't do it alone and you have got to want things to be different for us as well. We both may have to be willing to endure more pain in order for things to get better. I don't think we can make much progress without some outside help. At this point I think it is probably best that you not come home for a while. I think we both need some time to try and get to the bottom of what is driving us apart. . . . In the meantime, I want you to be in a safe, supportive environment. I have asked some family friends if you can live there until we can work out a plan to have you back in the family. I want that more than you will ever know. But, you have to want that too. Until you do, nothing I can do or say will matter.

There is a lot more that I want to be able to say to you, too much to try and cram into one letter. One last thing, I know that you are convinced that I kicked you out of the house that night. At this point whether I did or didn't doesn't matter. The fact is I want you back. All of us want you back. You are a part of our family and you belong here with us at home. I hope and pray that you will eventually feel the same way.

So where do we go from here? I guess the ball is in your court. I love you, I miss you, and I pray for your safety every time I think of you — which is often.

Love, Dad

---

9. How do you think Darcy would have felt receiving this letter? How did this letter affect you?

10. What did Phil try to communicate?

Remember

Despair plays a critical role in causing kids to lose heart and often deepens their rebellion. Despair is characterized by a loss of hope, which makes teens try to maintain self-sufficiency because they feel so powerless. Teens make two primary false assumptions about life: something is wrong with them (and needs self-reconstruction); God is intolerant and unpredictable like other people. Many parents try to alleviate despair by five inadequate strategies. The better way for parents to help their kids deal with despair is to do three things: enter their kids' pain, invite them to reflect, and model the fear of God.

Reflection

Below are several family scenarios. Your group assignment is to look at each of these and articulate what hidden pain might be behind the teens' actions. What might these kids be thinking and feeling?

1. Janet is forty-five and has a fourteen-year-old daughter named Deanna. Deanna is bright, sociable, well liked, and a model student. She is a perfectionist in academics and sports. Suddenly Deanna's grades fall, and she is no longer excited about school and her many extracurricular activities. She just stays in her room when she's at home, saying little to her mom. What might be occurring?

2. Robert, sixteen, suddenly explodes and starts yelling at you when his boss calls to see why he's late for work. (You happened to answer the phone.) His anger is too extreme for the incident mentioned. What might be going on in his heart?

3. Holly, eighteen, suddenly blurts out at the dinner table that she hates Dad's constant "third degree" while she's eating. Dad is stunned and speechless. Holly says she feels like he's a prison guard! What do you think might be going on?

Action Lab

As you observe your teen this week, look for areas in which you see rebellion (either open or subtle). Try to help your kid reflect on the possible purposes underneath the despair and rebellious behaviors you've noticed.

NOTES
1. Kevin Huggins, *Parenting Adolescents* (Colorado Springs, CO: NavPress, 1989), p. 66.
2. Huggins, pp. 212–213.
3. Allender and Longman, pp. 134–135.
4. Walt Mueller, "Marilyn Manson's Revenge," *New Man,* September–October 1998, pp. 32–33.
5. Allender and Longman, p. 141.
6. Huggins, pp. 230–231.

Fourteen

Challenging the Rebel

WE'VE talked a lot about the ministry model of parenting: asking questions that open doors to kids' hearts, speaking life words, increasing involvement in our kids' lives. These are vital concepts in the courageous parenting of adolescents. But at times, they're not enough. Even when parents put all of these concepts into practice, many kids simply will not respond. They persist in their rebellious behavior. This is because, as we learned in session 13, kids are committed to the foolish idea of making their lives work with no involvement from God or anyone else. How is a parent supposed to handle this persistent rebellion?

OBJECTIVE: In this session, you will learn how to challenge your teen's rebellion in a positive way.

Two Primary Ways to Confront Rebellion

Rebellion is resistance to authority, an inclination to resist authority, or a feeling or demonstration of anger or revulsion. Rebellious kids are inclined to resist our legitimate authority, often by extreme forms of anger. In a sense, rebellious kids see themselves as the only authority to which they need to answer.

In the last session, we looked at the sources of adolescent rebellion and learned that parents' first response must be *increased involvement* in their kids' lives. This involvement consists of entering their pain, inviting them to reflect, and modeling the fear of God.

In this session, we'll concentrate on the second primary way to confront rebellion: *uncompromising responsiveness.* Uncompromising responsiveness, which we introduced in session 6, is an active process. It means *to deal justly with teens' foolish thinking and to challenge it at every opportunity to promote maturity.*

As a parent takes whatever initiative is necessary to develop her teen's awareness of the true impact his choices are having on God, others, and himself, the child can begin to understand and appreciate the significance his life really has in God's eyes. Fools [including rebels] have little understanding of their own ways, especially of the impact or consequences that result from them. . . . Parents have the responsibility to respond to their kids' purposes and actions in a way that encourages kids to attach the same significance and meaning to them that God does.[1]

---

1. Put into your own words what "uncompromising responsiveness" means.

Uncompromising responsiveness empowers parents to challenge foolishness and rebellion. Huggins describes two primary tasks parents must pursue to confront rebellion constructively. First, parents must strengthen their teens' awareness and ownership of the purposes of their actions. Second, parents must call their kids to choose purposes that are directed to serving God and others.

1. Awareness and Ownership

Parents must actively strengthen their kids' awareness and ownership of the choices they make and the purposes of what they do. Taking ownership means acknowledging, "Yes, it's my choice. Nobody made it for me."

Maggie was a forty-five-year-old single parent who demonstrated remarkable courage to change the way she was dealing with her fifteen-year-old, Jason. Maggie had been a dependent parent, always giving in to Jason for fear of losing him to her ex-husband. She wept frequently during our parenting groups, was terrified of conflict, and had to leave the group often to compose herself. She was terrified to face her failure and the potential loss of Jason, and she was unwilling to confront her own heart. Over the weeks in our group, however, she began to look at the fears that controlled the way she related to Jason. Maggie began to demonstrate justice and care to Jason in ways he had never imagined!

Jason started using pot with other kids when he was eleven. He became an angry, demanding adolescent, often verbally assaulting his mom for not doing enough for him. He demanded that she take care of him, ignore his pot smoking, and give him whatever he wanted. Jason was a full-blown rebel at fifteen.

Maggie began to repent. She talked honestly to her son, telling him she would no longer be bullied by his anger and would be truthful in telling him of her disappointment. She challenged his purposes and actions more frequently. Over the months, she went even further. One evening, she laid out her thinking to Jason so that he could decide if he wanted to own his part of the family problems.

"I love you very much," she told him. "I realize I've failed you by being weak and cowardly. I've given you things you don't deserve or haven't worked for because I didn't want you mad at me. No more. I won't let you smoke pot in this house anymore, ever. I can't prevent you from doing what you choose outside these four walls, but not here. If you're going to be part of this family, I expect you to agree to go to school, do some chores that you and I agree on, and have the same basic rules your older brother has. I know this is a tough thing for you and me to talk about, but it's the best for you." Maggie was shaking when she got through talking with Jason, but she felt a freedom she had not known before.

Jason's reaction was predictable for a rebel. He raged. "No way, Mom! I won't agree to any of these rules! *I will smoke my pot whenever!* I'm not going to school, not working around here, and I will come and go when I want, just like always. Forget it. If you ask me to do this family thing, I will leave and you won't ever see me again!" Jason dropped the emotional bomb on his mom, expecting Maggie to give in as usual.

Maggie held her ground. "If you don't agree to these things, you're saying to me that you don't want to be a part of this family. You are saying, in reality, that you want to be on your own. I would be saddened by your choices. I can't stop you from leaving. I want you to know you are a part of my heart, and I want you home. But I also want you to know that you are the one doing this [increased awareness]. And I want you to know it will be your choice to stay or go from your home [ownership of Jason's choices]." Jason cursed, packed his duffel bag, and screamed that he would never return home again as he slammed the front door.

Maggie attached to Jason's actions the same consequences God did. She didn't avoid dealing with conflict; she dealt with her son honestly over the months before the showdown with him. She wept as she talked about Jason to the group, agonizing over his leaving home. Yet she knew she was giving her son a glimpse of justice and genuine love that she had rarely given him before. She was anxious, but felt stronger after the raging battle.

---

2. How did Maggie try to help Jason become aware of his foolish choices?

3. How do you try to help your kids take ownership of their choices?

---

2. Serving God and Others

Self-centered relating is normal for foolish kids. Parents must gradually call their kids to give up their foolish, selfish purposes and help them choose purposes that serve God and other people. Wise parents will encourage their teens to be other-centered (not self-centered) and to put the interests of other people before their own. In other words, *parents must call kids to other-centered relating* so they can mature. The apostle Paul said true joy is found in serving others:

> Do nothing out of selfish ambition or vain conceit, but in humility consider others better than yourselves. Each of you should look not only to your own interests, but also to the *interests of others.*" (Philippians 2:3-4, emphasis added)

Maggie had not heard from Jason for over a week when he finally called and asked to meet her in a Denny's restaurant. She was anxious to see him but knew his foolishness was far from gone. It was a tough meeting.

Jason: *(impatiently)* Well, are you going to let me back in the house under my conditions? I told you I can't live with your rules, so you have to change and back off. It's just too hard. I won't do it. Just because my brother agreed to your conditions, it doesn't mean I will. So can I come home?

Maggie: *(sorrowfully)* I want you to know what I last told you before you left a week ago. I love you. But I haven't changed my mind. I believe God is asking me to hold you accountable in ways I feared too much in the past. My own fears and needs kept me terrified to address the truth in our relationship. You are my son, and you need to decide if you want to honor me [serve others] in my honest requests for you to be a part of this family. You have said in the past that you care about God [serve God] and doing what He wants. I believe that coming home is what God wants for you in order to grow.

Jason: *(frustrated)* I won't come home under those conditions. I want my freedom, my friends, to come and go as I please. I'm not giving up pot either. I guess I'll be living somewhere else until you change, Mom. It's just the way I want it. I'm not telling you where I'm living for now. I don't want you to check up on me.

Maggie: I guess you'll be living somewhere else, based on your choices. I have one request. Can we meet at this restaurant every Saturday morning for breakfast to talk? I won't try to pressure you, and my decisions are still the same. But I want to try to at least stay connected to you as you have decided to live on your own.

Jason: This sucks. But yeah, I guess that would be okay.

---

4. How did Maggie try to call her son to a higher level of serving her?

5. In what ways do you try to call your kids to serve others and God?

Maggie communicated something powerful to Jason at the restaurant. She called him to serve her under godly family expectations. Further, she called him to serve God by honoring her and respecting her desires as the legitimate parental authority. Maggie was willing to enrage her son for the higher purpose of asking Jason to think more highly of others than himself. Maggie used powerful words, but parents must also use something else.

Mere Words Won't Do It

Proverbs 29:19 tells us:

> A servant cannot be corrected by mere words; though he understands, he will not respond.

Even when a parent speaks life words to his rebellious teen, the adolescent may not always respond. A teen's foolishness is often too deep-seated to be overcome by words alone. Jason didn't have any trouble understanding his mother's discussions with him about his foolish behavior. He simply didn't see how her words were meaningful for him. Proverbs 13:1 describes this tenacious tendency:

> A wise son heeds his father's instruction, but a mocker does not listen to rebuke.

Jason worked to dislodge Maggie's intervention. First he raged at her. Then he threatened. Finally, he just defied her. He would not "listen to rebuke." This is why wise parents need tools other than words to help their teens.

Punishment is usually ineffective, for reasons we'll address more fully in session 15. Essentially, the trouble with punishment is that it is usually arbitrary and based on momentary emotions, so it isn't logically related to the offense. While adolescents certainly don't enjoy punishment, they rarely learn from it either. They are more likely to be corrected by a more logical approach.

The logical approach we'll discuss here is *uncompromising responsiveness,* which is another way of saying "challenging and dealing justly with teens' foolishness." The avenues of uncompromising responsiveness in actions are the same ones we saw Maggie use in words: strengthening her teen's awareness of choice and inviting him to become a servant. We'll focus on choice for the rest of this session and session 15 because engineering choice is an art that requires considerable reflection and practice. In session 16, we'll look at inviting teens to become servants.

The Ability to Choose

In order to challenge their kids' foolish thinking, parents must first help to give them a sense of choice. You may be shaking your head and saying, "My kid *has* a sense of choice! Look at her weird clothes, the friends she chooses, and that obnoxious music. She chooses how she's going to do in school and what she'll do with her free time. She certainly doesn't let *me* have any input in those decisions!"

You're partly right. Adolescents do make choices. But they often don't realize they do. And they especially lack a sense of choice regarding the truly deep issues of life. "Will my parents value my contribution in the family? Do others respect me? Do they love me for who I am? Can I make a real difference in my world?" Many teens would answer no to these questions. They don't believe they can build meaningful relationships.

A kid like Jason, for example, who is unmotivated, angry, and fearful of life, might feel that he has no real choices because *nothing he tries ever really matters.* No matter how he tries to get a sense of security, love, or impact, he fails. He eventually settles on being a demanding, defiant bully with his mom and

others. At least he gets negative attention, rather than no attention at all. A foolish rebel may believe it's better to be the best of the worst than to be the best at nothing.

Foolish kids like Jason must learn they have the power to choose. Parents can encourage this direction by doing two things: (1) show teens that they make choices, and (2) create opportunities for choice.

Show Teens That They Make Choices.
Every time your teen makes a choice, *bring it to his or her attention.* By giving kids lots of feedback about their actions, parents can create a sense of ownership.

I have come to believe that many kids don't feel they make choices of significance.

> A teen must know of his power to choose. Every action an adolescent takes actually represents a choice he is making. However, a recent study of high schoolers found that kids do what they really want to do only about 20 percent of the time. At least 80 percent of the time these kids have no sense of choice in what they are doing.[2]

6. What do you think about the idea that kids don't feel they have a real choice? Do you think your own teen feels like this?

As simple as this may sound, it's important to assume that our kids don't fully make the connection between their actions and their inner choices. I talked to one father with a sixteen-year-old son who always mumbled, "I don't know," whenever his dad asked him about his choices. One evening, Jim, the father, asked his son Ryan to hurry and open the garage door so Jim could pull the car in. Ryan slowly strolled through the front lawn. Jim became impatient and tensely asked Ryan why he refused to run when Jim asked for his help. Ryan mumbled, "I don't know."

Jim began to help his son make a connection between his refusal to respond, his slow walking, and even his mumbling "I don't know" as choices to avoid his father. The more parents bring up the choices kids make in little as well as big actions, the more kids begin to connect their actions to their choices.

Create Opportunities for Choice.

As you point out again and again that your teen is making choices, she'll eventually make connections in her thinking between her choices and their consequences. Ironically, as kids begin to understand our efforts to connect their many actions to their choices, they may resist our efforts, because to understand their choices also makes them *more responsible for those choices.*

The adolescent thought process goes something like this: "If I don't have to own my decisions, I am not responsible for those decisions before others. But if I verbally acknowledge my decision, other people (like my parents) can hold me responsible." Beware: Kids will normally try to push away this sort of feedback because they realize they'll have to own up to their decisions. A wise parent will push in this direction to eventually discourage foolish thinking. Create as many opportunities as you legitimately can to show your teen that he's making choices.

Jim began to create many opportunities for Ryan to choose. Instead of manipulating Ryan into certain sports, Jim allowed him to decide what sports he tried out for at school. He gave Ryan more options of what chores he did at home. He allowed Ryan to set his own homework schedule by choosing what hours he

would study. Over time, Ryan began to be more responsive to making choices as Jim encouraged him.

---

7. Why is it important for parents to create choices for their kids?

8. How could you develop more choices for your kids?

Foster Cline and Jim Fay give a rationale for actively creating choices for our kids:

One reason choices work is that they create situations in which children are forced to think. Kids are given options to ponder, courses of action to choose. *They must decide.* Second, choices provide opportunities for children to make mistakes and learn from the consequences. With every wrong choice the children make, the punishment comes, not from us, but from the world around them. Then children don't get angry at us; they get angry at themselves. Another reason choices work is because they help us avoid getting into control battles with our children [as Jim did with Ryan]. Finally, choices provide our children with opportunities to hear that we trust their thinking abilities, thus building their self-confidence and the relationship between us and them.[3]

Logical Consequences: Illustrations of Choice

Real choices lead to consequences. If the same thing will happen to a teen no matter what he does, he will conclude that his choice doesn't matter. Consequences need to be related in some logical way to the choice, or they seem arbitrary. That's one of the drawbacks of punishment: It doesn't teach a teen to connect his choices to consequences that make sense.

When words alone are insufficient to confront a rebellious adolescent's behavior, wise parents *engineer logical consequences.* Logical consequences differ from natural ones in that natural consequences are outcomes kids experience on their own without our intervention. For example, a kid runs across a wet floor, falls, and hurts his knee; a kid fails to study for the math test and then fails the test; a teen yells at a friend and is not invited to a ski trip. Natural consequences are one way kids learn to deal with their foolishness. At times, however, natural consequences are inadequate in themselves to decrease foolishness because they lack power.

Engineered consequences, where parents actively structure kids' choices based on the reality of the situation, are more potent because they *alert teens' hearts to the power of pain in their choices.*

> The pain such consequences bring can be one primary thing God uses to get a kid to reevaluate and change the foolish strategies he lives by. . . . [Parents] should help him connect his pain to a choice he has made. Building this bridge between the purposes in a teen's heart and the disappointment he experiences in the world is essential to helping him become disillusioned with his own foolishness. Without this kind of help from parents, a teen will frequently fail to notice any relationship at all between the painful consequences of his choices and the foolishness of the choices themselves. He can continue to believe that his foolish strategy is really a source of life.[4]

Through a thoughtful, creative process, parents allow teens to fully experience the positive and negative impact of their choices. A parent must structure at least two legitimate avenues for the kid to choose between. Compelling teens to experience the logical consequences of their actions usually succeeds in helping teens push away from foolishness and gravitate toward maturity, even when words have failed.

Let's return to Phil, Marge, and Darcy from session 13. Darcy left the home in a rage over a power struggle with Phil. Phil was a maturing father and sent her a hopeful letter talking about his part of the conflict. Phil invited her to talk with him about returning home when she was ready. He acknowledged his deep sadness and sought her forgiveness. He wanted her back home, but not without constructing several choices she would need to make. Darcy's foolish strategy was to rage at her parents, shame them, leave home, make them pay emotionally, then seek a quick return home without any consequence. Phil and Marge were no longer buying such foolishness. Phil set the stage for her to choose a positive course or let her live with the painful choices she might make.

Think of a parent as providing a bridge, in a teen's mind, between her actions and their consequences. In the case of Phil and Darcy, Phil engineered a consequence with two options for Darcy to ponder. The first option was that for Darcy to come home, she would need to choose to seek counseling with her parents to work on their relationship. She would have to commit, honestly, to communicate with Phil and Marge and work through problems instead of raging and then leaving home to punish her parents. Darcy's other option was to refuse counseling or any ongoing communication, and so live outside the family on her own resources and bear the pain of her choice.

Obviously, this was a courageous, high-risk

approach that required careful thought. Yet, engineered consequences must *mirror the reality of the situation,* not ignore reality and allow the teen to decide what course of action to pursue. God allows us to choose our course of life with Him and allows us to live with our rebellious, painful choices for our ultimate good (Luke 15:12-14). *We shouldn't try to be better to our kids than God is to them.* Phil wisely provided a bridge between Darcy's actions and their logical consequences.

---

9. Explain in your own words why Phil was trying to connect Darcy's choices to a serious outcome.

10. How effectively are you bridging your teen's choices to the logical consequences of his or her actions? How could you do this more effectively?

Below is a parental bridge diagram that highlights the idea Phil was conveying to Darcy.

The parental bridge links Darcy's *foolish thinking* ("I'll rage at Dad and Mom, leave home, then return later and nothing will happen, as usual") to a *logical result* engineered by her parents ("You're free to choose to stay away from home, but it will cost you your family benefits and our care for you. It will be painful for you"). The purpose of the parental bridge is to make selfish and destructive choices so painful that it will not be worthwhile for the teen to pursue her course of action. Many parents fail at this stage out of fear of losing relationship with their kids. In reality, Phil and Marge knew they had been losing relationship for a long time under their former parenting strategy.

Another difficulty many parents have with logical consequences is that they have developed only one tool for dealing with rebellion, and they use it all the time. Some parents lecture, others hit, yell, plead, withdraw, or ignore. To challenge our adolescents' foolish thinking, though, we need to work at creating two or more alternatives for each situation. In the next session, we will deal in depth with developing logical consequences and offer more options for parents.

Remember

An important method of challenging rebellion is uncompromising responsiveness. Parents

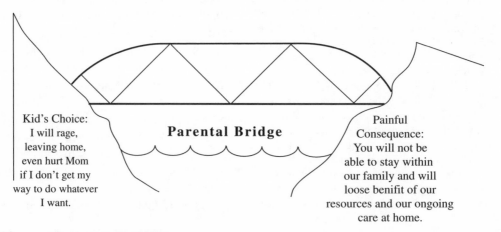

Kid's Choice: I will rage, leaving home, even hurt Mom if I don't get my way to do whatever I want.

Parental Bridge

Painful Consequence: You will not be able to stay within our family and will loose benifit of our resources and our ongoing care at home.

are to deal justly with their teens attaching the same significance God does to their teens' foolish rebellion. Parents have two primary tasks when challenging rebellion: creating awareness and ownership in kids' choices and calling them to serve God and others. Parents create a greater sense of choice for kids by helping them understand that they make choices. Parents also need to create choices in order to strengthen teens' sense of owning their choices. At times, words fail to affect rebellion. Parents must be willing to use both natural and, more importantly, logical consequences to connect kids' foolish choices to pain so they can mature in serving God and others. The parental bridge illustrates how we connect choices to painful consequences.

Reflection

On this page are four family scenes that depict rebellious teens' behavior toward parents. Your task as a group is to create two or more options that connect, or bridge, the kids' choices to logical consequences that could weaken their rebellious behavior and purposes.

Behavior	Parental Bridge
Tommy, 15, announces to his mom, "I will not be coming home until 6:00 a.m. I'll be at Jim's house." The weekend curfew is usually midnight. What consequence can a parent engineer to challenge his defiant behavior?	
Susie, 17, defiantly tells her parents: "I am not going to school any more. It's a stupid waste of my life! You can't make me!!" She's a junior with average grades and a big chip on her shoulder. What kind of logical consequence can her parents develop to challenge this behavior?	
12-year-old Sean has brought home several expensive electronic components that include a Nintendo, Sony Walkman, and all the attachments. He says a friend gave him the stuff; he has no money to buy the things. You suspect he stole the equipment. What do you do?	
Todd is 18, and constantly talks to his parents in a sarcastic, hurtful manner. His verbal attacks are getting worse, especially toward his mom. "You are such a stupid jerk. Can't you ever do anything right? This dinner tastes like crap!" How can Todd's parents challenge this rebellious behavior?	

Action Lab

What specific issues trouble you with your kid? Identify some areas of rebellion. Bring them up in the group to see if you can collectively create some logical consequences that will weaken your teen's foolish behaviors and purposes.

NOTES

1. Kevin Huggins, *Parenting Adolescents* (Colorado Springs, CO: NavPress, 1989), p. 131.
2. Huggins, pp. 239–240.
3. Foster Cline and Jim Fay, *Parenting with Love and Logic* (Colorado Springs, CO: Piñon Press, 1990), p. 78.
4. Huggins, p. 247.

Fifteen

Creative Consequences

IN session 14 we talked about creating logical consequences that help our kids see their foolishness. In order to do this effectively, we have to be aware of what we've been doing and what is going on inside us. We need to know where we are now in order to see where to head.

Let's return to Phil, Marge, and Darcy, back to the start of their conflict. What forces were operating in Phil's and Marge's thinking when they tried to confront Darcy? Remember, Darcy was angry and desperately wanted out of the house to see her friends and avoid her parents. The conflict was gaining momentum. Here is part of the conversation from session 12 when the conflict initially crashed in. Listen to the parents' real messages below the waterline, implicitly communicated.

Marge (pleading): Darcy, you know your father and I told you about your responsibilities at school and around home. Your grades are suffering; you need to study and you haven't this semester. You promise, but you aren't doing your work. Your friends can wait until the weekend. Come on, honey. Just do what your dad and I ask you to do tonight, okay?

(Marge's strategy is based upon weak natural consequences: she hopes Darcy will respond to her pleading to stay home, avoid the power struggle, and feel some desire to succeed in school. Sadly, Darcy is unlikely to be challenged deeply enough without direct parental intervention.)

Phil (tensely pacing): Darcy, I told you that you're forbidden to leave! You will do as your mother and I have said. Now unpack your clothes and get back to your studies!

(This strategy is *punishment:* Phil is using his power to force Darcy to comply with his demands. Ironically, his strategy only intensifies the power struggle with a powerful daughter. His strategy is illogical, arbitrary, and based on raw power to force compliance.)

Phil and Marge are frantically trying to cope with a difficult daughter. Yet they have too few tools to help Darcy. It's like playing golf with only one club. When parents have only one primary way of disciplining their teens, like yelling or pleading, kids' foolishness often remains intact and unchallenged.

OBJECTIVE: In this session, you will learn about creatively developing logical consequences as positive discipline options.

A Wise Father and a Rebellious Son

Rebellious kids are nothing new. In session 7, we looked at Jesus' story about the prodigal son. Let's return to see how the father in that story created a sense of choice for his wayward son. In the first part of the story, the father builds parental bridges between his son's choices and their consequences.

> Jesus continued: "There was a man who had two sons. The younger one said to his father, 'Father, give me my share of the estate.' So he divided his property between them.
> "Not long after that, the younger son got together all he had, set off for a distant country and there squandered his wealth in wild living. After he had spent everything, there was a severe famine in that whole country, and he began to be in need." (Luke 15:11–14)

The son in this story is wildly foolish and rebellious. He demands, not asks, that his father give him his inheritance early so he can spend it as he pleases. In our culture we fail to understand the sheer arrogance of this request. What is the young son really saying?

Henri Nouwen captures the full weight of the shocking request:

> Kenneth Bailey, in his penetrating explanation of Luke's story, shows that the son's manner of leaving is tantamount to wishing his father dead. Bailey writes: "For over fifteen years I have been asking people of all walks of life from Morocco to India and from Turkey to the Sudan about the implications of a son's request for his inheritance while the father is still living. The answer has always been emphatically the same. The conversation runs as follows: Has anyone ever made such a request in your village? Never! Could anyone ever make such a request? Impossible! If anyone ever did, what would happen? His father would beat him, of course! Why? The request means *he wants his father to die.*". . .

The son's "leaving" is, therefore, a much more offensive act than it seems at first reading. It is a heartless rejection of the home in which the son was born and nurtured and a break with the most precious tradition carefully upheld by the larger community of which he was a part. . . . More than disrespect, it is a betrayal of the treasured values of family and community. The "distant country" is the world in which everything considered holy at home is disregarded.[1]

---

1. In your own words, how would you describe the way the son views his father in this story?

2. Do you ever sense this level of contempt from your kids? If so, how?

We can now see the depth of contempt the son shows his father by his "heartless rejection" of his father's home. "Everything considered holy at home is disregarded." Our kids at times will exhibit to us the same intensity of foolishness.

Yet the story paints a powerful example of constructing a love response for foolish rebels. It shows us how God deals with us as rebels. This father would be perfectly within his rights to refuse his son, even to beat him and send him away. He knows his younger son is relationally distant, yet he agrees to give him the early inheritance. Why? He knows he needs to challenge the foolishness and rebellion at deep levels by engineering choices for the rebel. Normal discipline strategies have probably been tried and failed. Rebels do not develop overnight in any home.

The father wisely engineers a series of options for his younger son. His strategy is to confront his son below the waterline by allowing him to choose and to bear the painful consequences of his choices. In a sense, the *father actually accelerates his young son's foolishness,* knowing he will squander his resources quickly. This godly father anticipates that his son's foolishness needs a potent dose of reality. His son must choose to live in a painful world apart from his father's protection. Then the son will long for what is not available through his own foolish choice. It isn't until the son makes this discovery *on his own* that he considers repentance and returns home.

Some may ask, why didn't the father simply give the boy some well-deserved punishment? Let's look at punishment to see why it doesn't work to challenge foolishness.

What About Punishment?

Webster's defines punishment as "retributive suffering, pain, or loss; rough treatment." It usually has some component of *harming* the teen with "rough treatment" because of some rebellion. Usually, punishment doesn't *instruct* the teen toward maturity.

A parent of a rebellious teen will often be inclined to use punishment. In the face of obnoxious behavior, it's normal to want to hurt the teen as the teen has hurt us. Physical punishment, shaming, raging, threats, complete withdrawal of privileges, and generally "clamping down" are examples of punishment. At first it may feel good to get back in control. But ultimately, punishment always pushes kids away.

Consider the effect of punishment on Beth, a gentle sixteen-year-old girl living in a controlling, chaotic home with her mother. Here is a portion of her letter describing the destructive effects of punishment.

When I was 16, my mother burst into my room, stood over me, and said sternly, "You did what I always told you not to do, didn't you? You flushed something you shouldn't have down the toilet!" I denied it, knowing I had not. She said, "You did, and I know you did. Come into the bathroom." I followed nervously, as I always did when she accused me. She said, "Put this on," and she handed me a rubber glove. She said , "Now reach into the toilet and pull it out." I thought, "Okay, but you are going to be sorry." My heart was pounding as I pulled solid waste from the toilet. My mother calmly said, "Nine times out of ten I am right. This is the tenth time." She told me to take the glove off and then went to tell others of the family to be more careful and flush more often. I had always told myself that if Mom saw she was mistaken just once, she would face reality. All my lifelong hopes regarding my mother died right there.

Foster Cline and Jim Fay make a humorous yet potent case for avoiding punishment as we deal with our kids:

Imagine yourself banging a fender at the parking lot at work. You feel bad about it, and when you come home that evening, you explain the accident to your spouse. "What!" your loving mate shrieks. "That really makes me mad. You know how you wanted to go skiing this weekend? Well, forget it. You're grounded!" A ridiculous scenario? Of course. As adults, we don't get grounded when we mess up in life; nobody washes our mouths out with soap when we swear. Punishments don't happen in the real world unless crimes are committed. When people are punished for something, they seldom pause for self-examination. Resentment is the more common reaction. The same holds true for our children. . . . The *real* world by and large *doesn't operate on punishment.*[2]

3. What do Cline and Fay mean when they say, "The real world by and large doesn't operate on punishment"? How would you respond to this idea?

Punishment has several drawbacks:

The Parent's Attitude Is One of Personal Authority.

The underlying message is "I'm the parent, the one in power. You will do what I say or you will pay." For the teen, the likely result of this attitude in the long run will be anger, rebellion, and a sense of helplessness. Beth's mom demanded immediate compliance. That only caused Beth to feel exasperated (compare Ephesians 6:4).

4. Would you describe a parent's use of personal authority as destructive? Do you think it is a problem or not? How so?

Punishment Is Arbitrary and Barely Related to the Logic of the Situation.

When our teen comes home with Ds and Fs on his report card, what does not watching TV for several months have to do with his grades? We are not allowing his mistakes and consequences to do the teaching.

Punishment Is Often Personal and Dishes Out Some Form of Moral Judgment.

Beth's mom lacked compassion. She operated with an attitude of anger and moral superiority: "Nine times out of ten I am right. This is the tenth time." For many parents, being right is more important than loving.

Punishment Threatens the Teen with the Loss of Love and Respect.

Beth's mom often subtly threatened her with a loss of care if Beth failed to obey.

To sum up, punishment pushes teens away from their parents over the long haul. It produces distance, not love, in the relationship. It fails to teach teens to deal wisely with their choices.

Natural Consequences

The alternatives to punishment are natural and logical consequences. We introduced both of these in session 14, but now we'll look at them in more depth.

Natural consequences are simply the natural, unavoidable results of teens' unwise choices without our direct parental intervention. For example, in a home where only the laundry placed in the hamper gets washed, a kid who leaves his dirty clothes strewn all over his room will discover he has no clean clothes to wear. It's the natural result of his choice not to put his clothes in the hamper. However, a consequence like this is not adequate for challenging a teen's foolish behaviors. Natural consequences lack two critical characteristics: intensity and immediacy.

Intensity

To be effective, painful consequences must be intense enough to really affect the kid's choices. Often, natural consequences lack such intensity. Telling a kid that he'll have no clean Levi's if he doesn't put them in the hamper may not be a strong enough incentive (maybe he likes being a slob!). Or, if your daughter continues to bring home failing grades, being retained in the same grade level may make sense, but it will lack an intensity closely associated with the failed grades. She may be held back at the end of the school year, but she may not feel the consequence intensely enough to improve her grades during the year. Just because filthy clothes or repeating a year of school seems like an intense consequence to us doesn't mean it feels intense to a kid.

---

5. What is meant by the idea that natural consequences lack "intensity"?

Immediacy

Furthermore, for a consequence to be helpful, it must be *felt quickly* after the choice. Then the teen is able to make a mental connection between the act and the consequence. The problem with natural consequences is there is often a time lag before the consequence. When a teen gets drunk, for instance, he won't feel the hangover until morning. Homework not turned in may not be discovered until report card time. Sexual activity may go unno-

ticed until someone turns up pregnant. These consequences are too far removed from the deed to have much impact on foolish decisions when they are being made.

Logical Consequences

By contrast, logical consequences are both intense and immediate. They are structured choices that parents develop to impart training to kids. Huggins writes,

> Parents are thus responsible to engineer [logical] consequences for their adolescent's foolish choices whenever the natural consequences are not adequate to challenge his foolishness. Parents need to build an association in their adolescent's mind between his foolish purposes and the actual significance God attaches to them. To do this, engineered consequences should be designed to give a kid an immediate *[immediacy]* sample of the *ultimate* consequences *[intensity]* foolishness reaps: a loss of the freedom he deeply desires to impact the world and experience relationship in the way he chooses. Engineered consequences should always be designed to prevent a kid from successfully using his foolish strategies to satisfy these desires.[3]

---

6. Huggins says, "Parents need to build an association in their adolescent's mind between his foolish purposes and the actual significance God attaches to them." What do you think he means? How do you try to do this for your teen?

Parents usually want to challenge choices that are immoral, dishonest, immodest, sinful, or selfish. We can "engineer" logical consequences to reflect the impact of such deeds. These consequences are not arbitrary and anger-driven, like punishment, nor are they easily forgotten, like natural consequences. They are immediate, intense, and shrewdly chosen ahead of time when emotions are cool.

Let's return to the example of the prodigal son. The son asks his father for his share of the inheritance, leaves home, and blows the money. The father doesn't yell or lecture. Instead, he has engineered two choices: stay home (with the father's blessing) or leave home with the inheritance. He has structured his response to allow his young rebel to experience the full impact of his foolish decision. This wise father *connects his son's choice* to leave home with the money (Luke 15:12) *to the painful consequence* of the son's desperate need (Luke 15:14). The boy is starving and in misery. He feels the full weight of his choice's pain. As a result, he repents, or changes his thinking ("When he came to his senses"), and makes his way back home. The end result is a repentant son ("Father, I have sinned against you") whose foolish belief system has been confronted by a wise parent.

Pain also exposes a teen's sinfulness. As wise parents, we do not want only to alert our kids to their foolishness, but also to reveal their *hearts that committed the harm.* Second Samuel 24 describes God doing just this. King David wrongly takes a census of his troops during a time of national peace. Even David's commanders argue against such an unneeded census (2 Samuel 24:3). David's sin (24:10) appears to be pride, his desire to glory in his power. His foolishness is met by the Lord's prophet Gad, who brings a painful, engineered set of choices.

> Before David got up the next morning, the word of the LORD had come to Gad the prophet, David's seer: "Go and tell David, 'This is what the Lord says: I am giving you

> *three options. Choose one of them* for me to carry out against you.'"
>
> So Gad went to David and said to him, "Shall there come upon you three years of famine in your land? Or three months of fleeing from your enemies while they pursue you? Or three days of plague in your land? Now then, *think it over and decide* how I should answer the one who sent me." (2 Samuel 24:11-13, emphasis added)

Notice God's wisdom in engineering David's choices: the choices were limited ("three options"), painful, immediate, intense, and required choice ("choose one") so that David had to own the problem. While still loving David, the Lord didn't spare the painful consequences of David's actions. It was a life-lesson David would never forget.

---

7. How would you describe the way God dealt with David in this passage? In what ways does your teen experience your love in this manner?

In the logical consequences model, parents present kids with two or more alternatives for action. The teens are free to choose whichever option they wish. However, when they make foolish choices, *it is the kids,* not the parents, who must bear the consequences. "Because we live in a moral and physical universe, whatever we do counts," says Dan Allender. "The parents must create a universe that prepares the child by paralleling the larger universe."

Power struggles over money and clothes used to be the norm in our home at the start of the school year. Seth likes new school clothes. We struggled to help him own his decisions and get us out of the power struggle. Cathy and I decided to implement a new decision-making process when he went into middle school. It felt a little risky, but it demonstrated the strength of engineering logical consequences.

"Seth," I said, "Your mom and I want to give you all the responsibility for your school shopping this fall. You've said in the past that we were too controlling of your decisions, and we want to honor your request to decide for yourself what clothes to buy. From now on, you get to budget and buy your own school clothes. We have honestly calculated about what it will cost you to buy your favorite pants, shirts, shoes, and underwear. Here is all the money to buy your clothes. However, there is no more money when you're done, and you will have to live with whatever you buy." He readily agreed.

Seth thought he had struck gold! "Wow, that's great, you guys! Look at all this money. I can't wait to get my clothes." The next Saturday, we took him to the mall to visit his favorite stores. Within two hours, he had blown nearly all the money on clothes. Some of them were a little wild in color and style, but what came next was priceless.

"Dad, I have just twenty dollars left. I know I need underwear, but I always wanted silk underwear. They're really cool! But if I get them, I can only buy two instead of a whole bunch of other stuff and socks I need. I don't like these choices, because I have to decide." He was in extreme discomfort with what his next decision should be with the money. Cathy wisely responded, "Honey, it's your choice, do what you want. I believe you can make good choices."

Seth bought the silk underwear and didn't get enough socks for the school year. A week later he came to us, wanting us to get more socks. That was where it got challenging. "Seth," I told him, "I said no more money

when you were done buying, and you agreed. When I'm out of money, I can't spend any more because it's gone. I believe that's where you are now. I'm sure you'll think of some way to deal with this situation. So, want to play a little basketball?"

---

8. What were we trying to communicate to Seth?

9. In what ways are you trying to build a sense of ownership and choice in your teen?

Will our kids try to get us to take care of their messes? Absolutely. Was Seth frustrated with us? Of course. Did he try to persuade us to get the rest of his clothes? Yes, but not for long because he knew he had decided to live with his financial choices. It truly was his problem. We mirrored reality by not creating a false sense of reality—that he could demand and spend as much money as he wanted without consequences. It's important for kids to learn how the world works before they are adults and their wrong choices are truly disastrous.

It's not always easy to develop and use logical consequences to challenge kids. Let's look at some of the barriers we run into as we relate in this way.

Roadblocks to Using Logical Consequences

Logical Consequences May Be Seen As Punishment.

Phil, for example, might give Darcy several options without looking at his own desire to control her. She might see this as just another manipulation strategy. Without an open, caring attitude on the part of the parents, teens will see only punishment and will resist our best engineered consequences.

Kids Get Discouraged.

As a parent withdraws from negative involvement with his teen, there's a greater need for positive involvement. For instance, I knew Seth would struggle with truly owning his decisions in buying his school clothes. In the past I tried to lecture him ("I told you this would happen!") instead of just affirming that he was capable of living with his choices ("I'm sure you will think of some way to deal with this problem"). The decision to play basketball was not an attempt to avoid the problem but to acknowledge I wanted to continue to enjoy him while letting him resolve the clothing problem.

---

10. Do you sense your kids getting discouraged at times when you allow their choices to affect them? If so, how do you deal with their discouragement?

It's Easy to Bite Off More Than You Can Chew.

Many parents get gung-ho with the logical consequences idea and try to do too much too soon. It's important for parents to begin this process slowly, introducing logical consequences during conflict-free situations. Work on one area at a time, such as chores, transportation, homework, or requests. Slowly develop a repertoire of logical consequences for different situations. Then you'll be more prepared to apply the consequences in the heat of battle.

Sometimes It Just Fails.

When the strategy fails, parents must analyze the logical consequences they have devised to determine where they went wrong. For example, Phil's logical choices were to have Darcy either come home with counseling help or live on her own. If she refused to come home or speak to them, perhaps Phil and Marge would need to look at their own motives in order to ponder the lack of any change in Darcy.

What went wrong? Was Phil's attitude accepting and nonjudgmental? Was he actively looking for avenues of increased involvement with Darcy? Was the consequence logically related to her choices, or was it really a form of punishment? Were the parents truly together with the consequences? Had the consequences been fully thought through? Parents must honestly ask these questions, and many more, to make the corrections necessary to help promote maturity in their kids.

---

11. Describe why it is important to reexamine logical consequences when they fail. How can looking at logical-consequence failure be helpful to us?

The chart on the following page contrasts punishment and logical consequences. It may

The Major Differences Between
Punishment and Logical Consequences

PUNISHMENT			LOGICAL CONSEQUENCES		
Characteristics	Underlying Message to Child	Likely Results	Underlying Characteristics Child	Message to	Likely Results
1. Emphasis on power of personal authority.	"Do what I say because I say so."	Rebellion. Desire for revenge Lack of self-discipline.	**1.** Emphasis on reality of the social order.	"I trust you to learn to respect the rights of others."	Cooperation. Respect for self and others. Self-discipline. Reliability.
2. Rarely related to act; arbitrary.	"I'll show you." "You deserve what you're getting!"	Resentment. Desire for revenge. Fear. Confusion.	**2.** Logically related to the misbehavior; sensible.	"I trust you to make responsible choices."	Learning from experience.
3. Implies moral judgment.	"You're bad!" You're not acceptable."	Feelings of hurt, guilt, Desire to get even.	**3.** Treats person with dignity; separates deed from doer.	"You are a worthwhile person."	Senses he or she is acceptable even though behavior is not.
4. Emphasis on past behavior.	"You'll never learn," "I can never count on you."	Feels unacceptable. Feels can't make good decisions.	**4.** Concerned with present and future behavior.	"You are able to take care of yourself."	Becomes self-evaluating, self-directing.
5. Threats of disrespect, violence, or loss of love, either open or concealed.	"You'd better shape up!" "No child of mine would do a thing like that!"	Fear. Rebellion. Guilt feelings. Desire to "get back."	**5.** Voice communicates respect and good will.	"I don't like what you are doing, but I still love you you."	Feels secure about parent's love and support.
6. Demands, compliance.	"Your preferences don't matter." "You can't be trusted to make wise decisions."	Rebellion. "Defiant compliance."	**6.** Presents choice.	"You are capable of deciding."	Responsible decisions. Increased resourcefulness.

Systematic Training for Effective Parenting (STEP): The Parent's Handbook by Don Dinkmeyer and Gary D. McKay (1989 American Guidance Service, Inc. 4201 Woodland Road, Circle Pines, MN, p. 87. Reproduced with permission. All rights reserved.)

help you to engineer logical consequences for your teen.

Remember

Logical consequences are a positive discipline option for parents because they reflect the reality of a situation. Parents must help kids connect their choices to painful consequences. Punishment discourages kids from maturing because it is often based on parents' power, is not related to the situation at hand, uses patronizing judgment, and threatens kids with loss of love. Natural consequences do help kids make connections to their choices. Yet natural consequences often lack the intensity and immediacy needed to train kids. The strengths of logical consequences are fivefold: parents limit teens' choices to reflect reality; and consequences are painful when ignored, immediate, intense, and require our kids to own their personal choices. Engineered logical consequences permit parents to disengage from power struggles and allow kids to take responsibility for their own decisions.

Reflection

Below are some typical family scenes. As a group, brainstorm some logical consequences that might be appropriate for each situation.

Scene 1
Sara, fifteen, is starting to yell at her mom in the middle of a grocery store. She is angry because her mom refuses to allow her to go to the school dance. Sara's volume and sarcasm are increasing, and people are starting to stare.

Scene 2
Jeremiah, twelve, is sitting at the dinner table with his parents and his parents' best friends. He wants to stay overnight at the home of a school friend his parents don't know very well. Jeremiah takes advantage of his audience to put the pressure on his parents: "Tell me now! I want to know!" Mom and Dad are starting to feel embarrassed and want him to stop demanding an answer at the table.

Scene 3
Seventeen-year-old Sam wants the keys to the family car to go over to his girlfriend's house. It's Saturday morning, and his mom has planned for Sam to help with the chores along with the rest of the family. Sam says he had already made plans with his girlfriend and starts getting angry and demanding. He eventually loses his temper.

Action Lab

Identify a problem area you're having with your teen. Bring it up next week for the group to brainstorm some logical consequences.

NOTES
1. Henri J. M. Nouwen, *The Return of the Prodigal Son* (New York, NY: Doubleday, 1992), pp. 32–33.
2. Foster Cline and Jim Fay, *Parenting with Love and Logic* (Colorado Springs, CO: Piñon Press, 1990), p. 89.
3. Kevin Huggins, *Parenting Adolescents* (Colorado Springs, CO:NavPress, 1989), p. 248.

Sixteen

Words of Encouragement

REMEMBER *Leave It to Beaver*? After every episode of that 1950s TV show, life went on in a loving, fun way, with every tension worked out. We never saw hatred, swearing, or contempt, and rarely saw any conflict without quick resolution. Usually, the parents just shook their heads in a knowing way, laughing to themselves about the kids and smiling at their mild adolescent antics. Everything just seemed to work out well in Beaver's family.

Privately, most parents today want the same thing with their kids. Parents want predictability and order. Yet families don't live in the *Leave It to Beaver* home. Parents are called to offer rich encouragement to kids, not just in the good times, but in the challenging times of a chaotic, unpredictable world.

Phil and Marge are struggling but continuing to learn the ministry model of parenting. The following excerpt from Phil's personal journal shows him coming to grips with his relationship with Darcy. Phil and Marge have

spent a lot of time with other parents thinking through their stories with their kids. God is unseen yet powerfully at work within these two parents' lives. Phil would be the first to admit he is not a perfect father. Yet he's a maturing father, growing in godly passion through sorrow.

As I was praying for Darcy this morning, I found myself in touch with the disappointment in our relationship. I am struck by the parallels in my relationship with God. Darcy ignores me much of the time, disobeys me frequently, seems determined to have her own way and to do as she pleases . . . she wants life to be on her own terms. Am I any different? I am guilty of all the above. How does God relate to me in spite of my relentless determination? He loves me, He forgives me, He waits with open arms for me to come to Him, He disciplines me, He allows me to go my own way for a time, until I am miserable, until I realize that only He can fill the void in my soul. He pursues me regardless of how I relate to Him.

Should my love for my daughter, for my sons, be any different? Lord, I do want to love her differently, boldly, courageously. I am not even sure what that means, but I know it is the right thing. Help me, I cannot do it on my own. . . . I have tried, but it isn't working. Only in the strength of your Spirit can I love her the way that she needs to be loved. Father, soften my heart and my spirit toward my daughter. Help me to love her as You love her.

With Phil's heart as our example, we will conclude this leg of our parenting journey as we ponder what it means to be ongoing encouragers to our kids.

OBJECTIVE: In this session, you will learn how to encourage your kids toward maturity.

What Is Encouragement?

Webster's defines encouragement as "to inspire with courage and hope; stimulate, incite; to foster." Encouragement implies a thoughtful, active process to move others, including our kids, toward hope.

Larry Crabb and Dan Allender say, "Encouragement happens through the careful selection of words that are intended to influence another person [in this case, our kids] meaningfully toward increased godliness."[1]

---

1. Can you put into your own words what *encouragement* means?

Words and actions that encourage are motivated by the speaker's love and are directed toward the hearer's fear.

Larry Crabb tells of being a severe stutterer during his teenage years and of two traumatic experiences where he was asked to speak publicly. The first was in a junior high induction ceremony, where he stuttered his way through an agonizing speech in front of hundreds of kids. A short time later he was asked to pray aloud during a Sunday morning worship service. He became confused, embarrassed, and nervous, and internally vowed never to speak aloud again in front of a group. An older man, Jim, caught him on the way out the church door, put his arm on his shoulder and, as Dr. Crabb records, said these words to a very discouraged adolescent:

> "Larry, there's one thing I want you to know. Whatever you do for the Lord, I'm behind you one thousand percent." Then he walked away. Even as I write these words, my eyes are filled with tears. I have yet to tell that story to an audience without at least mildly choking. Those words were life words. They had power. They reached deep into my being. My resolve never again to speak publicly weakened instantly. . . . God intends that we be people who use words to encourage one other. A well-timed word has the power to urge a runner to finish the race, to rekindle hope when despair has set in, to spark a bit of warmth in the otherwise cold life, to trigger healthful self-evaluation in someone who doesn't think much about his shortcomings, to renew confidence when problems have the upper hand.[2]

Jim was attempting to speak, by words and physical touch, to Larry's disappointment and fear. Jim was communicating deep acceptance of Larry, even though the teen's faults lay exposed. By God's grace, we can have a similar positive effect on our kids. For parents, encouragement is a conscious decision to meet an adolescent's needs over the long haul.

Spurring One Another On

The book of Hebrews says this about encouragement:

And let us consider how we may spur one another on toward love and good deeds. Let us not give up meeting together, as some are in the habit of doing, but let us encourage one another. (Hebrews 10:24–25)

Let's look at three important words from this passage: "consider," "spur," and "encourage."

The word "consider" (*katanoeo*) means "to perceive clearly, intensively, to understand fully; or thoughtful considering of one another."[3] We are to give careful, intense thought to help meet others' needs. We are not to be haphazard or lazy in pondering how to help our kids. We are to ponder our kids' below-the-waterline lives with the same thoughtful perception.

---

2. What does "consider" mean to you as you think about your own teen? How do you actively "consider" ways to encourage him or her?

The word "spur" (*paroxysm*) means to "stimulate strongly, arouse, or incite to riot. . . . Christians need to spur or stimulate each other in two areas: *Love*: not [just] an emotion but a choice to act regardless of our feelings [and] *Good deeds*: works done for the good of others, and which attract others to Christ."[4] Although encouragement is thoughtful, to spur our kids on is also a strongly stimulating process, not a passive one.

Biblical encouragement is also exhorting or urging our kids to pursue some course of godly conduct. Let's look at what that means.

Thinking Deeply to Stir Our Kids Toward Love

Encouragement requires thought in order to be effective. It demands a pondering of what is best for each unique adolescent. Phil had to deal very differently with Darcy than with his other three kids. Each of our kids has different needs.

Think back to a time when, as an adolescent or adult, you felt encouraged by another person. What brought that sense of encouragement? People who truly encourage others are a breath of fresh air.

When my parents were going through their divorce, I felt confused, fearful, angry, and alone. My grandmother Ruth spoke to my heart and stirred me on to hope: "David, this divorce is going to hurt you deeply. But your dad and mom still love you. Honey, there is no way around the pain and fear. Regardless of where you are in life, know this house will always be a safe home for you. I want you to know you have a special gift, a 'feeling touch' you always have had in you. I cherish how you relate to others. Don't forget that I see your heart clearly and know good things will still be yours one day."

I vividly remember being in her yellow kitchen, smelling the chocolate chip cookies she was baking. In that moment, I felt Grandma Ruth a thousand percent behind me. Strangely, I felt an emotional rest in the midst of my chaos. An encouraging parent is one who actively, thoughtfully looks for ways to promote "love and good deeds" in her teen, even during the rough times.

Calling Forth Truth from Our Kids

Notice what my grandmother *didn't say* when she was trying to encourage me. She didn't pretend life was better than it really was for me. Imagine if she had said to me something like this: "David, your parents' divorce is a sad thing, but maybe they will get back together just like before, and you and your sister will be happy again. Just try and believe that they will get back together. Let's you and me think on the better days. It will help when you remember the sadness. Now give me a little hug, I want to encourage you."

What do you think I might have felt if my grandma had used those words to urge me to minimize the pain and fear of my parents' divorce? I might have enjoyed the chocolate chip cookies, but not the hug from her! I wouldn't have felt her coming alongside me in truthfulness. When parents, or parent figures, try to create an artificial reality for kids, it puts pressure on kids to hide the pain and fear. Her hypothetical words would have produced a movement away from the truth, toward deception, about what was occurring in my heart. The result would have been discouragement or a loss of heart.

The apostle Paul said that unrighteous people *suppress the truth* by their wickedness (Romans 1:18). Yet even believers can suppress truth if they are not careful. To *suppress* is an active process in which truth is forcefully submerged in a relationship.

Have you ever tried to sit on a beach ball at a swimming pool without the ball rocketing up from underneath the water? My sister and I used to go to swimming pools during the summer and sit on a sixteen-inch red beach ball in the middle of the pool. The trick was to slowly force the ball directly under your seat and maintain a tremendous amount of body control to keep the ball from moving upward. However, the ball always had an upward momentum. When I moved very far off the ball, it came up with a furious blast.

Suppression of truth is like the beach ball. When people deal with relationships untruthfully, they hold down the truth by pretending. For instance, if my grandmother had said, "Just try and believe your parents will get back together," her words would not have represented truth. I knew deep down that my parents' marriage was beyond repair, and I would

not have felt encouraged, I would have felt pressure to appear happy. The actual truth of the current relationship between my grandmother and me would have been suppressed.

But because Ruth called forth truth from me, I was able to rest in her words, gather strength, and continue moving forward in life.

---

3. What is meant by "calling forth truth" from our kids? How does it encourage them?

Parents must call kids to truth, even when it might be painful, because truth coupled with love always has a liberating effect upon the hearts of our teens.

Crabb and Allender illuminate three principles we need to think about when we use words to encourage others, including our kids:

> Acceptance is essential when a person's faults are exposed. The exposed person is in line to experience some form of rejection. Indifference, criticism, irritation, impatience, sarcasm, withdrawal, and disapproval are but a few of the many ways to reject someone as less than valuable. At the core of our beings we all fear rejection, whatever form it takes. . . . Encouragement depends fundamentally on *accepting* a person whose needs and faults lie exposed.[5]

---

4. Why is it so important to accept a person whose "needs and faults lie exposed"? How might that encourage your teen?

Seth came looking for me on a hot summer day after he was partway through mowing the lawn with our power mower. His eyes darted away from mine when he told me the bad news: "Dad, I just hit and destroyed one of the automatic sprinkler heads along the fence line. I couldn't see it because the grass was too high. I'm sorry."

My first reaction was irritation. I could envision our sprinkler man coming out, again, to fix sprinkler heads we had replaced just the previous month. Ten seconds later, Seth said quietly, "Wasn't it your turn to weed-whack that tall grass along the fence line where I hit the sprinkler head?"

He said it honestly, without a trace of anger or contempt. I found myself laughing out loud. "Yes, it was my turn to do the weed-whacking, and I didn't get it done for you. I messed this sprinkler head up by not doing the job before you mowed. I'm sorry; it was my fault. I bet you felt anxious to come to me, knowing we just spent money on the same problem last month. You've seen me get upset at this sprinkler system. It doesn't always work the best. You didn't hide your hitting it. You dealt honestly with me right away. That took courage on your part, given that you knew I could get frustrated, and even mad."

His fearful countenance changed to a smile. We both laughed at my having to deal with our sprinkler man once again! Seth experienced acceptance, even though it came a little slowly.

Understanding is sometimes better than advice.

A godly friend of mine once told me, "It is more important that we truly *understand* someone than that we listen only to seek *agreement* with us." Kids need us to understand them so that they feel we value them. We don't communicate value when we listen only to offer advice based on whether we agree with them or not. "Quick advice communicates disrespect and disinterest. The words *spoken* may be 'I think you should . . .' The words *heard* may be 'Your problem is simple. But you're too stupid to figure out a solution. So I'll tell you what to do.' "[6] Normally, when we offer quick advice to our kids without hearing their troubled hearts, they will experience it as some form of manipulative pressure to correct their deficiencies.

I have come to believe that kids intuitively know most problems don't have quick solutions that mere advice will solve. Some problems can be addressed quickly, but most deep issues won't just go away. When Seth approaches us about feeling lonely or feeling rejected by fickle friends, or wondering if others value him only because of his athletic abilities, he wants more than just a pat answer. He wants to be understood at deep levels in his heart, not given advice.

I remember one surprising scene after we dropped off a video rental late at night. He got in the car and was strangely quiet, with his head bent down toward his knees. Tears began to stream down his face. I had no idea what he was experiencing. "Dad, I really wonder sometimes if other kids in my class like me just for how I look and my ability to play basketball. Sometimes I wonder if I'm all that valuable to them." What do you think he wanted from me in that moment? Maybe something like "Come on, you're so popular! Everyone likes you—cheer up!" Or perhaps, "Seth, you're just making too big a deal out of this popularity thing. Lighten up, okay?" Seth wanted neither a pep talk nor minimizing of his troubled emotions. He wanted a *parent to understand* the depth of his anguish and fear.

The more precise our understanding, the more encouraging the words.

Teens fear two things above all else:

Loss of security (rejection)
Loss of significance (loss of value)

The essential fear that is locked deep in the core of fallen people is the fear of insecurity (rejection) and insignificance (loss of value). If encouragers clearly understand that these two deep longings lie beneath people's layers of self-sufficiency, their words may reflect a greater understanding of people's fears. Encouraging words identify the desire for relationship, penetrating beneath whatever layers are presented.[7]

Seth wanted me not just to understand him vaguely ("Oh yeah, I've been where you are, son"), but *to understand his pain specifically and speak to his fear.* To casually, half-heartedly understand our kids is to show weak love.

After a few minutes of listening to Seth talk about his anguish, I cautiously ventured into his heart. Remember, our kids' hearts are the sacred places where they *really* live. "You've talked a little about feeling 'different' at times from other kids at school. I don't think I really heard all you were saying to me. You are well-liked. I know your friends. But right now you're feeling terribly alone. I would guess you're feeling your only worth is tied to your ability to be handsome and athletic. But if you were neither handsome nor athletic, would others value you for who you are? That has to be a scary thought. Tell me more, if you'd like to."

Honestly, my knee-jerk inclination was to give advice: "Are you kidding? You're a great kid! Who doesn't like you—I've got a thing or two to tell them!" But I knew it would not be encouraging to Seth if I made it my mission in life to correct those who dislike him.

Strangely, two things occurred in the car as we sat in near darkness. His tears increased, and his body relaxed. He felt understood. Somehow my words touched a deep fear inside his heart that needed *specific words* as balm.

Our words need to be *precise* ("But if you were neither handsome nor athletic, would others really value you for who you are?") to encourage deeply. Parents are called to penetrate below the protective layers in their kids' lives to identify their desire for relationship and to move deeply into their hearts by words that encourage. If parents can show their kids that they understand, and speak to those fears, they will be more able to encourage their teens. This precise understanding makes parents feel more alive to kids.

Honest exposure of their hearts is extremely risky for teens. A parent whose true purpose is to encourage her adolescent will constantly monitor her own motives to be certain she accepts her kid's hurts. This is a never-ending process.

5. Think of a recent interaction you had with your teen. How could you have sought to understand precisely what he or she was thinking and feeling, rather than give advice?

The Special Words of Encouragement

Like so many of the ideas we've worked on, encouragement takes practice. The following chart gives four areas in which parents can use the concept of encouragement in a concrete way with their teens. These are just samples. As you work on encouragement, you'll have many more special words tailored to your unique kid's needs.

We started in session 1 with a story about Seth and me in a restaurant when I felt frustrated and confused. I would like to conclude with a personal story in which God gave us a glimpse of *mutual encouragement* in a most unlikely place.

Cathy's dad, Cloyd, died of cancer several years ago. Our family was still grieving when Seth, Cathy, and I were in a J. C. Penney store looking for clothing. Seth was about twelve. He decided to do something special for his Grandma Carol, in Cloyd's memory. "Hey Dad," he said, "come help me buy a gift for Grandma. It's Mother's Day next week, and I want to get her something special. I found a cool ring I want you to look at." I was startled because Seth went to the most costly gold and diamond rings in the display case. I knew he was planning to purchase the ring himself, and he didn't have much money at home. I thought I would be helpful and gently guide him to the less expensive section of the ring display about twenty feet away. What came next was dumbfounding.

Seth looked at me with disgust. "You have to be kidding if you think I would buy Grandma any of those cheap rings! I love Grandma and she's done a lot for me. I want to get her something really beautiful, a ring that is real gold and has a diamond in it, something really nice."

"But it will take over $150," I countered, "all you have at home and in your bank account. It will wipe you out." I wanted him to be practical and thrifty. What came next was said with as much conviction as an early adolescent can muster. "I don't care how much it costs. I know it will take everything, but because I love Grandma, I want to do this for her. It's my gift to her. You can buy her that cheap ring if you want. *But from me, I want her to have something of great value.*"

My mouth dropped. I had just had some self-righteous air let out of me. The jewelry woman helping Seth smiled with an edge of her eyebrow raised. I felt kindly rebuked yet profoundly challenged. I sensed Seth's lavish love for his grandma. My love, in comparison, was feeble. God used my son to challenge me in love.

Two weeks later, I was asked to speak to a church group on the subject of family relationships. Seth and Cathy were in the building as I spoke. The only thing I clearly remember from my talk was my concluding story of the ring. When I got to the end, I was finding it difficult to speak. I finished with these words: "God gives us amazing examples of his wild, lavish love for us through others. Our son, Seth, gave me such an example by his love for his grandma. I offered cheapness; he offered richness. I wanted practical; he wanted beauty. I desired to just get by; he gave all he had. I am amazed and humbled by my son's kindness. God gave me a rich glimpse of his lavish love that I will never forget."

I went to the back to greet the people. They offered kind words but not what Seth offered me next. He lingered until the crowd thinned, not making eye contact just yet. Then he had tears on his face as he embraced me. He fell into my arms as I held him up. "I never knew you *really* felt that way about me," he said. "It's so good to have you say it, and me to hear it out loud. Thanks, Dad."

Continuing Down the Path of Encouragement

Isn't that what all of us want—to deeply influence our kids' hearts in godly ways? To speak words of life to them? I wish I could say that one scene in the church foyer did the trick. Of course it didn't, because we still fail each other with more regularity than I would like to admit. Yet at the same time, I have a sense of growing hope in the midst of the disappointments in our relationship.

My heartfelt desire for each of us is to more fully realize that God has uniquely placed us, called us, and is in the lifelong business of equipping us to be parents of courage. My deepest passion is for Christ to richly surprise you at the good things He has in store for you as you grow to trust Him through the ups and downs with your kids.

We have come full circle in our thinking on what it means to be a ministry-oriented parent. Recall Mark's letter in session 1 and his final hopeful words: "But can I trust Him [God] to be good, wise, powerful, and working on my behalf, no matter what happens with my kids or in any other circumstance in my life? . . . Don't panic! Well, I can't help it sometimes, and neither can you probably. *May God use these uncomfortable times in our lives to reveal our lack of trust and to nudge us toward a deeper confidence in Him in the midst of uncertainty and upheaval.*"[8]

Don't Phil's concluding words from his journal entry at the beginning of this session sound strikingly similar to Mark's words? Both fathers have given us a glimpse of "God using these uncomfortable times in our lives to reveal our lack of trust and to *nudge us toward a deeper confidence in Him* in the midst of uncertainty and upheaval." Phil echoes Mark's hope: "Father, soften my heart and my spirit toward my daughter. Help me to love her as You love her."

Truly, the key to being ministry-oriented parents is allowing God to nudge us and soften our hearts toward our kids in the midst of life's uncertainties. *The real key to influencing our kids is, ultimately, becoming godly parents ourselves.* Continued blessing on you in your ongoing journey parenting your kids with a growing sense of grace, hope, and confidence.

Remember

Encouragement means inspiring others with a sense of courage and hope, to excite and spur our kids onward to love and good deeds. Encouragement depends fundamentally on accepting a teen whose needs and faults lie exposed. Calling forth truth, or putting words to the reality of the current parent-adolescent relationship, helps encourage kids by making sense of their relationships. Three principles help us to speak deep words to encourage our kids: (1) the essence of encouragement is exposure without rejection, (2) understanding is sometimes better than advice, and (3) the more precise the understanding, the more encouraging our words will be.

Reflection

Below are some family scenes with questions for your group to answer after each.

1. Your seventeen-year-old son was nominated for class vice president. He lost the election and is now very discouraged. What might he believe about himself? How can you encourage him?

2. Your thirteen-year-old daughter spent the day waterskiing with a group of friends. She's not very athletic and was never able to get up on her skis. She's ashamed of her lack of ability. What might she believe about herself? How can you encourage her?

3. As a group, bring up several examples of times when your own teens have been discouraged. Brainstorm together and come up with ways to encourage them.

NOTES

1. Larry Crabb, Jr. and Dan Allender, *Encouragement: The Key to Caring* (Grand Rapids, MI: Zondervan, 1984), p. 20.
2. Crabb and Allender, pp. 24-25.
3. W. E. Vine, *An Expository Dictionary of New Testament Words* (Old Tappan, N. J.: Revell, 1940), p. 230.
4. Bruce Barton, Dave Veerman, and Linda K. Taylor, *Hebrews Life Application Bible Commentary* Edited by Grant Osborne, (Wheaton, IL: Tyndale, 1997), p. 163.
5. Crabb and Allender, *Encouragement: The Key to Caring,* pp. 104–105.
6. Crabb and Allender, p. 106.
7. Crabb and Allender, p. 107.
8. Mark Dorn, *Pilgrim's Journal* newsletter, April 1998, The Navigators, 4438 S. Alkire Street, Morrison, CO 80465. Reprinted with the author's permission.

Leader's Notes

LEADERSHIP is essential to the success of a parenting group. The leader's job includes the following tasks:

- To begin and end the meeting on time
- To ask people to read aloud key portions of the session's reading
- To periodically tell stories from their own experience as parents, stories that illustrate the points being made in the session
- To select the questions that are most important for the group to discuss
- To ask questions
- To listen closely to answers and ask follow-up questions as appropriate
- To express opinions at appropriate moments
- To set a tone of respect and free exchange of ideas
- To make sure everyone who wants to speak gets adequate air time
- To help the group keep track of the big picture in the material
- To phone parents who miss meetings or are struggling and need one-on-one support
- To decide how to divide the group into subgroups for discussion

The ideal group will have two leaders and twelve to twenty parents. If the group is smaller than twelve, it can manage with one leader. However, a group larger than twelve needs two leaders because in the second hour of the meeting, the group breaks into smaller groups of six to ten parents for more in-depth and personal discussion. Also, two leaders can share responsibilities for guiding the first hour's discussion, telling personal stories, keeping track of time, and checking in with struggling parents during the week.

What Makes a Good Group Leader?

Three attitudes are vital for group leaders in order to provide an open atmosphere for parents.

FLEXIBILITY: A leader needs to be flexible with a diverse group of parents coming from varied backgrounds. Many parents today do not come from the typical two-parent household of earlier generations. It is estimated that nearly 60 percent of all young people today will be raised in a single-parent household at some time during their childhood or adolescence. Divorced, single-parent, blended, and even grandparent-led homes with adolescents are becoming more the norm in our culture.

Also, some of the most wounded people in our churches are parents confronting issues with their adolescents that have no easy answer. The leader must be willing to enter into another parent's world with a redemptive, grace-filled mood. A leader's black-and-white thinking is often lethal when building a sense of community in a group with parents who may not know each other well or at all.

SELF-REFLECTION: The group's success depends heavily on the leaders' abilities to self-disclose appropriately about their own struggles and victories in parenting. To "self-disclose" means to tell brief stories of interactions with their teens. The text of each session contains many such stories from the author's experience as a parent of his own adolescent son and as a counselor of other parents. It will be helpful for leaders to tell similar stories occasionally, perhaps once per session. Leaders' stories should be brief but illustrate a main point of the session. Leaders' stories should reflect both successes and missteps in relating to their teens.

If leaders have an honest sense of their strengths and weaknesses in parenting, parents more easily feel part of a growing, safe place in which to think honestly about their own kids. Self-disclosure by the leader helps parents to feel safe. Also, along with the stories in the text, leaders' stories offer parents a model by which to tell their own stories about themselves and their teens. Such models will be especially useful during the second half of the course when parents want to talk about troubling, hurtful, or shameful situations in their homes.

Leaders must limit their self-disclosure to the parenting experience. The group is not a forum to discuss marriage or unrelated issues. Leaders need to have some growing sense of their own style of relating—that is, how they come across to their own kids and how they respond to what their kids do.

INTEGRITY: Integrity is the leader's ability to adhere to sound moral principles, and to be honest and transparent with others. Leaders need to be willing to admit when they don't know an answer, to receive group feedback that may be troubling to them, and to dialogue with parents about issues that can't be fit into easy solutions. The leader has the role of "fellow parent traveler," as opposed to "parent expert," within the group. If leaders present themselves as nonstruggling "parent experts," other parents will often be reluctant to talk about their own struggles because the leader has not modeled an open atmosphere. Leaders who wisely share some struggles as well as successes foster integrity and open communication with the other parents.

It should be emphasized that leaders do not need to have perfect families or professional training as counselors to be effective. They do not have to have all the answers to parents' questions. In fact, giving parents advice about what to do with their kids is emphatically *not* the leaders' job. Any parent who is flexible, self-reflective, and genuine can be effective as a leader.

Stages of Group Life

The following is an outline of four stages your group may go through:[1]

Stage 1: *Hesitant and dependent.* The decision to trust is based on the participants' confidence and attraction to the leader. They may hesitate to believe that the other members have anything of value to contribute to their situation. They will be dependent on the group leader. In the early stage of group relating, members may be constantly sizing each other up. They search for similarities and often give and receive advice. This armchair counseling will be obsolete later in the group. In stage 1, it lessens people's awkwardness and is a vehicle for expressing mutual interest and caring. Thus, you need not confront advice-giving during the first couple of weeks; it may be just a conventional way of breaking the ice.

Stage 2: *Conflict and rumors of mutiny.* During this stage, group members become preoccupied with dominance, control, and power. The "peer court" is in session. People try to establish a pecking order. They criticize other members in order to obtain status. There may be a certain degree of hostility toward the leader because the unrealistic expectations of his or her abilities to create change are dashed. The magical aspects of the leader are shrinking to life-size proportions.

Also, members feel disillusioned. They sense the leader will not reward them as the favored member of the group. Some participants may attack the leader, while others rally to defend him or her. Some may doubt the entire process at this stage.

Stage 3: *Group cohesiveness.* In this stage the morale of the group improves. There is a sense of cooperation and a desire to unite so that the bonds of intimacy can be built. The group will enjoy a rich experience of self-disclosure. In a sense, they have forgiven the leader for falling from his or her pedestal, and they are ready to see what support and feedback the group members can offer. Be aware that there is a potential for negative feelings to be suppressed in order to maintain the cohesiveness. The gamut of emotions must be open for expression. The group's hostility must emerge if the group is going to mature. When you cross this barrier, the group will be able to address deep issues about their parenting styles.

Stage 4: *Termination.* The ending of a group is an integral part of the process and should never be overlooked. If closure is handled well, it can be an important force in promoting change. Closure reveals to group members the meaning of continuing to love in spite of the sadness of separation. For some group members, the thought of ending the group is threatening. Their defense against this transition often is to resurrect former issues in order to legitimize their need to stay in a support group.

The group labors mightily to construct a bridge that is durable enough to bear the weight of sadness. Once the bridge is in place, the members must face the sorrow so that it transports them to the task of loving new people. Ideas for constructive termination of the group are included in the leader's notes for session 16.

Session 1: An Internal Shift

The first group meeting sets the tone for the course. People who attend will be deciding whether they want to be part of the group. Your goals for this session are to:

- Create excitement about this course so people will want to continue
- Give people an overview of the course so they know what to expect

- Begin to build relationships so that a sense of community starts to develop
- Encourage people to commit to the group and to the group's covenant

Before people arrive for the meeting, arrange chairs in a circle so that everyone will be able to see each other's faces. Consider providing something to drink and/or eat.

Greet people as they arrive. Let them know you're glad they've come and that you look forward to being with them. Consider handing out name tags.

Describe how the process of the group will work. In most sessions, the group will spend the first hour going over the teaching section of the session and the second hour applying those ideas to their own relationships with their kids. In this first session, however, the teaching section is brief, and the bulk of the session will be devoted to an exercise that will help parents get to know each other.

You might want to go over some or all of the questions in "How Does This Course Work?" on pages vii-viii.

Discussion: Each session in this course begins with several pages of text interspersed with a few discussion questions. There are several ways in which you can help the group digest this text. At times you may want to have someone in the group read a section of the text aloud. For example, it might be useful to have someone read Mark's letter aloud. It's a good idea to ask someone ahead of time if they would mind reading a section, rather than asking a person in front of the group. Some people are uncomfortable reading aloud.

After the reading of Mark's letter, invite the group to respond to question 1. As the leader, you should be the first to answer this question. Your answer will model for the group how brief or lengthy an answer you are looking for. It will also model the degree of honesty and vulnerability you hope others will show. As a rule of thumb, plan to be slightly more honest and vulnerable than you would like group members to be.

Instead of reading aloud the section entitled "Not in the Concrete!", you may prefer to let the group read it silently and then summarize the highlights of this section. With each section, it will be up to you whether to have it read aloud, provide time for group members to read it silently, summarize the main points, or ask the group to summarize it.

You can let people read my [Dave's] story silently, or you can ask someone to read it aloud. Then invite the group to respond to question 2.

Stories like Mark's and mine greatly help parents grasp the abstract concepts they are learning. One of the most important things you can do as the leader is to tell stories like these yourself. Before each meeting, try to think of a story from your own life as a parent that illustrates the material for that session. When have you been in a situation similar to what I describe with Seth in the restaurant? When have you felt like Mark? Take a few minutes to tell one of your stories. Be clear about the goal of your story; you are not trying to impress the group with your expert parenting skills or your spiritual depth, nor are you trying to prove how badly you have suffered at the hands of your kids. Rather, you are trying to show that you are more like the members of your group than you are different, that you still need God to help you as a parent. You are trying to set an example of focusing on what God is doing with your heart, rather than on what your kid ought to do. Your story should illustrate a time when you needed God or when you learned something about yourself from an interaction with your teen.

Parenting Pairs exercise: Parents need a chance in the first session to get acquainted with each other. They also need equal opportunity to talk.

This introductory exercise begins immediately to model nonthreatening topics to help parents communicate with each other. The one-hour exercise is called Parenting Pairs. Because some parents are reluctant to talk about themselves, this simple exercise is designed to have the entire group, including leader(s), divide into pairs. People should pair up with someone they don't already know. Each parent will use the Parenting Pairs worksheet on page 5 to record his or her partner's responses. After the pairs have talked with each other for twenty minutes, they will gather as a whole group. Each parent will verbally introduce his or her partner to the rest of the group. By introducing their partners, people need not feel shy talking about themselves in front of a group.

You will need to watch the clock while the pairs are discussing their answers. Let them know when ten minutes have passed and they should switch roles, and when twenty minutes have passed and they should gather as a group.

You will also need to monitor the time each person takes to introduce his or her partner. These introductions should not take more than forty to sixty minutes, depending on the size of the group. Some people are naturally talkative, so you may need to gently interrupt and move the group on if someone talks for more than five minutes. You can model the length and tone of a good introduction by being the first to introduce your partner. Your partner should be someone other than your coleader, ideally someone whom you do not already know well. If you introduce that person warmly in about three minutes, the group will take their cue from you.

When all introductions are complete, thank the group for coming and ask if anyone has any questions about the group. Ask parents to read session 2 and think about the questions before coming to the next meeting.

The Parenting Pairs exercise replaces the Reflection portion of the meeting that all other sessions include. If your group contains more than eleven parents, you will divide into two subgroups for Reflection in sessions 2 through 16. You should come to session 2 with a list of names for each subgroup, rather than letting people group themselves. Give some thought to the composition of these subgroups. For example, encourage couples to attend the same subgroup unless there is a compelling reason to divide them. Try to distribute men and women evenly between the subgroups; do the same with married and single parents. In this way, people will get to hear the perspectives of both the same and the opposite sex— this diversity is especially helpful for single parents. If possible, avoid having too many loud parents in the same group, or they will dominate the quieter ones. Beyond these basic guidelines, grouping people is more an art of compatibility than a science.

Session 2:
A Look at Ourselves

OBJECTIVE: At the beginning of the session, read aloud the objective. At least for the first several sessions, have someone read the objective aloud in the group to make sure everyone is tracking with the overall purpose of the particular session. It is also a good idea to give the group an overview of what to expect in this session: they'll spend an hour going over the content for the session, then spend another hour on the Reflection section.

How the group will go through the materials: Before the group meets, read the entire session in order to think through the main ideas. Mark the key sections on which you want to comment. Use the workbook as your personal guide, and feel free to write, underline, or highlight sections for quick recall. Think about the amount of time you have to cover the material, and decide which sections are most important.

To help parents feel included, it would be good to ask people to read aloud the italicized dialogue that begins each session. In session 2 you will need three readers: Mom, Dad, and Graham. It's wise to preselect members, ideally a week in advance, rather than springing this job on people at the last minute. Choose people who you think will feel comfortable reading the roles realistically.

The section entitled "An Estranged Son" lays an important scriptural foundation for the ideas of nonreflection versus biblical reflection. These ideas recur throughout the course, so it's essential that people understand them. Have parents turn to 2 Samuel 13–14 to follow along as you read. (Don't assume that people know how to find 2 Samuel in a Bible. You might direct the whole group to the table of contents at the front of their Bibles and note where 2 Samuel is located.) This narrative about King David is used as a contrasting picture on how a nonreflective parent relates to his kids. Highlight how David related to his son Absalom, specifically after the rape of Absalom's sister, Tamar. Draw out the themes of David's parental silence, his refusal to deal with the distance developing between him and Absalom, and the results of this refusal in his family.

Discussion: Ask yourself the discussion questions ahead of time and rephrase them in your own language. Think about how you would answer the questions so you will have some idea of what to expect from the parents. Also, the questions will help you think carefully through the content. When you ask the questions in the group, the discussion will help you to ensure that parents are grasping the initial concepts being presented.

Allow about five to eight minutes for the group to discuss each question as you move through the session. Not every parent will need to comment on the questions; probably two or three parents on each question is a realistic number. Most sessions have five to seven questions. In sessions with up to nine questions, you may want to select just one question out of those from the same section.

Areas of potential misunderstanding: Session 2 emphasizes how nonreflective parenting develops. From Scripture and parents' stories, you will highlight the "Causes of Nonreflective Parenting." This section contains the themes of parental disappointment, failure, and fear.

Parents may try to say these realities don't exist for them. They may have some level of resistance to talk at this stage. It will be enough for you to put these ideas on the table for parents to think about as they proceed. You can then move below the surface in the coming weeks. At this point, you might want say something like "These are hard things for most parents to acknowledge fully, or much at all, but these emotions can be barriers to our becoming more effective parents. We will try and look at these things in the weeks ahead."

Sharing your personal story: It will be vital for you to share progressively deeper parts of your own parenting journey in the group. At this forming stage of the group, even short personal stories can help make parents feel they are not alone in their concerns. They also need to know you are a fellow struggler, not a resident expert. In session 1, I described the struggle between my son and me in the restaurant in which my nonreflective parenting ended in frustration, confusion, and anger. Perhaps you can share a three- to five-minute story in which you were nonreflective with your son or daughter.

As a rule of thumb, three to four self-disclosure stories by the leader per session would be the maximum parents can hear effectively. The group is for them, not for the leader to work out his or her issues. Too many self-disclosing stories from you will make parents start to wonder about your boundaries and potential neediness.

However, you need to be willing to "prime the pump" by sharing first if parents hesitate to answer a discussion question. Your personal stories let the parents know you are in this thing together.

Reflection: Before the group meets, think about how you would personally answer the Reflection questions. Specifically, the desires you are feeling with your kids and the ways you have been most disappointed are the key applications in session 2.

Further reading: Also, the supplemental book *Parenting Adolescents* by Kevin Huggins is a great resource to further develop your thinking. The section entitled "The Causes of Nonreflective Parenting" on pages 95-110 explains in detail the process of nonreflective thinking by parents.

Group process issues: In the initial stage of any group, members are getting acquainted with each other. Typically, parents in this stage are somewhat hesitant, maybe even trying to figure out the leader and the other members. The often unspoken questions parents have at this stage are "Is this group safe for me to talk?" "Will I be accepted and valued for my contributions?" "Can I honestly relate to these parents, and they to me?" "Can this group of parents really help me grow?" Understand that in the first stage of the parent group, people will be feeling each other out in terms of these expectations and questions. (For more, see previous section, "Stages of Group Life.")

For next week: Ask someone if he or she would be willing to read the italicized opening section of session 3 at the beginning of your next meet-

ing. No preparation is necessary, but it's a good idea to ask someone ahead of time.

Session 3:
How Teens See the World

OBJECTIVE: At the beginning of the meeting, read aloud the objective. Emphasize that the point will be to take a realistic look at how kids experience their world. Remind the parents that they'll spend an hour going over the content and an hour on the Reflection section at the end of the session.

How the group will go through the materials: Before the group meets, everyone should read the entire session to grasp the main concepts. With a yellow highlighter, mark the sections and questions that need to be emphasized during the meeting. Leaders and parents have found it helpful to write in the margins alongside the text to emphasize and remember key thoughts.

Have someone read aloud the italicized story about Aaron that opens this session. (At the end of session 2 you asked this person if he or she would be willing to read.) From this account, ask aloud question 1. This question enables parents to actively engage the content right away.

Emphasize how important it is for parents to learn how to figure out their kids. Read the italicized words that come before the first bold subhead: *kids aren't impossible to figure out.* This is a foundational thought. Many parents feel confused and uncertain when their kids reach adolescence. Therefore, helping parents come to believe they can, over time, learn to understand the forces shaping their kids is an important focus.

Read aloud Proverbs 19:8: ". . . he who cherishes understanding prospers." The proverb emphasizes that becoming people of understanding is a God-honoring direction for life. Parents are called to become more understanding in order to encourage their kids toward maturity.

Discussion: Again, get in the habit of rephrasing each discussion question ahead of time to make sure you have a clear understanding of how the questions fit with the preceding content materials. You have only six discussion questions in this session, so you should have time to cover them all. Each one should take around five to eight minutes for parents to discuss. It's not necessary for every parent to answer each question, because these questions are intended merely to make sure parents understand the material. The Reflection time is when every parent needs a chance to answer each question.

Areas of potential misunderstanding: Session 3 revolves around the themes of how the world expects kids to change and the big changes kids notice in their lives as they move through adolescence.

Expectation #2, "How They're Supposed to Think," can be confusing to parents. The notion of moving from "concrete" to "formal" thinking processes is somewhat sophisticated. Also, kids don't move all at once from one stage to the other. Help parents understand that for older children (age 9–12), "concrete" (black-and-white, rigid rule-keeping) thinking is often the norm. Yet even older children have some capacity to think in abstract concepts, to make subtle cause-and-effect connections with their worlds. At the same time, even older adolescents (age 17–19) shift back and forth from more advanced "formal" thinking processes to "concrete" thinking. This shifting can frustrate parents.

The other area of potential confusion is teens' observation #3, "How Things Can Be Avoided." Parents need to start to come to grips with the thought that their kids do, indeed, have

great capacity to be deceptive. This reality is tough for most parents. Many parents assume kids just need a little emotional "tune-up" and they will be forthright and honest in all their relationships. Proverbs 26:23-26 hits clearly on the theme of deception in relationships. Read this passage aloud to highlight this section as you comment upon it.

Sharing your personal story: It will again be necessary for you in this early stage of the group to prime the pump by sharing a three- to five-minute story from your own past. For instance, you might tell a story about "How They're Supposed to Look." The story of Seth's ritual of grooming his hair in front of the hall mirror is an example of how kids feel the need to look good. Perhaps you can share a story from your adolescence or your kids' adolescence to help parents connect to how important it is for kids to look, think, or relate in a certain way for acceptance in their worlds. Talk about how needing to look good or fit in with others caused you to feel as an adolescent.

Reflection: Before the group meets, think about how you would answer the Reflection questions personally. It's especially important for each parent to answer questions 3 and 4. By reflecting on their own adolescence, parents will find it easier to understand their kids' struggles. In some ways, adolescence is much tougher in today's world than it was a generation ago, but in other ways, the issues and feelings are similar.

Ideally, you will take ten minutes at the beginning of each Reflection time to invite feedback on the previous session's Action Lab. In reality, you may feel pressed for time and be tempted to skip this conversation. However, people are much more likely to do the Action Lab if they know they will be invited to talk about it in the group.

Further reading: Read pages 49-68 of *Parenting Adolescents.* Kevin Huggins goes into greater detail about "concrete" versus "formal" thinking processes. He also expands the ideas of how kids develop new insights into their world as they move into adolescence.

Group process issues: The group is still in the initial phase of getting acquainted. Parents are getting some sense of who you and the other parents are. Some parents will emerge as wanting to talk more; others will be fairly quiet at this stage, observing your leadership and integrity. Some may be reluctant to talk, wanting to hear more from you before they are willing to risk sharing their lives in the group.

You may sense that many people are hesitant to share very deeply at this stage. Yet you may have two or three parents willing to risk revealing a little more of their struggle. Even a few parents willing to share early on will be positive role models for other parents, and they will come to talk more over time.

Session 4:
Why Teens Do What They Do

OBJECTIVE: Read aloud the objective at the beginning of this session. Emphasize the importance of truly learning about the hidden forces that drive kids to behave in very foolish ways. This session is one of the foundational pillars the course is built upon; it is central to becoming parents of deeper understanding. Our kids' deep foolishness affects all of their lives and relationships in profound ways.

How the group will go through the material: As you read the content ahead of time, look for the overall flow and allow yourself to be affected by the stories. Again, think about your time limitations and the key topics you will want to spend more time on.

Have one parent read the italicized story about the *Titanic.* Have parents recall how the *Titanic* sank, the details of how a small, narrow rupture below the waterline because of an unseen iceberg caused catastrophic damage to the vessel. Highlight the below-the-waterline dangers to which parents need to respond.

Have a parent read Proverbs 20:5, the central text for this session. You will return to this scriptural metaphor of issues below the waterline throughout the rest of the course, so be sure to give this image a lot of discussion in the group.

The story of my adolescent foolishness should help parents grasp what adolescent foolishness is. Help parents trace the themes of disappointment, basic beliefs, and guiding strategies through this story. It's important for parents to make the connection between outward behavior and relational disappointment that starts below the waterline, out of parents' sight. Kids' disappointment often grows slowly, beginning at levels far below the surface. Kids' behavior then reveals bits of their foolish thinking processes.

Areas of potential misunderstanding: Session 4 emphasizes how foolishness develops in kids' thinking and relating. The focus is for parents to learn how to help their kids connect their behaviors to foolish purposes.

The disappointment kids experience with parents and others may need some additional explanation. Proverbs 20:6 speaks of the relational disappointment that all people experience. Read this verse aloud. Stress that relational disappointment is a part of all relationships. No parent can prevent kids from feeling some level of disappointment in their worlds. In fact, as parents, we want to allow kids' disappointment to surface honestly. We don't want kids to minimize or ignore it. Kids' disappointments enable parents to point their kids toward God as the real healer of relationships. Be sure to allow significant discussion in this area of disappointment.

Also, parents can fail to make connections between their kids' disappointment and small, subtle violations of relationship with others. Often, parents can read my story of my parents' divorce and say to themselves, "Well, my kid hasn't experienced such a heartache, so obviously disappointment doesn't apply to my kids." A parent who fails to listen to his kids' struggles, who dismisses his pain, or who is just too busy and ignores his kids can in the long run be just as disappointing as a parent who leaves the home. Help parents see that all disappointments, large and small, fuel foolishness in our kids' thinking.

Sharing your personal story: In addition to using my story of the growth of my foolishness, you have an opportunity to connect to parents by using a short personal story of your own. Perhaps you could share an early disappointment you experienced in your own home or in other significant relationships as a teenager. The disappointment you share need not be catastrophic. It might be an ongoing, nagging issue like feeling ignored, minimized by others, or excluded from your parents' lives. Your goal in sharing this story will be to encourage parents to take greater risks in the group.

Be willing to ask a few parents to share some of their own disappointments as well. These stories will connect the parents to each other and promote a growing atmosphere of openness and safety.

Reflection: Before the group meets, think about how you would answer the Reflection questions personally. Specifically, you will want to emphasize questions 2 and 3. Focus on helping parents develop hunches about how their own kids might answer question 3: "Life works for me when . . ." Have parents share aloud with the group how their kids might answer this question.

Further reading: Read pages 41–45 of *Parenting Adolescents.* Huggins does a good job of helping parents understand how all of us, parents and kids alike, struggle with relational disappointment while living in a fallen world.

Group process: The group should start to move into some initial levels of conflict. It will begin to deal with harder issues that may have been minimized or ignored in the first few sessions. People may begin to question the leader ("Who says you are right?") or even other parents. This questioning is a normal part of the group process. You may find some parents trying to control the time by sharing excessively and some unwilling to talk much at all. Some form of pecking order can begin to develop at this stage. Remember, a willingness to struggle with issues or with you is a healthy sign for the group members at this stage.

Session 5:
Drifting Apart

OBJECTIVE: Read the objective aloud at the opening of this session. Emphasize the theme that relational drifting is an inevitable process unless parents take creative and thoughtful steps to slow it.

How the group will go through the materials: Parents should always read through the entire session ahead of time. Most parents should be getting on track with the reading by now, but it still is good to remind them that reading the materials before the group meets is critical.

Ask someone ahead of time to read the italicized story of Grandpa's boat. The boat drifted out into the lake because of Susie's lack of vigilance and energy to prevent it. The boat metaphor introduces the idea of relational drifting: As waves subtly moved the boat, so subtle forces will move parents and kids apart. Make this connection clear. Lack of awareness and energy to combat drifting will have the same effect in relationships as it had for Susie and the boat.

Summarize the story of David and Absalom. Specifically, the story in 2 Samuel 14 deals with the drifting David allowed with his son after Absalom returned to his home in Jerusalem. Emphasize 2 Samuel 14:24: "He must go to his own house; he must not see my face." This Scripture captures the essence of David's struggle with his son—he refused to *fully* bring his son back into ongoing, restored relationship. He merely brought his son home *physically,* but not from a forgiven heart, because of his own unaddressed struggles.

Have a parent read the last paragraph from the section on David and Absalom. Repeat the question from this paragraph aloud: "What was happening to make David respond in this way?" Draw to the parents' attention the three forces that maintained drifting in David's family: continuing to justify his anger toward his son, ignoring his own past failures, and avoiding the truth of his own angry heart by building a self-protective wall to avoid feeling pain. Make the connection between David's problems and those that parents today have with their own kids.

Discussion: Now ask aloud question 1: "When have you felt or acted out defensiveness toward your teen in ways that maintained an unhealthy distance?" This question opens parents to recognize their own unique defensiveness. They may be utterly unaware of defensiveness that maintains distance with their kids. Give parents plenty of time with this question so they can ponder and hear other parents respond to this issue of distance. Draw out several parents to discuss the unhealthy distance they overtly or covertly use with their kids. This question is a tough one because it asks parents to look at their own hearts, so expect some resistance. Yet if the group is beginning to open up more, you

should have a few parents willing to discuss it in some depth.

Give special attention to the section "Five Stages of Drifting," because this process is a problem for many families. Summarize Jay's struggle with his parents and school teachers. Give some time to the development of power struggles in the last part of the drifting process. Most parents will be able to make the connections to power struggles with their own kids as well.

If parents have trouble identifying the drifting in their own families, the warning signals and question 3 should help them think concretely about their situations. There are only three discussion questions in this session, so you should have plenty of time for all of them. Again, though, it's not necessary for everyone to answer each question. Some parents will benefit most at this stage from listening to how others answer the questions.

Areas of potential misunderstanding: In the section "It's Easy to Create Distance," parents need to know these are only sample distancing strategies. There are many more strategies than the eight mentioned. Be willing to talk about other styles of maintaining distance, such as the "angry parent" or the "shaming parent." Think about the strategies you have used to maintain distance with your kids or others.

The third distancing strategy mentioned (avoidance of emotional interaction) deserves special attention. Parents who relate to their kids in a heavily justice-oriented way ("There is no problem as long as my teen obeys me.") may struggle with the idea that emotional interaction is even important. These parents may resist truly acknowledging their kids' anguish or troubled hearts. Read aloud the paragraph about Sam, the father who used power to force his kids to agree with him while avoiding their troubling emotions.

Stress that as hard as it is, parents must be willing to acknowledge their distancing strategies deeply and to let God deal with their hearts.

Sharing your personal story: Share a longer story from your own life about the five stages of drifting you have experienced with your kids. A five- to seven-minute story would be appropriate to give parents a glimpse of your personal journey. It could be a story of mild drifting or of more significant drifting. Talk about how, as you witnessed changes in your kids, you felt anxiety or fear. You might have felt anything from mild anxiety to full-blown fear during these adolescent changes. Then share with the parents some of the strategies, however ineffective, you used in an attempt to regain control. Talk about how you saw your kid begin to harden with the subsequent power struggles.

Reflection: Again, before the group meets, think through all four of the Reflection questions. Mentally highlight question 2 about how drifting was handled in your family so you can think through your adolescent experiences. It's important to help parents remember their struggles by looking back, as well as to help them look at their kids today.

Question 3 is the main application question for this session, so give a much longer period of time for parents to respond to this question.

Further reading: Pages 95-99 of *Parenting Adolescents* highlight David and Absalom's distancing process. Huggins expands on the wrong goal of reducing our own pain, which is the driving force behind distancing strategies.

Group process: If the group is working well, it should begin to move from conflict or tension to an initial stage of cohesion. However, even the best groups will move back and forth between stages. The group process is never completely smooth or without tension from one stage to the next.

Thus, parents may retest limits and the leader at times, and at other times they may feel more connected with each other. Your job after the group is functioning is to maintain as much as possible a consistent and positive relationship with the group members by being accepting, genuine, and open to their feedback.

Session 6:
How the Home Affects Kids

OBJECTIVE: Have one of the parents read aloud the objective.

How the group will go through the materials: Preselect two parents to read the italicized story about Allen and Lilly. Make sure the readers you select will be comfortable reading realistically and with emotion.

Read aloud the section "Two Forces That Shape the Home Environment" with emphasis on Jeremiah 31:20. Help parents see that the Lord is passionate both to "delight" and "speak against" His children. God always operates, simultaneously, with both justice and mercy. Make sure parents understand this key principle so that the next section about uncompromising responsiveness (justice) and unconditional involvement (grace) will be clear. Be willing to summarize this section for the parents.

Discussion: Remember to ponder ahead of time how you would answer each discussion question. Feel free to rephrase the questions.

There are four discussion questions, so you will have plenty of time to ask parents for their feedback. Perhaps three to four parents could discuss their thoughts on each question. Question 3 moves into the area of parents combining love and justice with their own kids. Make sure you spend a longer period of time with this concept because it can be a challenging truth for parents to really grasp.

Areas of potential misunderstanding: The section after question 3 emphasizes the two primary forces, *uncompromising responsiveness* and *unconditional involvement,* that shape a kid's home environment. The more difficult of the two concepts to explain will be uncompromising responsiveness (justice), so be willing to elaborate with the text example and maybe a personal story of your own. One of the key sentences in this section to be read aloud is, "We are to attach the same significance to our teen's heart and choices that God attaches to ours." Make sure parents see that all of the things kids do, their choices and actions, have significant consequences in life.

Read Seth's basketball story from the "Uncompromising Responsiveness" section to highlight this truth. Seth asked me a question all kids really want to ask their parents. Ask the parents the question at the end of Seth's story: "Do you and other adults really take notice of me and see my contributions as significant?" Underscore the idea that this question is at the heart of what kids want to ask every parent. Each adolescent has a deep longing to have others, particularly parents, see their contributions as significant, lasting, and even eternal.

Sharing your personal story: The group should be willing to take greater risks in telling their personal stories with their kids. It would be helpful if you could tell a personal story about using uncompromising responsiveness with one of your kids (or having experienced it when you were a kid) and another story about unconditional involvement. For example, share a story from either your adolescence or adulthood in which you felt enjoyed for who you were by another person. Talk about feeling alive and safe within such relationships, and how that feeling helped you to mature.

In the section on unconditional involvement, I use my grandmother Ruth to flesh out the idea of "delight." Take the time to sum-marize my story about my grandmother delighting in me and how her love encouraged me. Ask the parents to talk about feeling delighted in by others (or perhaps not feeling that) and the impact such relationships had upon their lives. Help parents to think more deeply about the power of just enjoying, or delighting in, their kids. When kids feel we truly enjoy them, with no strings attached, it is a potent force to move them toward maturity and away from foolishness.

Reflection: Ponder how you will respond to the Reflection questions prior to the group. Focus most of your time on question 2. Have parents try to identify where their kids likely fit within this chart. Ask them to share why they think their kids fit within the particular section of the chart from the descriptors given.

Also, ask parents where they see their parenting style. They may not see their styles clearly now, but this will lay the groundwork for further reflection on parenting styles as the group proceeds.

Further reading: Pages 129–140 of *Parenting Adolescents* help parents think clearly about uncompromising responsiveness and unconditional involvement. Huggins also goes into significant discussion about how the different parenting styles from the "Home Environments" chart tend to shape teens' foolishness.

Group process issues: The parents should begin to feel more of a collective sense of "we-ness": we are in this parenting journey together. Hopefully, a sense of connection and cohesiveness is developing among the members. Parents will begin to feel a greater sense of freedom and intimacy. As a leader, you will recognize group milestones when you hear parents willing to share themselves without much prodding or share deeper parts of themselves than they have before.

Again, negative emotions toward others may resurface, yet if the group is growing, these negative emotions will not derail the parents' overall sense of connection to one another and commitment to the group purpose. As parents begin to risk more at this stage, the potential for deeper community develops and gives God freedom to work in their hearts in rich ways.

Session 7:
Influencing Our Teens

OBJECTIVE: Have someone read aloud the objective for the session. Help parents understand that increased influence is an ongoing, positive force they can begin to use in all areas of relating with their kids. Explain that you're going to look at five levels of increased influence parents can begin to build.

How the group will go through the materials: Have one of the parents read the italicized story about Robby and Cal. Be sure to comment on Robby's deep disappointment and his feeling of failure as a parent—these are the feelings that have led him to move away from his son emotionally. Ask the rhetorical question, "Who can blame him?" Then state to the group, "Most of us ask this question, subtly in our hearts, when we experience deep, unrelenting pain with kids." Help parents see how Robby is a consumer parent, forfeiting his influence with own son. That word *consumer* is strongly negative and may feel threatening. Is Robby really using his son as a consumer item? Yes, because he's in the relationship only for what he can get out of it, not for what he can give when he's getting nothing he likes.

Read Galatians 5:13,15 aloud to highlight the biblical idea of people actually consuming one another in selfish relationships. Summarize the consumer parent section. Read aloud the italicized sentence at the end of the section to punctuate this consumer parenting theme: *"Nothing is to be gained by staying in a painful relationship if it doesn't benefit me."*

Have the parents look at the chart about the five levels of influence. Talk through each of the five levels of parenting influence to be sure everyone understands each one. Clearly state the difference between consumer parents and godly parents of influence.

Discussion: You have five discussion questions in the content section, so you'll have adequate time to give up to eight minutes per question should the parents need the time.

Focus on questions 3 and 4 about material involvement. Give parents plenty of time with this area to make sure they understand material involvement well. It's easy to hear "material" involvement as financial provision, whereas the kind of active involvement in kids' lives described in this section is scary or even distasteful for many parents. They don't like their kids' worlds! Why would they want to get involved?

It will also be important for you to summarize the section about empathetic involvement and ask parents to respond to question 5. In addition, you might have parents give examples of how they experience empathy *from* their kids. These questions move parents to understand *personally,* not abstractly, the forces motivating their kids to respond as they do.

Areas of potential misunderstanding: Consumer parenting is a hard idea for parents to "buy into" when they think of themselves with their kids. Most parents rarely view themselves as "biting and devouring" their own kids, for it is a repulsive thought. Yet Galatians 5:15 teaches that people, even parents, can "consume" others in selfish relationships. Parents can be worse than we think we are! Parents need the strength and courage only

God Himself can offer them. You will need to develop the concept of consumerism by discussing how it plagues all parents at certain times in our relationships.

The second area needing clarification might be the "Level 4: Dynamic Involvement" section. Highlight the idea that only parents willing to pursue their kids patiently, over the long haul through weeks and months, will be able to challenge kids' thinking and actions effectively at this stage. Understandably, parents often want quick results with kids when they feel discomfort. Parents can't quickly skip from level 1 to level 4 influence without doing the tedious work of developing increasing levels of involvement.

When they read question 1, some parents may reply, "My teen never seeks forgiveness." That's a fair response and may be true. There are several possible reasons why this may be the case, and you could lay out some or all of them for the parent to consider. Perhaps the teen has been self-willed and defiant for a long time. Look back at the home environment of the defiant teen (page 38 in session 6) to see if there is a connection. Perhaps the parent has not been receptive to apologies, so the teen has stopped making any. Perhaps the parent has not set an example of seeking forgiveness when he or she is wrong, so the teen has never learned to do so. This course focuses on the kind of person the parent is becoming, so it might be worth asking the parent what he or she does when he or she is wrong. Everyone hurts people sometimes; do we seek forgiveness when we do that?

Sharing your personal story: You should be able to share more and risk deeper parts of your personal journey at this stage. Perhaps you can share a more emotional, thoughtful story about how you were able to move beyond superficial issues ("How's school? Any tough classes?") to more of a heart issue with your teen.

You may start by rereading the story of Robby's willingness to invite his son's anger in the Dynamic Involvement section. Robby's words to Cal illustrate a parent willing to risk more of himself, even inviting his adolescent's disappointment, when Robby asked, "Why do you feel like you have to fight me all the time?" Robby allowed Cal to vent his deepest anger and disappointment honestly in order to ultimately deepen his influence with his son.

Reflection: Think through the Reflection questions before you arrive at the group. Help the parents use the levels of influence chart in this section. Help them honestly evaluate where they are with each of their kids, as well as think about ways in which they want to work on deepening their levels of influence.

Further reading: Pages 176–186 of *Parenting Adolescents* offer a more detailed description of developing levels of influence with kids. Huggins' levels of influence are clear, thoughtful, and applicable.

Group process: Ideally, the group will be moving to greater levels of cohesion and self-disclosure over the weeks together. One of the road markers here is the solidarity group members will continue to feel toward not just the leader, but also the other parents. This solidarity, or "we-ness," reveals itself in more consistent voluntary attendance, active participation, and parents helping each other in the group. You should not have to prime the pump as much at this stage by directly asking parents to interact. However, cohesion fluctuates up and down during the group process because it is a dynamic, not a static, relational process.

Session 8:
Building Bridges, Not Walls

OBJECTIVE: Have a parent read aloud the objective. Comment that examining our goals is an ongoing process as we learn to shift to ministry-oriented goals.

How the group will go through the materials: This session is longer and contains more discussion questions than most sessions, so it will be important for parents to be prepared by reading the content carefully ahead of time.

Read aloud the paraphrased "Carpenter Story" by David Wilcox. The story conveys the idea of building "bridges of forgiveness" in our relationships. The bridge metaphor, which will be used again in this course, provides a visual picture parents can identify with. Restate the last sentence in this story to connect it to the thrust of the session: "Like the wise carpenter, it takes brave parents willing to build bridges, not walls, with their kids."

Ask someone to read the italicized story of Tim and Judy. This is not a dialogue but a narrative that requires only one person to read.

The section "Unmet Desires, Foolish Goals, and Consumer Parents" is complex and challenging, with multiple concepts that parents need to grasp. You will need to summarize this section for the parents, slowly moving through each paragraph to make sure parents are tracking with you. Be sure to differentiate between parental *goals* and parental *desires* by using Tim and Judy's story as an example. Summarize the three types of desires parents experience with their kids. It's necessary for parents to understand these three desires, as we will build on them over the rest of the course.

Discussion: There are nine discussion questions, so you will want to think through them in advance, even putting them into your own words to convey them to the parents. The discussion questions are grouped into three sections, so you may want to pick just one or two questions from each section to ask the parents aloud.

Be sure to allow more time for the questions around desires and goals in the early part of the content. Specifically, questions 1 through 4 deal with the differences between critical and crucial desires. Parents need to recognize when they have crucial desires about their kids and to understand how those desires affect their kids. Focus on question 4 about how parents may be controlled by a crucial desire in ways they may not like with regard to their kids. Allow plenty of time for parents to process this question aloud in the group. Crucial desires are a central thought in this session — parents need to learn how to recognize crucial desires and then shift to a ministry goal.

Areas of potential misunderstanding: Casual, critical, and crucial desires are key to understanding this session. The *crucial* desire is the most challenging concept for parents to understand with regard to their own kids. You may best help parents by reading aloud the paragraph quoted from Kevin Huggins on page 50. Parents run into trouble when they believe something that seems vital to their own well-being is at stake in their kids' behavior. One can't control another person's behavior, but if one's own well-being seems to be at stake, one will surely try! Try to help parents see areas in which they believe their own well-being is at stake. Parents can feel some level of emotional resistance about this concept, so be willing to allow them to dialogue informally about this idea, to let it slowly sink in during the group discussion.

Self-sacrifice is another important truth needing extra discussion. Read the paragraph that describes how Judy risked with her daughter Janice so Janice could know God more honestly. Ask parents to think of ways in which their own kids might see their self-sacrifice on an ongoing basis. Be sure parents understand that true self-sacrifice is actively helping their kids know God, not just sacrificing for their physical needs (which may be necessary in some cases) or giving in to their demands (which is actually harmful).

Sharing your personal story: You should be able to share at a greater depth your own story about desires and goals that you have pursued with your kids. Perhaps you could share in about five to eight minutes a story of a time when you realized your desires had moved from seeming critical to seeming crucial. Describe how your own parental well-being seemed to be at stake with your adolescent, and how that feeling moved you to use your kid to meet your needs instead of first meeting his or her needs.

Be willing to share some of your own personal discomfort, as well as ways, perhaps, that God freed you to shift to a ministry goal to better love your own kid as a result of looking at your own heart first. You will convey a real hope to struggling parents when you become more aware, and repent more deeply, of your own foolish crucial desires. As parents glimpse your own honest struggle and hope in the Lord, it will encourage them to share more of their own stories.

Reflection: The four questions elicit a deep understanding of the content. Focus on questions 3 and 4. Ask in what ways parents can be involved in ministry goals with their kids in a practical way.

Further reading: Pages 80-85 of Larry Crabb's *Inside Out* develop the topics of casual, critical, and crucial desires. Also, pages 73–75 of *Parenting Adolescents* lay out a thoughtful understanding of these different desires.

Group process issues: The cohesive stage is an ongoing opportunity to see the parents being useful in each other's personal growth. In all likelihood, not all the parents will be best friends. Parents may come from varied life experiences, differing maturity levels, and vastly different upbringings. Yet each member needs to sense they have a place in the group, to feel they are accepted as a person and their contributions valued by the members. The overall purpose—learning to be more godly parents—is what continues to bind the parents together in the group. Without this overall purpose, there is no meaningful group.

So by sharing your story, you will continue to model for the parents what a maturing, honest parent looks like. In this way you will encourage parents to risk in the group process.

Session 9:
Asking Questions That Open Kids' Hearts

OBJECTIVE: Have someone read aloud the objective. Briefly comment that moving into kids' hearts is a central component of becoming parents of godly influence. Understanding what the heart is and how to move into it will be the focus of this session.

How the group will go through the materials: Ask three parents to read aloud the italicized dialogue between Dad, Mom, and Renae. Preselect parents willing to read creatively and with appropriate emotion.

In the section "The Art of Listening to a Kid's Heart," read aloud Luke 10:26-28. Stress that loving God and our kids from our hearts is our foremost job. It's essential to love God fundamentally with your *heart,* not just with your soul, strength, and mind. This material about listening to our kids' hearts should get the greatest emphasis in this session because listening is foundational to asking heart-directed questions. Likewise, asking heart-directed questions is essential to having godly influence with kids.

Use Proverbs 4:23 and the story of the artesian well to help parents understand the image of the heart as wellspring. Outward behavior—indeed, all of a kid's life—flows from the innermost places in his heart. Read aloud the quotation that begins, "The inner life, the story of the heart . . ." Underline the sentence in this section: "Listening carefully to the language of our kids' hearts and responding wisely is one of the keys to godly influence." It would be easy in this session to focus on the techniques of asking questions, but parents must first cultivate the skill of listening before they will be able to think of effective questions.

Read aloud Ray's story in the section entitled "Open-Ended Questions." Ray honestly struggled with his daughter not wanting to spend the summer with him. His story captures the struggle of a father willing to look at his angry, demanding heart. He was willing to offer his daughter grace by a heart-directed, open-ended question. His story is laced with an honest hope that will be a good model for parents.

Discussion: Ask yourself the questions ahead of time, especially pondering the issues of the heart. The session emphasizes listening carefully to our kids' hearts. The secondary theme is that heart-directed questions need to be open-ended, non-defensive, and biblically perceptive.

Allow extra time to discuss open-ended questions. Of the three qualities of questions, open-endedness is the most basic. The chart demonstrates some examples of open-ended questions. Focus on question 5. Help parents to think about and practice some open-ended questions that might get at the heart of their kids' below-the-waterline thinking.

Areas of potential misunderstanding: Session 9 emphasizes how parents must ask questions that open up the deeper issues of their kids' heart passions. Some parents may have learned to focus on managing kids' external behaviors, not on asking heart-directed questions. Make sure the parents clearly understand that Luke 10:26-28 tells us to love God and others first and foremost from our hearts.

Make sure parents make the connection that their kids' hearts, or control centers, can't be managed like a corporation. The Curtis and Eldredge quote is a beautiful picture of what all people, including our kids, long for in relationship: "The heart does not respond to principles or programs; it seeks not efficiency, but passion. Art, poetry, beauty, mystery, ecstasy: these are what rouse the heart. Indeed, they are the *languages that must be spoken* if one wishes to communicate with the heart." Highlight this theme by stating that kids won't be managed into relationship as a CEO would run a corporation. Instead our kids, ultimately, will respond to parents who learn to speak the language of the heart wisely.

Sharing your personal story: You might want to share a brief personal story about how God has used you to ask questions to open the heart of your own kid. Be willing to give some detail, whether it was a struggle like Ray's or something that went more smoothly, to help parents understand the principles of asking questions that open up kids' hearts. If the idea of asking questions to open your kid's heart is new to you, try it before the group meets and tell the group what happened.

Reflection: Before the group meets, think through what closed and open-ended questions you would use to fill in the chart. Write down your own answers in the blank spaces in the chart so you can quickly recall them during the group time.

You will have five "Kid's Remark" responses to walk the parents through here. Be sure to give plenty of time to have the parents focus on coming up with open-ended questions. Allow extended time for parents to practice developing questions directed at the hearts of the kids in these scenes.

Further reading: Pages 201–205 of *Parenting Adolescents* explain how to develop open-ended, nondefensive, and biblically perceptive questions. Brent Curtis and John Eldredge's *The Sacred Romance* is a deeply penetrating look into the passionate heart of God and our hearts' deepest desires. Though not directed specifically at parenting, their book eloquently describes how a heart moves richly toward loving God.

Group process issues: Ideally, the cohesive stage will continue to encourage parents to share deeper parts of their parenting journey with each other. As you continue to model your own parenting story, it should continue to encourage parents to risk deeper struggles and, hopefully, to see glimpses of joy. This stage can still move back and forth into areas of conflict, but by now members will engage in conflict with a more redemptive mood, not out of malice, to help each other grow.

Session 10:
Speaking "Life Words" to Your Teen

OBJECTIVE: Have someone read the objective aloud. Emphasize that the focus is for parents to learn to speak *into the heart* of their kids, not just to their minds.

How the group will go through the materials: This session is a longer one with more content and discussion questions, so plan plenty of time to digest the material ahead of time,

and be willing to highlight the key concepts you want to impart.

Preselect two parents, and assign them the roles for the italicized dialogue between Dad and Lee. Have them read the dialogue aloud to the group to dramatize the idea of how potent, and truly devastating, death words can be.

Proverbs 15:2,4 and 18:21 need to be read aloud in the group to have a contrasting idea of the power of "life" and "death" words. Parents need to grasp that their words have the power either to heal or to harm their kids' hearts.

Summarize aloud the section "Life Words Communicate Unconditional Involvement to a Teen." Specifically, focus on the story about Cathy speaking life words directed toward Seth's heart during a troubling time. Cathy was willing to explore Seth's personal struggles, offering him hope in the midst of his strained relationships. You can use this story as an example to talk about parents in the group offering unconditional involvement by speaking life words to their kids. As parents talk about this story, and perhaps their own, ask them how their kids might experience "hope" in relating to them personally.

Discussion: Ask yourself the six discussion questions ahead of time, putting them into your own words. Allow about five to eight minutes per discussion question. Parents should be willing to share more freely, and not every parent needs to answer each question. Question 2 is the most challenging question in this session, so be willing to give more time here for the parents to dialogue with each other. Also, allow sufficient time for parents to give examples of speaking life words into their kids hearts.

Areas of potential misunderstanding: Session 10 emphasizes understanding the heart and learning to speak into kids hearts. The section "Seeing our Kids' Hearts as Stories to Be

Entered" is very complex and challenging, but it is essential for parents to grasp. You will need to slowly summarize this section aloud, using the examples. Read 2 Corinthians 3:2-3 aloud to help parents see that kids' hearts are stories to be entered. Then read aloud the quotation of Daniel Taylor on page 65. Make sure everyone understands what the heart is and how it can be thought of as a story. Read aloud the story on page 64 of the man's misdirected words, "I just *love you guys*," as a contrasting, negative example of trying to speak into a person's story. He failed to speak meaningfully, so he didn't enter his friends' hearts. You may want to share a brief personal story where you were able to speak into the hearts of your own kids.

Further, use the example of Smokey the Bear as a concrete, specific, and compelling story that conveys speaking to people more powerfully by engaging people's *minds and hearts simultaneously.* Emphasize the idea that parents must appeal to both the minds and hearts of their kids at the same time, if directed life words are to have their full influence.

Sharing your personal story: Increasingly at this stage, the parents are likely to share more detailed and emotionally richer parts of their parenting story. You should need to prime the pump less and less. You might tell one personal story about ways you are learning to speak life into your kid's heart.

Reflection: Review the chart in the Reflection section before the meeting. You may want to write your own life-word responses in advance to help parents if they get stuck trying to corporately come up with responses during the group reflection. Assure them that this is not an easy exercise for beginners; that's why they're working together. Consider the difference between the vague question, "What's wrong?" (which can elicit no more than the reply, "Nothing"), and the question, "You look really

down. Did something happen at basketball practice?" The second question shows we're noticing the teen's body language and are genuinely interested in him. Of course, no inquiry will be received well if the teen perceives us as intrusive rather than caring. Some parents want to be their teens' best friends and know every detail of their lives. That's excessive involvement; it usually occurs when a parent is trying to get her own need for love met through her teen.

If the parents complete this chart before the hour is over, ask them for personal examples from their own family, so the group can corporately develop life-word responses to help individual parents in their own homes.

Further reading: Pages 205–210 of *Parenting Adolescents* will help expand the theme of speaking life words to develop greater parental influence. Further, Daniel Taylor's *The Healing Power of Stories* conveys powerful ways our stories can bring healing to our relationships. Though not a book on parenting per se, it emphasizes the necessity of knowing our "stories" to help shape disconnected lives into real meaning and personal plots, and ultimately, to promote change in our life stories.

Group process issues: The cohesive stage should be continuing to develop. As the group continues to work on real-life parenting issues, the parents will have the opportunity to continue to connect to each other more deeply.

You will want to build on not just the growing emotional climate of "we-ness" ("we are in this parenting journey together"), but also the sense of overall parental collaboration. Hopefully, parents will solve problems through mutual support, not by competition with each other. As parents continue to be authentic, open, and increasingly vulnerable, greater personal growth will take place for each individual.

Session 11:
What Lies Behind Kids' Emotions

OBJECTIVE: Ask a parent to read the objective aloud. Emphasize that the group will look at three primary negative emotions so that parents can trace kids' negative emotions to their below-the-waterline disappointed goals and strategies.

How the group will go through the materials: Ask two parents to read aloud the italicized dialogue between John and Keith. Preselect two parents willing to read the angry scene with realistic emotions.

In the section "The Primary Negative Emotions," read aloud Genesis 3:8-10,12. This passage highlights the three primary negative emotions you will develop in the rest of this session: anger, fear, and shame. It will be important for you to summarize this section for the parents to emphasize the powerful, destructive changes taking place not just between God and the humans, but also between the man and the woman. Sadly, Adam and Eve began hiding from God and each other. The negative results of the Fall continue today, as people develop intricate hiding strategies that affect all relationships, including those between parents and kids.

Restate the quotation at the end of this section to focus on looking at negative emotions—rather than running from them—in order to become mature in loving others: "The reason for looking inside is not to effect direct change of negative emotions to positive emotions. Instead, we are to listen to and ponder what we feel in order to be moved to the far deeper issue of what our hearts are doing with God and others." Again, emphasize that parents need to focus on the issues of their own hearts, not just on developing good skills of looking at their kids' negative emotions. You may need to reorient parents repeatedly to

look at their own hearts first before looking at their kids'. In this session, that will mean looking at their own emotions, as well as their kids', in order to pursue their kids' hearts with growing courage and integrity.

From "Shame: An Unreached Goal," read aloud the story of Tim and his dad. Our kids' sexuality may be uncomfortable for us, but it is a vital area in which we need to encourage our teens. When Tim was emotionally vulnerable and felt extreme shame, his dad spoke life to him. Highlight the fact that parents have great opportunities to encourage their kids even through the most potent negative emotions, like Tim's shame.

Discussion: Ask yourself the questions ahead of time and put them into your own words. The session emphasizes tracing our kids' negative emotions, but tracing our own emotions is also essential. Parents need to learn how best to use these negative emotions in order to move below the waterline into their kids' hearts. In this way they will move toward their kids' foolish goals with a growing sensitivity and wisdom.

There are nine discussion questions, so you may want to ask one question from each section in which there are several questions. Be sure to give time to the discussion questions on fear and shame. Shame, in particular, is a challenging topic for parents to apply with their kids, so spend more time with this section. Go over the content and invite parents to answer the discussion questions.

Areas of potential misunderstanding: Focus on the section on shame. Parents often misunderstand shame, and it's hard for parents to learn how to draw it out of their kids' hearts in an encouraging way. Read Tim's story slowly to make sure parents are connecting to what the dad was trying to accomplish by allowing Tim to speak his painful words. This dad went much further than just listening, for he drew out Tim's likely heart purpose of wanting to hide from feeling dirty, ugly, sickening, and unspiritual. The dad put words to his son's shame, helping Tim make sense of his negative emotions and thereby reducing his shame. Underscore the dad's powerful, healing words so the parents can clearly see what the dad was attempting to accomplish with Tim. Some parents will find this story embarrassing — in other words, it will trigger feelings of shame in them. Shame is the hardest emotion for parents to draw out of their kids because it so often touches areas about which parents, too, feel shame. Thus, it's important to stress that parents need to look at the emotions their kids trigger in them. Parents need to address the shame in their own hearts in order to respond effectively to their kids' shame.

Sharing your personal story: You might want to share a brief story — like Tim's — about how your teen struggled with anger, fear, or shame and how you were able to trace his or her negative emotions to heart purposes and goals. Further, talk about how God is helping you to see your own anger or fear. Tell how you have begun to discern what might be going on in your kids' hearts by looking at your own negative emotions first.

Reflection: Be sure to look over the chart with the three sample situations before the group meets. It would be a good idea for you to fill out the chart on your own ahead of time in case the group needs extra help from you.

Further reading: *The Cry of the Soul* looks to the Psalms to explore how people's emotions reveal their deepest struggles with God, themselves, and others. The chapters on anger, fear, and shame will help you think about how emotions are windows into people's hearts.

Group process issues: As the group continues to grow, the cohesion parents feel can at times make it more difficult for them to express negative emotions about the leader, the members, or the process. Sometimes the group can restrict certain members' negative emotions in order to sustain the feeling of group closeness. At this stage, all members likely feel good and lighthearted. Yet this stage must be slowly worked through in order for the group to be productive. Only when parents' emotions, both positive and negative, can be expressed and worked through will the group continue to be most useful and productive for the remainder of the group experience.

Session 12:
Conflict: Surviving the Tsunami

OBJECTIVE: Ask a parent to read aloud the objective. Briefly comment that you will be dealing with how to address even severe conflict with your kids in a positive way.

How the group will go through the materials: Ask three parents to read aloud the italicized dialogue between Darcy, Phil, and Marge. This is a powerful scene, so be sure to select parents who are willing to read dramatically. The primary metaphor of Darcy as an adolescent "tsunami" will be used in the rest of this session and mentioned in upcoming sessions. Summarize the unseen force of a tsunami's power below the waterline.

Be sure to highlight the chart entitled "The Way Conflict Is Handled in a Family." It is a visual way to help parents identify their responses to conflict. Allow people some time to look over this chart and talk about which response is most typical for them.

Read Proverbs 14:26 aloud. Comment that parents are to model the home as a "secure fortress," creating an emotional "refuge" in which kids can stand secure even in the devastating conflict they can generate. Our kids need this sense of spiritual "refuge" if we are to weather conflict well with them.

Focus the majority of the content time on the section, "Handling Conflict in a Positive Way." Briefly summarize Nehemiah 5. Read aloud Nehemiah 5:6-7, which describes how Nehemiah handled those under his care in a strong yet kind way. Read aloud the first principle, "Nehemiah Encouraged Emotional Vulnerability When His People Were Hurt and Angry." Help parents to understand that they too are to encourage their kids to be emotionally vulnerable by drawing out their kids' pain and anger, even when it is directed toward them. Parents need to let themselves feel their kids' hurt, not just dismiss their struggles. It's essential to seek truth over comfort in relationships. Read aloud the quotation that begins, "Christians are never angry enough. . . ." Comment that parents can have a righteous anger that contains strong components of sadness, desire, and hope for good things for our kids even in the midst of conflict with them. If kids sense parents have the courage to allow them to be deeply angry, even with their parents, kids feel safe to let their heart complaints surface and, ultimately, be healed.

The first principle is the most important, but do allow time for the parents to interact with the other two principles as well.

Discussion: There are seven discussion questions; you may not get to all of them. The session emphasizes three myths, as well as three values, about relational conflict. Discuss question 4 by asking parents to reflect upon what myths might be operating in their family. Ask several parents to comment on this question. Also, summarize the story of Seth dyeing his hair (under the third value). This story illustrates how a parent needs to deal first with himself after an episode of conflict. Comment

that even conflict can help parents and kids grow in their ability to love. Questions 5 and 6 help parents to look at using conflict in a healing way.

Areas of potential misunderstanding: Dealing with conflict brings up strong feelings in parents about their kids and themselves. Very discouraged, frustrated parents may blame their kids ("It really is *their* fault I got furious!") when you point out that parents need to look at their hearts first, as in the story about Seth's hair. Minimally, some level of finger pointing at kids ("Come on, you're letting these kids off the hook!") may occur as the most discouraged parents try to keep the spotlight off themselves. So be willing to talk honestly about the struggles parents might have in owning their part in a conflict.

Sharing your personal story: You might want to share a brief story about how God used a conflict, perhaps a severe one, with your adolescent. Talk about how you allowed your kid to be deeply emotionally vulnerable. Perhaps your teen shouted a painful, angry outburst, but you were willing to allow him or her to vent the heart complaint, as Nehemiah did. Or maybe it was a conflict where you completely blew it by getting angry, as I did with Seth, and you were willing to own the angry damage you dumped on your kid. Perhaps at a later time you were able to work through the conflict with your teen. Either type of story will be helpful for parents as they learn to look honestly at themselves.

Reflection: There are three Reflection questions to preview before the group meeting. Give yourself time to think about these questions and answer them in your own words. Allow extra time for question 3 because it calls for serious reflection and application of exactly how a parent will move toward his or her kid's heart.

Further reading: Pages 163–175 of *Parenting Adolescents* explain the process of handling conflict in a positive way. His section on Nehemiah is an engaging story about how people can influence others by encouraging vulnerability, allowing impact, and helping relieve others' emotional pain. Pages 65–77 of *Cry of the Soul* address the righteous anger parents are called to boldly live out.

Group process issues: The sense of connection should be progressing, yet positive conflict will continue to be an ongoing part of the group. It may be helpful to think of the cohesive stage as a two-part process: cohesion (in which members feel positive and connected) alternating with productivity (in which parents actively work on the issues that brought them into the group in the first place).

Session 13:
Rebel with a Cause

OBJECTIVE: Have someone read the objective aloud. Briefly comment upon the necessity of thinking honestly about our kids' rebellion and of moving into kids' despair to model hope for them.

How the group will go through the materials: Ask three parents to read aloud the italicized dialogue between the Counselor, Phil, and Marge. Again, preselect parents willing to read with appropriate emotion. Comment upon Darcy as an illustration of the adolescent despair you will examine closely in this session.

In "Despair Is the Culprit," read aloud the quotation in which Kevin Huggins describes the relational disillusionment kids experience first with parents, then with peers. Reread the last sentence for emphasis: "This constitutes another crisis for the adolescent: he must find the love he longs for while stranded in a sea of relationships that offer more disappointment, rejection, and heartache." Comment upon the betrayal and disillusionment that lead to a crisis in kids' worlds and provoke, at times, even despair.

In "How Kids Respond to Despair," read aloud the quotation, focusing on the italicized sentence, *"his basic assumptions about the events of life are always designed to maintain his illusion of self-sufficiency."* Self-sufficiency always, ultimately, backfires and fails kids. Summarize the story of Winner as an example of despair's often unseen relational damage. Parents must be alert to kids' personal disappointments to better minister to them.

In "A Sick Heart," read aloud Proverbs 13:12. Read the story of food poisoning as a metaphor of spiritual heartsickness. Read aloud the quotation describing the process of how heartsickness develops.

In the third biblical approach to dealing with despair, "Model the Fear of God," read Proverbs 14:26 aloud and then read Phil's letter to Darcy. It is an honest, poignant letter of hope in the midst of his daughter's despair. Allow the parents to interact with Phil's letter at length.

Discussion: Ask yourself the ten questions ahead of time, pondering the issues of despair and hope in them. Focus on helping parents think about potential adolescent despair by highlighting questions 2, 3, and 5 for parents' personal applications.

Phil's letter to Darcy communicates in thoughtful detail how a parent invites his daughter to look at God for herself through her dad's growing heart. Be sure to give plenty of time to discuss questions 9 and 10 to help parents personalize hope and communicate grace while kids may be in the midst of despair and rebellion.

Areas of potential misunderstanding: Parents experiencing high levels of anger and frustration with rebellious kids may struggle with personalizing their kids' rebellion and, after honestly pondering, connecting it to despair in their adolescents' heart. Parents may want to shift blame to kids, accusing them of creating the mess they are in. This may be mostly true, but it won't be helpful if parents move no further than just blaming kids for their messes without getting involved themselves.

Emphasize that truly ministering to despairing kids is not primarily about parents' pain, but about modeling relationship and God to kids in the midst of pain. Emphasize the biblical theme of "A Sick Heart" in Proverbs 13:12. A sick heart often drives adolescent despair into hopeless places. Be sure to give plenty of time to Phil's letter to help parents see how Phil incarnated the principles of biblical influence: his vulnerability, sorrow over his rage, speaking truth in their relationship, allowing his daughter to have a personal impact on him, and longing for a restored relationship. All of these stances were likely to move Darcy away from despair and toward hope.

Sharing your personal story: You might want to follow Phil's letter with a story of your own in which God showed you areas you needed to address in your relationship with your own kids. Perhaps, as with Phil, it came after an angry explosion. Or perhaps something less severe moved you to deal with your own failure and led you toward a more repentant heart. Be willing to share for several minutes about your struggles and the ways you are allowing God to move you to minister more deeply into your kid's heart. If you have seen despair in your teen, describe what you've seen and how you have responded.

Reflection: Review the three family scenes before the group meets and think through the questions posed at the end of each scene. You may want to write down your own answers to

the Reflection questions to help the group if they get stuck.

Encourage the parents to ponder what might be going on in these kids' hearts as they listen in on each family scene. By now, parents should be able to make more subtle, below-the-waterline hunches about what is likely occurring in these kids' lives and their own kids' hearts.

Further reading: Pages 221–231 of *Parenting Adolescents* explain how parents deal with kids' despair and describe a biblical approach for responding well to adolescent despair. Pages 133–145 of *Cry of the Soul* look biblically at despair's corrosive effect upon the human heart.

Group process issues: Ideally, the cohesive stage will go beyond parents merely feeling positive and connected to each other. For growth to occur in the group, a sense of productivity should begin to emerge in which parents engage in new thinking and risk-taking actions outside of the group in their kids' lives. Real parental maturity ultimately has to occur with greater frequency in the real world, beyond the group, where parents live and interact with their kids on a day-to-day basis.

Session 14:
Challenging the Rebel

OBJECTIVE: Ask a parent to read aloud the objective. Comment briefly that your main focus will be learning to wisely, thoughtfully challenge deep levels of rebellion in positive ways and so strengthen kids' ownership of their problems.

How the group will go through the materials: Ask two parents to read aloud the italicized dialogue between Jason and Maggie. Preselect parents willing to be creative in the reading of this scene, because it will be developed more in this session.

In "Two Primary Ways to Confront Rebellion," the main thrust is using *uncompromising responsiveness,* or justice, to weaken kids' foolishness. Read aloud the quotation from Kevin Huggins to help parents understand the concept of uncompromising responsiveness. Underscore the last sentence of the quotation: "Parents have the responsibility to respond to their *purposes* and *actions* in a way that encourages kids to attach the same significance and meaning to them that God does" (italics added).

For "Serving God and Others" (under "Two Primary Ways to Confront Rebellion") read aloud Philippians 2:3-4 and connect it to other-centered relating. Summarize the two tasks (ownership of choices and serving) that are absolutely necessary for kids to mature beyond their rebellion. Highlight the way Maggie shifted away from being a fearful parent to becoming a mother of deep strength with Jason as she dealt wisely with his rebellion. Make sure everyone sees how she fulfilled the two tasks.

For "Mere Words Won't Do It," read aloud Proverbs 29:19: "A servant cannot be corrected by mere words: though he understands, he will not respond." At times even our kids won't respond, though they too clearly understand what we desire for them. Parents need tools more powerful than just words.

In "Logical Consequences: Illustrations of Choice," read the sentence aloud: "*Engineered consequences,* where parents actively structure kids' choices based on the reality of the situation, are more potent because parents want to *alert their kids' hearts to the power of pain in their choices.*" Also read aloud the quotation from Kevin Huggins that begins, "The pain such consequences bring. . . ." Make sure everyone grasps the idea of the "parental bridge" that connects

foolish thinking to a logical, painful result that is likely to deter kids from pursuing destructive choices. Help parents see the logical connection between teens' choices and the consequences. Use the "Parental Bridge" diagram in this section so parents can picture this concept.

Discussion: There are ten discussion questions; you may not get to all of them. The session emphasizes creating awareness and ownership of our kids' choices, helping kids to serve God and others, and engineering logical consequences for foolish choices in order to weaken rebellion. Question 6 is important because parents may not be aware their kids feel they have no real choices. Use the bulk of your time on Phil and Darcy's struggles and the "Parental Bridge" diagram with questions 9 and 10. Your goal will be to help parents grasp the concept of connecting kids' choices with painful consequences. This concept is foundational for session 15 on creative consequences.

Areas of potential misunderstanding: When logical consequences are introduced, there will likely be a strong pull for parents to jump ahead to session 15 and develop many examples of logical consequences to deal with their respective teen situations. You will feel this pressure, too, for it is normal for parents to want to solve the problems they are facing.

However, it's important for parents to grasp the theory of logical consequences before they leap to applying it. Session 14 introduces the concepts and gives some examples of logical consequences, but you may need to redirect parents to come back next week with their personal struggles. Also, help the parents to see that their task is to *alert their kids' hearts to the power of pain in their choices.* Your focus continues to be pursuing kids' *hearts* first and foremost, not just engineering choices to weaken their foolishness.

Sharing your personal story: Perhaps you can share a brief story of how you have been developing logical consequences with your kids, jumping off from the story of Darcy and Phil. Talk about how you've tried to develop at least two logical options for your kids in a parenting situation. In sharing your story, don't focus exclusively on the *skills* you are developing in terms of creating good consequences, but continue to focus on the *hearts* of your kids that need to be penetrated by God's truth.

Reflection: There are four family scenes depicting rebellious teens' behavior toward parents. Be sure you review the questions ahead of time and think through the answers. It's not easy for parents to come up with logical consequences for these four family scenes, so go slowly and allow the group to brainstorm each scene. Scene 2 about Susie is a particularly hard case. Allow more time with this scene to let parents think creatively together. School is a common teen struggle, so this example should be relevant to many parents.

Further reading: Pages 233–254 of *Parenting Adolescents* explain the process of responding to a rebellious teen's purposes and creating logical consequences. Also, pages 71–85 of Cline and Fay's *Parenting with Love and Logic* build a logical rationale with an easy reading style. Cline and Fay explain why developing choices works well with kids and helps extract parents from unwanted power struggles.

Group process issues: The cohesive stage will continue to develop. However, it is not too soon to talk about the upcoming termination of the group within the next two weeks. Often, if parents have allowed themselves to become personally invested, they will begin to feel the need to "pull away" from the group members

prematurely to lessen the sorrow of having the group end. (See "Termination" stage described on page 130.) It will be important to encourage parents to continue to be an active part of the group until the end of the group experience.

Session 15:
Creative Consequences

OBJECTIVE: Ask a parent to read aloud the objective. Briefly comment that the focus of the session will be developing creative logical consequences to continue to weaken kids' foolish and even rebellious behaviors.

How the group will go through the materials: Ask two parents to read aloud the italicized dialogue between Marge and Phil. Comment on Marge's inadequate strategy that used *weak natural consequences* and Phil's strategy that used *punishment* to attempt to get Darcy back in line.

Under "A Wise Father and a Rebellious Son," read aloud Luke 15:11-14 to show how the father created a sense of choice for his rebellious son. Summarize Henri Nouwen's point about the shocking request the young rebel made to his father: the son actually wanted his father dead! Yet instead of punishing him, the father created several choices for his son. Read aloud the paragraph that begins, "The father wisely engineers a series of options for his young son."

"What About Punishment?" helps parents look critically at the downside of punishment. Read aloud Cline and Fay's advice on avoiding punishment. Emphasize their statement, "Resentment [toward punishment] is the more common reaction. The same holds true for our children. . . . The *real* world by and large *doesn't operate on punishment.*" As parents, we are to model the real world to our kids as we creatively challenge their choices at deep levels.

Focus on the "Logical Consequences" section by using the quotation from Kevin Huggins that begins, "Parents are thus responsible to engineer [logical] consequences . . ." Summarize this longer section to help parents understand clearly that they will weaken foolishness by connecting their kids' choices to painful, real-world realities. Read aloud the sentence, "As wise parents, we want not only to alert our kids to their foolishness, but also to reveal their *very own hearts that committed the relational harm.*" Again, our focus must be to direct parents, not merely to challenge kids' behaviors. Continually exposing kids' hearts is essential to spark repentance and deepen kids' movement toward God.

Highlight the section, "Roadblocks to Using Logical Consequences." It will help parents evaluate why logical consequences fail and to rethink how to apply the principles within their own families.

Discussion: There are eleven questions, so you might not be able to get to all of them. The session emphasizes thinking through a biblical model of developing logical consequences, and parents will attempt to develop introductory applications with their own kids. Focus on question 6 about building an association between a kid's foolish purposes and the significance God attaches to them. Question 8 will also be helpful because Seth's story is a practical, understandable example of parents developing logical consequences. You can use Seth's story as a model when you move on to thinking through logical consequences in group members' families.

Areas of potential misunderstanding: Make sure the parents see how the material in this session connects with that in session 14. You might go back to the "Parental Bridge" diagram from session 14 to help parents picture

how to engineer choices that relate to painful real-world consequences. Parents need to make the mental connection between engineering or "bridging" kids' choices and letting kids live with their own consequences. It is challenging for most parents to think up logical consequences, so be willing to go slowly. Let parents ask what logical consequences might look like in a given situation with their own kids.

Be sure to talk about developing logical consequences *in advance of a conflict,* not during the heat of the battle. In a two-parent home, it's important for spouses to agree on the logical consequences ahead of time. Again, the focus must be seeing kids mature in relationships, not using logical consequences as subtle punishment.

Sharing your personal story: Perhaps you can share a brief story of how you've been working on developing logical consequences with your kids. You might want to summarize the story about Seth, then move to one of your own. In this way, you will help parents connect your story to their own situation.

Reflection: There are three family scenes describing rebellious kids' behaviors. Again, it will not be easy for parents to come up with logical consequences for these kids, so allow them to brainstorm as a group. Scene 3 is an especially difficult situation, so give parents more time on this one. Hopefully, you will have time for parents to bring up situations with their kids and brainstorm creative consequence options.

Further reading: Pages 245–254 of *Parenting Adolescents* address very difficult kids who need creative intervention and real-world logical consequences. Also, pages 87–99 of *Parenting with Love and Logic* give several creative stories of parents developing consequences.

Group process issues: Remind parents that next week is the last session. Mention how important it is for all parents to attend because during the termination stage parents may be tempted to pull away. They may want to find something else to do on the last night to avoid the sorrow of saying goodbye. However, their corporate involvement is necessary to allow closure, or saying goodbye. Even if saying goodbye is hard for them, they need to understand that the other group members need them to do it. Parents also deepen the learning for themselves by giving and receiving feedback about the group during the last session.

Session 16:
Words of Encouragement

OBJECTIVE: Ask a parent to read aloud the objective. Briefly comment that the focus of this session is finding ways to continue to encourage your kids, over the long term, on the road toward deeper maturity.

How the group will go through the materials: Ask one parent to read aloud the italicized section of Phil's journal entry. Comment that this entry captures the growing heart-attitude of long-term encouragement that parents are called to develop.

Under "What Is Encouragement?" read aloud Crabb and Allender's definition of encouragement. Summarize Crabb's story of the man in his church who encouraged him ("Whatever you do for the Lord, I'm behind you one thousand percent"). Be willing to describe the positive impact true encouragement offers hurting kids.

For the section "Spurring One Another On," ask a parent to read aloud Hebrews 10:24-25. Be sure to focus on the words "consider," "spur," and "encourage" to highlight what biblical encouragement really means. It is a creative, intensive, thoughtful, and active process.

Summarize the story of my grandmother's involvement in my life from the section, "Thinking Deeply to Stir Our Kids Toward Love." Focus on Ruth's creative, thoughtful words that spoke to a hurting kid's heart. She used a deep knowledge of my pain coupled with truthful words. Remember, parents can't easily "fix" kids' problems, especially losses like death. Our ministry is to speak life into kids, often in the midst of life's uncertainty, and thereby offer hope.

Summarize Crabb and Allender's three principles under the section, "Calling Forth Truth from Our Kids." Be sure to read aloud the quotation under the third key concept: "Acceptance is essential when kids' faults are exposed . . ." Highlight the concept that when parents truly accept their kids' deep faults, when kids are most emotionally exposed, this acceptance always develops encouragement and influence.

Be willing to summarize the story of the ring in order to talk about how *kids can minister* to us. It is a poignant story of mutual encouragement, a glimpse of the maturity parents long to see in their kids.

Conclude by reading aloud the entire section, "Continuing Down the Path of Encouragement", as a final summary of the course. This section encourages parents to continue the journey. Read the last paragraph as a call to reflect and then continue their growth forward.

Discussion: You have only five discussion questions, so you can allow more time for each question. Give extra time to question 3 about "calling forth truth from our kids." It is a challenging concept, yet central to kids' needs. Question 4 asks parents to reflect upon the importance of truly accepting a teen whose needs and faults lie exposed. Ask how this acceptance would encourage their own kids and what it might look like within their own families.

Areas of potential misunderstanding: Make sure parents clearly understand the biblical definition and personal applications of encouragement. Encouragement is an active process where we creatively, actively, and consistently find ways to speak to the *unique* needs of each of our kids. Each one may require a different way of encouragement, not a one-size-fits-all.

Spend time on the concept that "acceptance is essential when kids' faults are exposed." Parents can misunderstand this idea as just bland acceptance of kids' shortcomings: "You want us just to overlook their mistakes and not deal with the problems?" Discouraged parents may see exposed faults in this way. Be sure they understand the concept. Acceptance does not conflict with uncompromising responsiveness and logical consequences. We offer kids warm, loving acceptance *even while* allowing them to experience the consequences of their choices. Acceptance means not punishing, not raging, not shaming kids when their faults are exposed.

Sharing your personal story: This session includes several poignant stories about my son. Be willing to springboard from one of these stories to talk about a time when you felt your words truly spoke to your teen's heart. This is the last session, so allow your personal story to "punctuate" the experience for the parents as they conclude the group.

Reflection: There are three discussion questions about different family scenes. Focus on question 3, which invites parents to bring their own stories and get the group's help in brainstorming creative words of encouragement. Most of your time will be spent on parents bringing their own family needs to the group for help.

Further reading: Crabb and Allender's *Encouragement: The Key to Caring* is a great primer on thinking through the basic components of encouragement. Though not directly about parenting, it offers a wealth of insight into how we can become better encouragers of others.

Group process issues: The group is now at the termination stage (see "Termination" stage on page 130), where it is possible to deepen parents' personal gains from the group. Though not a pleasant topic, ending the group is a built-in reality from the start. For some parents, the thought of ending is fearful because they will lose the group's support. If closure is handled honestly and courageously, though, the group can continue to be an agent of positive change even when it is only a memory. Parents are starting to see much of what they have learned in the real world of life at home.

Termination activities: Here are several options as you facilitate the group's healthy termination. Think through the personality of your group and choose one that suits it best.

- Letter to the group: Before the last session, each parent writes a letter to the group members to be read at the last session. Participants write about the things they will take away from the group. What have they learned? What thoughts or feelings do they have about the other parents? What would they say to someone beginning the process of courageous parenting? What desires do they have for the others in the group?
- Cards of encouragement: Each parent writes his or her name on one side of several index cards. During the last group session, these cards are passed around to all the other parents. The parents write a sentence or two of appreciation about the person or the hopes they have for that person's

future. The cards are then given to the appropriate parents at the end of the meeting.

- Regrets: During the final meeting, parents are asked to imagine leaving, getting into their cars, and driving away. They are to imagine looking in their rear-view mirrors back at the place they are leaving and let surface what they would regret not having said before they left. Then they begin talking through any unfinished business or emotions they have about the group and its members.

Here are some questions to consider addressing during your final session:

- What are your feelings about ending the group?
- About what do you feel loss and sadness?

- What is it like to say goodbye? How have you departed from loved ones in the past? Do you believe this goodbye will be different or the same?
- How would you long for others to say goodbye to you?
- Do you believe you accomplished the personal goals you set out with when you started the parenting group? Can you explain your thoughts?

NOTES

1. Adapted from Irvin D. Yalom, *The Theory and Practice of Group Psychotherapy* (New York, NY: Basic Books, 1985); and Dan B. Allender, *The Wounded Heart Workbook* (Colorado Springs, CO: NavPress, 1992), pp. 187–188.

Glossary

The following are key terms used in this workbook, along with their definitions.

Basic beliefs: A core belief system that shapes an adolescent's responses to other people and to his world. The teen is generally unaware of his basic beliefs and how they drive him to act with others.

Contempt: A powerful form of anger intended to intimidate or control others, provoking others into emotional battle or retreat. Contempt is best understood metaphorically, as an "emotional scab" worn to protect a wound from further damage in a relationship. Contempt functions to keep teens at a safe distance, where they can't be hurt by the parent. The more pain a person feels, the thicker the emotional scab he develops to protect himself.

Desire: A deep longing on the part of a teen and parents for unfailing love. This longing is often unmet in relationships between parents and the teen when problems begin to develop. For our purposes, there are three types of desire:

> **Casual desire:** Parents' casual desires are often expressed as *preferences,* such as how kids should dress, keep their rooms, or spend their leisure time. The final decision is left up to the adolescent because the parent does not see the outcome as threatening to the teen or the parent.

> **Critical desire:** Parents usually express critical desires to teens as *clear directives.* Schoolwork, friends, choice of schools, entertainment, and spiritual commitments are typically seen as critical. These areas legitimately affect the

159

well-being of the adolescent, and parents see them as vital. Usually, parents will provide direct feedback in these areas critical to kids' development.

Crucial desire: Parents experience crucial desires when they believe something vital to their *own well-being* is at stake. When parents believe the fulfillment of these desires depends on their teens, nearly everything that happens to these kids becomes a crucial concern for them. Crucial desires are virtually a matter of emotional life and death and can blind parents to their destructive impact upon their kids.

Emotional gas tank: A metaphor of relationship demonstrating how teens "drain" parents emotionally. Teens' "gas levels," or their emotional reserves, change constantly when they encounter relational disappointments. A parent's role is to initiate relationship, or "fuel," her adolescent.

Foolishness: An active thinking process about which kids are often not fully aware. A foolish thinking process flows from the teen's decision to trust in his own efforts to get the deepest desires of his heart met without relying on anyone else but himself. This process of adolescent self-trust is an inevitable reality of living in a disappointing world. It results in relational failure and increased anger toward God, oneself, and others.

Heart: The center or focus of a person's inner life. In biblical usage, the heart is the source or spring of motives, the seat of passions, the center of the thought processes, the spring of conscience. Heart is associated with what is now meant by the cognitive, affective, and volitional elements of a person's life.

Impact: Otherwise known as "significance." This is another crisis kids face on the road to adulthood: wondering if their lives can have a substantial, lasting effect on others. Teens want to know that significant people will stand up and take notice of their accomplishments. Usually during adolescence their sense of impact begins to fall because they sense they can't seem to meet other people's expectations.

Influence: The capacity of a parent to produce a positive effect on his kids by indirect, sometimes intangible, means without using force. It is the opposite of *control,* whereby the parent can affect an adolescent's behaviors and/or attitudes by employing force or power. Control usually leads to decreasing parental effectiveness.

Misguided focus: When a parent encounters disappointment with a teen, the focus of the parent's mental energies often moves to "fixing" the situation or relieving the pain. The focus of a disappointed parent too easily moves toward changing or controlling his kid's outward behaviors. A key characteristic of a parent's misguided focus is an insistence that the solution to the problems in the family involves changing something or someone besides himself.

Parental reflection: An ongoing process in which parents actively look at the hidden motives (dynamics) that guide their outward behavior toward their adolescents. Parents are often unaware of the motives that drive their behavior, so a new way of thinking and relating in the context of other people is essential to discern hidden motives and move the parent toward a deeper level of love.

Stability: One of the major crises that teens must overcome to make a successful transition to adulthood. As they enter adolescence, kids find they have less control over their worlds than they did as children. Their parents can't control things (school, friends, failures) for them, and teens have a great sense of unpredictability. Much of their behavior is intended to bring predictability and safety into their lives.

Uncompromising responsiveness: One of the two basic ingredients (the other is unconditional involvement) a parent must incorporate into a relationship with a teen in order to give the kid a taste of what God is like. It most closely gives a picture of God's *justice*. Uncompromising responsiveness teaches teens that everything they do has lasting impact because of who they are as young people. Parents must help kids begin to understand their own motives and behaviors, and attach the same significance to them that God does.

Unconditional involvement: Together with uncompromising responsiveness, unconditional involvement helps parents to demonstrate to teens what God is really like. Unconditional involvement gives teens a taste of God's grace, or *unconditional love*. A parent who boldly takes whatever initiative is necessary to stay relationally near his kid during problem times is demonstrating God's involvement toward her.

Unfailing love: Adolescents face another life crisis as they relate to others who ultimately disappoint them and fail to love them unconditionally. A challenge faces the teen: she must find the unfailing love she longs for while stranded in a sea of relationships (with parents and peers) that offer the disappointment, rejection, and heartache of a fallen world.

Author

DAVID HUTCHINS is cofounder and executive director of the Gensis Institute, a nonprofit biblical training and counseling ministry in Spokane, Washington. He also coordinates counseling programs for adolescents and parents through churches and Spokane County Juvenile Court. A twelve-year veteran of Youth for Christ, he developed *Courageous Parenting* in response to parents' request for more formal, biblical help to positively influence their children. He completed his master's degree in Biblical Counseling under supervision of Dr. Larry Crabb at Colorado Christian University.

David and his wife, Cathy, and son, Seth, live in Spokane, Washington.

About Genesis Institute

Our Mission
Genesis Institute exists as part of the Body of Christ to care for human souls, guided by the fixed point of biblical revelation. All Genesis training ministries seek to enable and encourage the Christian community to this end.

Our Training Ministry Opportunities
Training opportunities are scheduled throughout the year for Christian leaders, workers, and learners wanting to grow in caring for others.

Courageous Parenting Seminar: A one-day seminar for parents of adolescents exploring the content of the *Courageous Parenting* workbook. The seminar is designed to help parents and youth workers creatively think through a biblical model of influence in the life of their teens.

Courageous Parenting Leaders Training: A two-day, highly interactive, small group experience designed to help Christian workers and volunteers become more effective mentors to parents of adolescents. An overview of the *Courageous Parenting* workbook is the primary focus. Other topics include: beginning and developing small groups, understanding group process/dynamics, avoiding relational pitfalls in the small group, and developing a vision to encourage parenting leaders for the long haul.

Core Concepts in Biblical Mentoring: A three-day training experience designed to help Christian workers and volunteers develop a broad and cohesive understanding of mentoring. A biblical and theoretical model of people, problems, and solutions is examined initially. Thereafter, personal storytelling is explored by video and group participation as a means of helping others.

How to contact Genesis Institute regarding these training opportunities in your area:
Phone: (509) 467-7913
Mail: N. 10220 Nevada, Suite 280, Spokane, WA 99218
Web Site: *WWW.GENESISINSTITUTE.ORG*

MORE HELP TO IMPROVE YOUR PARENTING SKILLS.

Raising Adults

Are your children becoming adults, or just adult-aged children? Jim Hancock challenges assumptions and creates common ground to allow parents to train their children to accept responsibility and gain an adult perspective on life.

Raising Adults
(Jim Hancock) $11

Becoming the Parent God Wants You to Be

Written by best-selling author Dr. Kevin Leman, *Becoming the Parent God Wants You to Be* is a real-life parenting curriculum that helps you discover you can be a great parent–without being perfect!

Becoming the Parent God Wants You to Be
(Kevin Leman) $12

BRINGING TRUTH TO LIFE
www.navpress.com

Get your copies today at your local bookstore, through our website, or by calling (800) 366-7788. Ask for offer **#6005** or a FREE catalog of NavPress resources.

Prices subject to change.